Chronicle of a Failure Foretold

COLOMBIA

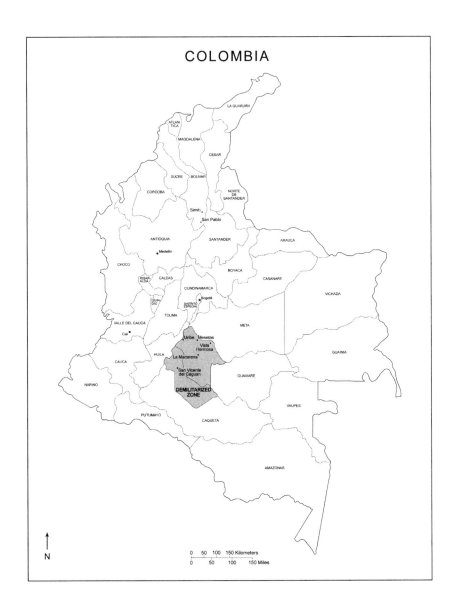

Chronicle of a Failure Foretold

The Peace Process of Colombian President Andrés Pastrana

Harvey F. Kline

THE UNIVERSITY OF ALABAMA PRESS
Tuscaloosa

Typeface: Minion

∞

The paper on which this book is printed meets the minimum requirements of
American National Standard for Information Sciences-Permanence of Paper for
Printed Library Materials, ANSI Z39.48-1984.

Kline, Harvey F.
Chronicle of a failure foretold : the peace process of Colombian president
Andres Pastrana / Harvey F. Kline.
p.   cm.
Includes bibliographical references and index.
ISBN-13: 978-0-8173-1556-6 (cloth : alk. paper)
ISBN-10: 0-8173-1556-X
ISBN-13: 978-0-8173-5410-7 (pbk. : alk. paper)
ISBN-10: 0-8173-5410-7
1. Colombia—Politics and government—1974– 2. Negotiation—Colombia. 3. Peace.
4. Pastrana Arango, Andrés. 5. Fuerzas Armadas Revolucionarias de Colombia.
6. Ejército de Liberación Nacional (Colombia) I. Title.
F2279.K53 2006
986.106′34—dc22

2006028161

In memory of my brother
Edward Alvin Kline
1938–2004
separated too soon but sure to be reunited
¡Adios querido hermano!

Contents

Dedication   v

Preface   ix

Part One / The Context for Failure   1
1. Colombia before the Presidency of Andrés Pastrana:
   The Context for Failure   5

2. The Immediate Context for the Pastrana Negotiations:
   The Government of Ernesto Samper (1994–1998)   27

**Part Two / The Negotiations between the Government and the
Guerrilla Groups**   47
3. The FARC Negotiations Begin: June 1998–January 1999   49

4. The First Agreements of the FARC Negotiations:
   January 1999–January 2001   67

5. The Negotiations in 2001:
   Agreements on Process but Not on Substance   90

6. The FARC Negotiations End: January–February 2002   112

7. The ELN Discussions through the Declaration of Geneva:
   September 1998–July 2000   126

8. The Failure of the ELN Discussions   147

Part Three / Conclusions   167
9. Why the Pastrana Peace Process Failed   169

Notes   187

Bibliography   213

Index   223

Preface

This book is a study of the attempts of Colombian president Andrés Pastrana to negotiate peace with guerrilla groups during his administration (1998–2002). To paraphrase Colombian Nobel laureate Gabriel García Márquez, it might be called a "chronicle of a failure foretold,"[1] and indeed it might be useful to state the conclusion from the very beginning: Despite all the efforts, all the rhetoric, all the well-written documents, and all the meetings, in the end the bargaining failed. Fighting in the countryside remained as before, with increasing attacks in the cities. It also led to the 2002 election of Álvaro Uribe Vélez, a hard-liner who insisted that peace negotiations could only follow demobilization and surrender of weapons, the opposite order used by Pastrana.

It would have been scientifically more productive (and personally more pleasing) to write a book about a successful peace process, such as the ones that apparently were achieved in Nicaragua, El Salvador, and Guatemala. I hope to write that book about Colombia some day. However, based on the premise that "Those who cannot remember the past are condemned to repeat it,"[2] there is also merit in analyzing a failure. Indeed one of the conclusions from this study, stated and defended in the final chapter, is that the Colombian government had not learned from failures prior to 1998.

In a sense I began this book when I first lived in Colombia in 1964. As I was reading about Colombian politics, when *La Violencia* between the Liberal and Conservative parties was ending, one day I asked a Colombian friend how he explained the terrible condition of the country. He replied simply, "It's simple. The Spanish screwed us."

Later in graduate school I learned that such an independent variable did not work in explaining Colombian violence, whether it was between the parties or as it was later between the Marxist guerrilla groups, the paramilitary squads,[3] and the government. If it had, all eighteen Spanish American countries would have been equally violent. I have written a series of books about how different presidents tried to end the endemic brutality. This book is the sixth book I've written on Colombian politics and the second of the series on attempts to end the violence, the first having been published in 1999 by The University of Alabama Press as *State Building and Conflict Resolution in Colombia, 1986–1994.* I began the third in 2004 when, thanks to a fellowship from the Fulbright program, I was able to spend two months in Bogotá studying the peace program of President Álvaro Uribe.

More specifically I began collecting information for this book from the very first conversations that representatives of Andrés Pastrana had with guerrilla groups, even before he was elected president. This was made possible by the miracle of Internet. While in the previous books I had made trips to Bogotá, not only to interview individuals, but also to collect very basic information from libraries and newspaper files, in 1998 I could read daily newspapers and homepages of the government, the guerrilla groups, and the paramilitary squads while in the United States. Hence, when I went to Colombia to work on this book in June 2003, the major purpose was to conduct interviews. During that trip I was able to interview eighteen people, with a nineteenth added by telephone after my return. During the 2004 trip, although my interviews were specifically about the Uribe government, two new interviewees added information about the Pastrana peace process. A new method, similar to having access to the Internet, has been the ability to communicate through email. A description of those individuals and the dates of the interviews are at the end of this book, noting not only the dates of face-to-face interviews but also of telephone calls and electronic correspondence.

I would like to thank many people who assisted in this study. Nothing I do would be possible without Dottie's support. Space does not allow me to mention all the others. Invaluable help came from chair Ann Mason and my colleagues in the Departamento de Ciencia Política of the Universidad de los Andes. They have been good colleagues on six occasions, always listening to my thoughts and suggesting other ideas, and equally important, they have been very good friends.

A singular *gracias* goes to my friend Fernando Cepeda Ulloa. Fernando was chair of *Ciencia Política* when I first arrived at the Universidad de los Andes in 1968. We have occasionally been colleagues and always students of Colombian politics and friends ever since. In 2003 he introduced me to the *Fundación Ideas para la Paz,* a foundation which had saved all of the peace process documents of the Pastrana presidency on computer. The *Fundación* allowed me to search through the documents and copied all that I wanted onto CDs. My footnotes in the chapters below demonstrate how valuable those documents were.

Also thanks to Ashley Kline whose combination of artistic and computer abilities gave order to the charts in chapters 3–8. Likewise my appreciation goes to good Colombian friends, Armando Borrero, Francisco Leal, and Julio Pérez. Debbie Posner was an excellent copyeditor. Her queries made this a better book.

Finally a word about the dedication. As I was nearing the end of the preparation of this book, my brother, Edward Alvin Kline, died unexpectedly. I find it hard to imagine two brothers, brought up by loving North Carolina parents, who were so different in so many ways. I played sports in my youth; he did not, probably because he was challenged by being almost deaf. I married a wonderful woman and we had children and grandchildren; he remained single, staying with our mother as she lived well into her nineties. I went to Latin America on trips; he went to bird shows all over the southeast of the United States.

He once gave me a plaque that says "It's nice to have a brother who cares." I know that he was right, because he did care. I'll always miss him.

¡Adiós, querido hermano!

Chronicle of a Failure Foretold

PART ONE
The Context for Failure

In this book I argue that the peace process of Colombian President Andrés Pastrana was doomed from the beginning. While many Colombian experts would place the blame for that failure on the Pastrana administration itself (with various arguments as I show in the following chapters) I believe that there was a more fundamental reason: that the Andean nation is made up of many political archipelagoes, in many of which the national government is not the strongest actor.

The Colombian government has never enforced laws in a large part of the country. The diverse topography of the country, with three ranges of the Andes as well as the Amazon rainforest and the Orinoco grasslands, led one study to conclude that it was the third most geographically challenged country in the world. In his excellent book, Eduardo Pizarro Leongómez reports that, "According to the Index of Geographical Fragmentation constructed by the Center for International Development of Harvard University, Colombia was in third place of the 155 nations studied."*

The economic implications of this are shown by Frank Safford, who besides the variations caused by the three ranges of the Andes, the Orinoco and Amazon basins, and the Caribbean and Pacific coasts, adds the complication of altitudes in the mountains:

> This means that most major regions of the country are capable of producing, at one altitude or another, virtually all of the crops that might be grown in any other major region. . . . The combination of mountainous terrain and tropical climate thus makes possible a good deal of *local* complementarity among economic niches at different altitudes. By the same token, however, these geographical features, until well into the twentieth

*Eduardo Pizarro Leongómez, *Una democracia asediada: Balance y perspectivas del conflicto armado en Colombia* (Bogotá: Grupo Editorial Norma, 2004), footnote 20, p. 307.

century, obstructed the development of much of a national market or even very vital regional ones.

Safford concludes, "Colombia's mountainous terrain and tropical climate combined to make the country, in the words of Luis Eduardo Nieto Arteta, a series of economic archipelagoes."**

For similar reasons there are political archipelagoes. Just as the Andes have various ecosystems, depending on altitude, rainfall, and other variables, and hence economic archipelagoes, Colombia has an assortment of regional political systems, with a variety of "disorganized organizations," including the guerrilla groups, the paramilitary squads, and the government itself. While there might be national FARC, ELN, and AUC organizations, their unity many times is more apparent than real. Decision-makers of the central government have never constructed a strong army or national police force. This, in turn, led to a tradition of private justice and a violent national history. Then the final element was added: Colombia became the leading drug-producing nation in the world. The accompanying money and firearms further weakened the state and strengthened private protection arrangements.

Within each region different groups accrue wealth in ways that would not be possible if Colombia were a peaceful country with a national constabulary force capable of enforcing laws. Some do it through the drug trade, others through selling their abilities to threaten or punish with violence. The two dimensions mix, with groups killing each other over drugs, with ideology perhaps playing a secondary role or possibly none at all. People are killed when harvesting coca simply because they are working for another group. When a guerrilla group demobilizes in an area, either through military defeat or through peace treaty, some of its members join paramilitary squads. On the face of it this seems paradoxical since they are going from a Marxist to a "right-wing" group, but they really are selling the only ability they have—to make violence—to another party.

In this book I argue that Andrés Pastrana failed in his efforts to bring peace to Colombia, not only because of the many errors that his government committed, but more basically because of the very complex political economy of the country. Colombia had never been effectively integrated economically, socially, or politically. While the transportation and communication advances of the

---

**Frank Safford, "Agrarian Systems and the State in Colombia," in *Agrarian Structure and Political Power: Landlord and Peasant in the Making of Latin America,* eds. Evelyne Huber and Frank Safford, 177 (Pittsburgh: University of Pittsburgh Press, 1995), citing Luis Eduardo Nieto Arteta, *El café en la sociedad colombiana* (Bogotá: Ediciones Soga al Cuello, 1971), 115.

twentieth century brought Colombians closer together, power bases that were regional in nature made a national peace process impossible.

I approach the work of analyzing an "announced failure" through three major parts. The first section includes two chapters to place the Pastrana government in context. In the first chapter I evaluate Colombian history before 1994, beginning with a description of Colombian political history before 1960, followed with a description of the origins of *Fuerzas armadas revolucionarias de Colombia* (FARC) and the *Ejército de liberación nacional* (ELN), as well as the "third player" (in addition to the government and the guerrilla groups)—the private justice groups or "paramilitary squads." The chapter concludes with description and analysis of two major peace processes, the first during the presidency of Belisario Betancur (1982–1986) and the second during the presidencies of Virgilio Barco (1986–1990) and César Gaviria (1990–1994).

In the second chapter I turn to the presidency of Ernesto Samper (1994–1998). Although for reasons analyzed in the chapter there were no formal peace negotiations, I analyze four actions that later affected the Pastrana presidency—some actions with the FARC, the beginning of conversations with the ELN, the growth and reorganization of paramilitary groups, and the change of the FARC strategy from guerrilla warfare to a war of movements. I also argue that the Colombian political system reached a low point in its integration, approaching the "partial collapse of the state" or a "failed state."

The second part of this book chronicles the Pastrana government's peace efforts with the two guerrilla groups. Chapters 3, 4, and 5 describe and analyze the negotiations with FARC, while chapters 6 and 7 do the same for the attempts to have negotiations (or perhaps "pre-negotiations") with the ELN. Within chapters 3, 4, and 6, in addition to description, I present lower level generalizations. Chapters 5 and 7 conclude with midrange generalizations for the two specific cases.

The final part of this book contains the conclusions. In chapter 9 I present higher level generalizations of two major kinds. The first type is comparative: why was the Pastrana process in Colombia a failure when peace processes in Nicaragua, El Salvador, and Guatemala were apparent successes? The second sort has to do with basic characteristics of the Colombian state, society, and nation that were the more fundamental causes of the failure of the Andrés Pastrana peace process.

Colombia before the Presidency of Andrés Pastrana

The Context for Failure

Every chief executive makes his or her decisions within the context of the history of the nation and at least to a certain degree is restrained by it. In this chapter I introduce a number of major themes that served as limitations on the Pastrana peacemaking process, including the political patterns of the first 138 years of Colombia's history, the emergence thereafter of guerrilla, paramilitary, and drug groups to constrain decision-makers, and the peace processes of presidents before Andrés Pastrana. I conclude the chapter with an analysis of the themes seen both before and during the Pastrana presidency.

Decisions Made (or Not Made) in the First 138 Years of National History (1820–1958)

Colombia began with a weak central state. Nothing was done for most of the first 138 years of independence to change that sense of weakness. As a result a number of "political archipelagoes" emerged, with different control systems.

Spanish and Portuguese colonies in the New World brought a governmental system that appeared to be centralized, but that functioned poorly. In theory, political authority in the Iberian colonial fragment came from the king. The Council of the Indies issued rules for the colony, which were carried out by viceroys, *audiencias* (judicial administrative areas) and *cabildos* (town councils), none of whom were selected democratically. What on paper was an efficient, centralized bureaucracy, in practice functioned under the policy, "I obey, but do not comply." This phrase, John Phelan argued, reflected a centralization of authority among the viceroys and governors that was more apparent than real.[1]

Studying what today is Ecuador, Phelan found that the coastal areas were never subjugated as intensively as the Sierra. In fact, many coastal areas remained unconquered until the nineteenth and twentieth centuries. Nor was the administration particularly centralized. Many administrative decisions were actually made in the Americas by several competing agencies; local conditions and local interest groups played a significant role.[2]

There are no comparable studies of colonial Nueva Granada (as Colombia was called until 1852); the Spanish crown might have had substantial authority in Bogotá (as it did in Quito) but that did not mean that it had authority in Medellín (any more than it did in Esmeraldas). David Bushnell argues, "This political disunity was to some extent inevitable. Certainly no part of Spanish America had so many natural obstacles to unity—so many obstacles to transportation and communication per square kilometer—as New Granada, with a population scattered in isolated clusters in various Andean ranges, not to mention other settlements along the coast."[3]

In Nueva Granada, the process of independence was regional, with Cartagena and Bogotá often going separate ways. If the fall of the Spanish crown led to the lack of a legitimate political regime, it also led to a more decentralized and weak state bureaucracy. *Patrias chicas* ("little fatherlands"—vast territories dominated by a local family) became stronger, as did individual large landholdings. Large numbers of landowners held power within their territories, in effect existing as private governments.

Three key clusters of decisions in the first years of the independent history of Colombia both reflected this decentralized power array and further produced a weak central state in the political regime.[4] Although no specific individuals can be given credit or assigned blame for these decisions, they were the seeds from which the failing state was to germinate.

The Legal System

The first set of decisions had to do with the nature of the legal system: the decision not to construct a strong law enforcement branch of government, since it might be a threat to civilian government (1830 to the present) was one. The decision to allow private groups to take the place of official law enforcement (from the landowners of the nineteenth century to the paramilitary groups called on to fight the guerrillas along with the military in the period from the late 1960s to the late 1990s) was another.

The government never attempted to construct a large police force that would allow it to enforce its decisions. Nor were the national armed forces or the police allowed to have much power. As former president Alfonso López Michelsen pointed out in 1991, private landowners in the nineteenth century made the rules for the areas of their landholdings, chose some of their employees to enforce them, and imprisoned workers who misbehaved. López argued that the country had made a trade-off. Unlike many other Latin American countries, violence did not originate from the government, but rather from the lack of government.[5] These decisions eventually resulted in powerful "self-defense" or "paramilitary" groups.

Although it is questionable whether a strong national police force was feasible in nineteenth-century Colombia, the basic reasons for this decision included the Colombian leaders' fear of the institutions of a strong state, especially the armed forces and the police. Many other Latin American countries had seen such institutions end elective governments. In addition, Colombian leaders, primarily from the upper economic groups, did not want to raise the taxes necessary to maintain a strong military and national police. Better to let those who needed a police force (i.e., the large landowners) do it themselves, and pay a sort of "users' fee." Not constructing a national police force left effective power in local hands, instead of delegating it to some distant national government.

The federalist period of nineteenth-century Colombia (1853–86) was one of even less central authority than the previous period. During this stage, law enforcement rights and duties reverted to the states, although most likely real legal power remained with the owners of large estates.

The Use of Violence in Politics

The second set of decisions had to do with the use of violence in politics, often in the name of party (from 1838 until at least 1965). It began when parties that lost elections took up arms to win power, almost always failing in that endeavor. The violence intensified when the Church became part of the partisan conflict, even though nearly all Colombians were Catholic. The Church sided with the Conservative Party, which favored the maintenance of its responsibilities for education and social programs, while the Liberals proposed that the government take over those responsibilities.

The consequences of using violence were made potentially less serious for individuals at certain times when partisan violence was amnestied (most recently in 1953 and 1958). It was also decided that, given the relatively closed nature of the political regime during the National Front (1958–74), even Marxist guerrilla violence was justified (late 1950s to the present) and might be amnestied.

As a result, political competition in Colombia was never limited to peaceful means. There were eight civil wars during the nineteenth century, six of which pitted all (or part) of one party against the other party. In the course of these civil wars, the peasant masses "participated" in national politics, and knew of the national political system. This participation did not mean that the masses had influence on the policies of the elites. Most of the mass participation was originally because of their affiliation with a large landowner, who instructed them when and against whom to fight. In those civil wars, thousands of *campesinos* (peasants) died.

The tradition continued into the twentieth century, with a short period of partisan violence in 1932 and then *La Violencia*. This period was so intense that Colombians refer to it as "La Violencia" (The Violence), even though the word in Spanish refers to *any* violence. It began in 1946, with the Conservative Party leaders initiating a campaign to eliminate Liberals. The Liberals reacted, leading to at least 200,000 deaths during the period which ended in about 1964. As a result of all this, Fabio Zambrano Pantoja interprets the history of his country as one in which "the *real people,* that is to say, the majority of the population, learned politics through the use of arms before they did through the exercise of the suffrage." Peasants learned to fight before they learned to vote, causing the exercise of politics to be conceptualized as a conflict before it was conceptualized as a place of concord. In this way, as Zambrano states it, most people were "applying the generalized idea that *war is the continuation of politics by other means.*"[6]

The frequency and intensity of violence in the nineteenth century had effects that lasted at least until the end of La Violencia. The numerous civil wars and the widespread participation in them of the campesinos led to a strict and intense partisan socialization of the masses. Many campesino families had "martyrs," family members who had been killed, disabled, or raped by members of the other political party. While original party identification of campesinos came from instructions of their patrons, at some point this identification developed a life of its own, based on the past. Eduardo Santa said that Colombians began to be born "with party identifications attached to their umbilical cords."[7]

As a result of this system of violence, other cleavages, such as social class and regionalism, became secondary to the primary party one. Third parties were notably unsuccessful until the early 1990s. Violence became the normal way to handle things. As a Colombian sociologist said in an interview for a previous book, "We have no ways to channel conflicts. Probably because of the traditional, oligarchic set up of the Liberal and Conservative parties, we never developed peaceful ways to resolve conflict. If we have disagreements we only think of violence as the way to solve them."[8]

The Elite Political Game

The final set of decisions had to do with the rules for the elite within Colombian democracy. While the members of the parties were allowed and even encouraged to take up arms against the members of the other party, the party leaders generally got along quite well with each other. They came from the same economic groups, belonged to the same exclusive social clubs, and at times entered into governing coalitions—most notably the National Front through which the two parties constitutionally shared power equally from 1958 to 1974.

There were twelve occasions between 1854 and 1949 when one political party at the elite level entered into a coalition with all or part of the other political party. These elite coalitions tended to take place when presidents assumed dictatorial powers, when party hegemonies shifted, and, especially in this century, when elite-instigated violence got out of control.[9]

The longest, most formal coalition was the National Front (1958–74). In a consociational agreement first proposed by leaders of the Liberal and Conservative parties but later approved in a national referendum and as a constitutional amendment, power was shared equally.[10] The presidency alternated between the two parties (no other was legal), while all legislative bodies were divided equally, as were executive cabinets at all levels, governors, mayors, and non-civil-service bureaucrats.

One might have expected the Colombian state to finally develop in a more modern way under the National Front, since the old party hatreds had been discarded. However, as Francisco Leal Buitrago argues, during the years of the National Front, Colombia lost that opportunity. Clientelism replaced sectarianism as the source of support for the political parties. While this change was important, "The long-lasting political weakness of the state was not significantly altered. The bureaucratization of the dual party system and the transformation of clientelism into the axis of the political system prevented the widening and modernization of the state from significantly increasing the extent of the state.[11]

Rather than building a state that would have been better prepared to deal with current and future problems, Colombian policymakers were subjected to what Barbara Geddes has called the "Politician's Dilemma."[12] Similar to politicians in other developing countries, when Colombian leaders had to choose between their need for political survival (clientelism) and longer-term interests in regime stability (building the state), they chose the former.

Background: Violence and the Origin of the Guerrilla Groups and Paramilitary Squads

While Marxist guerrilla groups emerged in most Latin American countries after Fidel Castro's 1959 victory in Cuba, the influence of Marxist revolutionary groups in the Colombian countryside goes back to the final years of La Violencia. After 1960 violence had different motivations, as Marxist revolutionary groups, paramilitary squads, and drug dealers used violent tactics. In the 1960s and 1970s, four main guerrilla groups were operating in Colombia: the Armed Forces of the Colombian Revolution (FARC), the Army of National Liberation (ELN), the Nineteenth of April Movement (M-19), and the Popular Army of Liberation (EPL). The latter two demobilized in 1990; the FARC and the ELN remain in combat today, sometimes collaborating but at other times fighting each other. The FARC, the largest, most militant, best-armed, and best-trained guerrilla group, had roughly 20,000 active combatants in 2003.

The Armed Forces of the Colombian Revolution (FARC)

In 1966, the Communist-dominated Armed Forces of the Colombian Revolution was founded, although Communist-oriented peasant defense groups predated it by more than fifteen years.[13] As early as 1949, the Communist Party urged the proletariat and others to defend themselves. In 1964 the Colombian military tried to wipe out the insurgents who became FARC, based in the area called Maquetalia. The government termed this an "independent republic" and President Guillermo León Valencia was quoted on more than one occasion as saying "Tomorrow we are going to capture 'Tirofijo' " (Manuel Marulanda Vélez, the FARC leader). At this writing Tirofijo still leads FARC.

Since its origins in the self-defense forces of campesino villages during La Violencia, the FARC has had close ties with the Communist Party and remains dominated by Marxists today. FARC strongholds have tended to be frontier regions neglected by the national government and plagued by general lawlessness. FARC has acted as a de facto state in such areas and also served as a gendarmery for squatters and peasants growing illicit crops. Tirofijo, FARC's septuagenarian leader, is a former Liberal campesino who took up arms in the 1940s and has been fighting the government ever since.

During the 1990s, popular support for the FARC diminished for several reasons. The fall of the Soviet Union brought an end to some of the FARC's financing, and made its Marxist ideology seem anachronistic. The FARC increasingly relied on protection rents from the cocaine and heroin sectors, and intensified its longstanding practices of kidnapping for ransom and extorting ranches and

tionally affected by disputes over land between landless campesinos and large landowners, especially ranchers. In the mid-1970s the guerrilla group began using kidnapping and extortion as a means of financing itself. In the late 1980s its most active fronts were in the banana-growing areas of Urabá.[15]

The M-19 appeared after the April 19, 1970, presidential elections, in which former General Gustavo Rojas Pinilla appeared to have won, only to have later government returns show that he had lost. It made its first public appearance in 1974 when it stole a sword that had belonged to Simón Bolívar. Its membership included dissidents expelled from the Communist Party and the FARC and others from the socialist wing of the *Alianza Nacional Popular* (ANAPO, National Popular Alliance) that Rojas had founded. They shared a belief in their struggle as a continuation of the crusade for freedom—a "second independence"—and a tendency to substitute audacious political-military feats for the patient work of building a movement.[16]

The M-19 was always somewhat of a romantic, Robin Hood–type movement. Originally an urban guerrilla group, the M-19 also participated in rural activities in Chocó and the Nariño-Putumayo areas in 1981. It began to be considered a serious urban guerrilla threat when it kidnapped and murdered the leader of a national labor federation in early 1976. It received international publicity when it tunneled into a Bogotá arsenal and stole arms in 1979, when it kidnapped all the guests (including the U.S. ambassador) during a cocktail party at the Dominican embassy in 1980, and when it kidnapped and executed a missionary from the United States in 1981. Its most audacious act came on November 6, 1985, when the M-19 seized the Palacio de Justicia on the Parque Bolívar in downtown Bogotá. The army reestablished control the following day, but only after the palace had been gutted by fire and more than 100 deaths had occurred, including the deaths of eleven of the twenty-four Supreme Court justices.

The EPL and M-19 both reached demobilization agreements with the government in 1990. Each became legal political parties, the M-19 became the Alianza Democrática M-19, while the majority of the EPL created a legal political movement called *Esperanza, Paz y Libertad* (Hope, Peace, and Liberty). Other members continued their guerrilla conflict.

Paramilitary Groups

Private justice began early in Colombian history; the country has been rife with paramilitary groups since its inception. In the nineteenth century they first appeared as large landowners established their own justice system on their lands. Private justice appeared in a different form in the twentieth century during La Violencia. The first self-defense groups to organize themselves then were businesses. These tactics financed the guerrillas' military expansion, but did not win them new sympathizers. In addition, the FARC faced greater pressure from paramilitary groups and the increasingly U.S.-fortified Colombian military. In response, the guerrillas grew more inclined to engage in actions that harmed civilians, such as using land mines and the notoriously inaccurate gas-cylinder bombs, hijacking commercial jets, assassinating elected officials, murdering peace activists, and attacking an upscale family recreation center in the heart of Bogotá. Despite losing whatever positive image the FARC had with the general public, the group continued to gain territory and combatants throughout the decade.

The Army of National Liberation (ELN)

The first guerrilla group to emerge, towards the end of La Violencia in 1962, was the pro-Castro *Ejército de liberación nacional* (ELN, Army of National Liberation). The ELN arose after a group of Colombian scholarship students went to Cuba at the height of the Cuban missile crisis in 1962. Some of the group asked for and obtained military training and began a series of discussions about a *foco* (focus) strategy for Colombia. The ELN was officially born on July 4, 1964, and was initially comprised primarily of university students.[14]

Originally based in Santander, for many years the ELN controlled large tracts of oil-rich lands in the eastern plains of the Orinoco river valley. In the early 1980s, the large sums that the ELN reportedly extorted from an oil pipeline construction operation allowed the guerrilla group, which had dwindled in size a that point, to rearm and expand its ranks dramatically. The coal and oil sector were lucrative targets for the ELN's kidnapping and extortion activities unt the mid-1990s, when the ELN lost territory to paramilitary challengers. Firm in the energy sector were more likely to pay protection money to security se vices with paramilitary links than be extorted by the ELN. Also, U.S. particip; tion in the Colombian conflict increasingly prioritized the energy sector, whic further placed the ELN on the defensive.

The EPL and M-19

Two other guerrilla groups later emerged. The first was the *Ejército popular Liberación* (EPL, Popular Liberation Army), a Maoist group which never gain signification strength. The second was the *Movimiento 19 de abril* (M-19, 1¢ of April Movement).

The EPL was founded in 1967 as an armed organization of the Maoist w of the Colombian Communist Party. In the 1960s and 1970 the EPL was es cially active in the Departamento de Santander, an area of the country tra the "peasant self-defense" groups in Tolima, with a concentration of a thousand families. In the 1950s, similar groups appeared in other places. Ironically, FARC originated in one such group.

After the end of La Violencia, in 1965, then-President Guillermo León Valencia issued Decree 3398 and in 1968, during the presidency of Carlos Lleras Restrepo, Law 48 was passed. Both the decree and the law gave legal status to paramilitary groups. The basic clause said that the government could use any citizen in activities to reestablish normalcy. In this way, the weak state could enlist the help of private groups to battle the guerrillas. The national army was to arm and train the private individuals, and close ties developed between many paramilitary groups and the military.

This was a crucial decision by the Colombian government. As Philip Mauceri states, "The state response to insurgent groups in Colombia can best be characterized as 'abdication and privatization,' a process in which state actors provide the legal framework, legitimacy, logistical support, and on occasion armaments to private societal actors in order to combat insurgents."[17]

This process was especially seen in the 1970s, when with the growth of the FARC and its progressive hostility toward the civilian population (especially ranchers and large farmers who could pay protection money), those with traditional political affiliations adopted the "self-defense" structure to repel the guerrilla attacks. Many of the self-defense groups arose "in response to the constant demands of the guerrillas because it was clear that the government could not guarantee to protect honor, life, and property across all the national territory."[18]

During the presidency of Virgilio Barco (1986–90), paramilitary groups experienced a dramatic change. Earlier the groups were comprised of individuals who produced legal agricultural products. However, as the drug lords became wealthy, they bought more land. While at first they bought land to become "gentleman farmers," later the land was used to grow coca. Soon, drug money began supporting paramilitary squads.

Two other important things occurred by the end of the Barco presidency. First, according to some sources, the number of deaths attributed to paramilitary group activity exceeded those from guerrilla activities. Second, the connection between the Colombian military and the paramilitary groups was officially ended. Nevertheless there is no doubt that the relationship continued to exist to a degree.

The presidency of César Gaviria (1990–94) was one in which many efforts were made, albeit most unsuccessful in the end, to limit violence in Colombia.[19] With a new policy for the drug dealers, his government made it very clear that paramilitary groups and drug dealers would be grouped with common delinquents for any judicial processes. They would not be given any political status, as the guerrilla groups had. The Gaviria policy change included the discretionary use of extradition (which really had no relevance at that time in the paramilitary case) and the reduction of sentences, which did affect the paramilitary groups, if they surrendered and confessed at least one crime.

Specifically the Gaviria government used the same decrees as it had with the drug dealers to encourage the surrender of members of the paramilitaries. As a result of this new policy the self-defense groups tried to clear up their image. They argued to the government that, having been the invention of military, they were then abandoned to their own luck after having lent enormous counterinsurgency services to the army. In one memorandum they demanded to be treated like the guerrillas, who were allowed to turn in their arms, demobilize, and enter into national political life. They assured the government that they had nothing to do with the *narcotraficantes* (drug traffickers) and, on the contrary, said that they were threatened by an alliance between Pablo Escobar and the ELN. This was yet another case in Colombia of various, conflicting statements being made, with no reliable way to reach a conclusion about their truthfulness.

Henry Pérez and Fidel Castaño were the two great leaders of the paramilitary groups in Colombia. The army of Castaño was operating in Córdoba; that of Pérez in the Magdalena Medio. In the Magdalena Medio, perhaps the most successful of the groups surrendered and turned in weapons in May 1992. Ariel Otero, who had become the leader of the Magdalena Medio paramilitary group after the death of Henry Pérez, made it clear that there had been no negotiation with the government.[20] Further, Otero was optimistic that the paramilitary group's war was over. Even if the conversations with guerrillas failed, "We definitely will not return to arms. That has no meaning. The only crazy people who remain in this country are those of the guerrilla coordinating group." They had demobilized because "we understood that war was not the best route to solve the country's problems. . . . The solution was not in the guns but at the political level."[21]

While there was perhaps progress during the Gaviria years in demobilizing paramilitary groups, this is not to suggest that all were demobilized or that all the weapons were turned in. Yet matters were to become more complicated during the following presidency because the Colombian government again began backing private groups, albeit with the hope that they would be more over the government's control than they had been in the previous period of legality. Further complicating the situation, the private paramilitary groups, especially those led by Carlos Castaño, formed a national organization.

The Drug Groups

The final ingredient in the Colombian political archipelagoes was added with the drug trade. Colombia began a major role in the international marijuana trade in the 1970s. However, it developed its key function in that industry when drug leaders from Medellín first decided to diversify to cocaine and then to initiate large shipments of the drug. As a result a new economic group grew up around the illicit drug industry. While later the cartels of Medellín and Cali became internationally known, as early as December 1981 the Colombian drug industry held a secret national convention, at which 223 drug-gang bosses created a paramilitary group called *Muerte a Secuestradores* (MAS, Death to Kidnappers). The drug lords pledged US$7.5 million to the squad, whose goal was to kill all kidnappers and to end the guerrilla practice of kidnapping people, including the "honest, hard-working drug gang bosses," for ransom.[22] During the late 1980s the Medellín group brought the nation to its knees through bombings in the major cities.

In the 1980s and 1990s there were three competing groups of drug traffickers: the Medellín cartel, the Cali cartel, and the Atlantic Coast cartel. During the Pastrana government there were dozens of trafficking organizations. Abundant evidence exists documenting the investment of drug earnings into legitimate businesses in Colombia (including a professional soccer team), politics, the military, and the police forces. Drug traffickers have used bribes and intimidation to corrupt individual Colombians of every rank. In a 1988 warning, they told a judge who was contemplating bringing Pablo Escobar to trial in connection with the assassination of a newspaper editor, that she should be "absolutely certain that in calling Mr. Escobar to trial you will remain without forebears or descendants in your genealogical tree."[23]

Drug traffickers murdered tens of thousands of Colombian judges, police officers, soldiers, journalists, and public functionaries. At times any Colombian who opposed the power of the traffickers, regardless of stature, was at risk. High-profile assassination victims include a justice minister, an attorney general, three presidential candidates, the publisher of one the nation's largest newspapers, and a beloved comedian.

In addition to their direct contribution to violence in Colombia, drug traffickers have played a key role in the rise of paramilitary violence. In the 1980s, newly rich drug traffickers purchased extensive ranches, often in areas with a guerrilla presence. The drug lords equipped and trained private armies to guard their assets and deter kidnapping or extortion by the guerrillas. The traffickers shared with other large landowners a deep hatred of not only the crimes of the guerrillas, but also their goal of massive land reform. Drug traffickers thus joined other elites in creating paramilitary groups in certain regions. Before long, some of the trafficker-created paramilitary groups became directly involved in drug trafficking, grew autonomous, and amassed great wealth and power. While it is true that drug traffickers sporadically seek accommodation with guerrilla groups, more frequently the two groups clash over turf, the division of profits, and the size of the share to be paid to campesino growers.

In August 1989, drug traffickers assassinated Senator Luis Carlos Galán, a dynamic reformer who was leading in the preference polls for the 1990 presidential election. Galán was an articulate advocate of stronger action against the *narcos,* as the narcotraficantes had come to be called. The day after Galán's murder, President Barco declared all-out war on the traffickers and received forceful U.S. backing. Key elements of the government offensive were to confiscate the property of suspected drug kingpins and extradite individuals under indictment in the United States. The drug dealers responded with a massive urban bombing campaign in Bogotá and Medellín. By the end of 1989, several mid-level narcos had been extradited and one of the leaders of the Medellín cartel, José Gonzalo Rodríguez Gacha, had been killed in a battle with government troops.

Based on the argument that Colombia could do little about the drug trade (an international matter) but had to deal with the drug terrorism, President Gaviria initiated a kind of plea-bargaining with traffickers that had little precedent in Colombia. Traffickers who surrendered and confessed to at least one crime received reduced sentences. Extradition was no longer possible. A Constituent Assembly rewrote the constitution in 1991 prohibiting it. Gaviria's policy brought the surrender of the three Ochoa brothers and Pablo Escobar of the Medellín group. The notorious Escobar, however, escaped after a little over a year in prison, and he evaded capture for fifteen months. When Escobar was killed by government troops in December 1993, it marked the end of the Medellín cartel, the most brazen, violent, and politically ambitious trafficking group. The leaders of the Cali cartel either surrendered or were captured during the Samper years.

The end of the Medellín and Cali cartels, however, did not mean the drug trade disappeared. Drug exports did not decline as new leaders and smaller groups replaced the dismantled ones and global demand for illegal drugs continued to rise. The U.S. Drug Enforcement Agency commented that the lower-profile groups were even tougher to combat than their predecessors. Considering that drug trafficking has produced at least six Colombian billionaires and some 160 millionaires, there will always be a large pool of would-be traffickers, no matter how many individuals the government might capture or kill. One potential source of change—a transformation of the prohibitionist approach—

is highly unlikely on the U.S. side, though Colombian elites have openly debated decriminalization. Finally, while direct contribution of drug trafficking to violence in Colombia may have declined by the Pastrana years, its role in undermining the rule of law remains a crucial problem.

The drug dealers' connection with a paramilitary group is far from the only interrelationship among the various armed actors. The government also had a relationship with the paramilitary groups, until the Barco years. In addition, guerrilla groups developed relationships with drug dealers, first by protecting their fields and factories, later by "taxing" them, and in some cases by entering the drug enterprise directly. Finally, there seems to be little doubt that drug groups entered into politics, not only in the national congress but by influencing the presidency, even before the years of Ernesto Samper.

The First Two Attempts to End Guerrilla Conflict through Negotiation

The Pastrana attempts to negotiate the end of guerrilla violence in Colombia were the third major effort. The first came during the presidency of Belisario Betancur (1982–86), and the second came in the later years of the administration of Virgilio Barco (1986–90) and the first years of César Gaviria (1990–94).

The Betancur Attempt

In the first six weeks after he became president on August 7, 1982, Belisario Betancur announced that he would name a Peace Commission. Law 35 of 1982 granted amnesty to all those in armed conflict with the government before November 20, with the exception of those who had committed non-combat-related homicides, those who had committed homicides including "cruelty," and those whose victims had been in a position of "inferior strength." Guerrillas already imprisoned for the pardoned crimes—whether indicted or convicted—would be released. In the first three months some four hundred guerrillas accepted the amnesty.[24]

The peace initiatives of Belisario Betancur were based on the assumption that guerrilla violence would be understood as the product of objective circumstances of poverty, injustice, and the lack of opportunities for political participation. As a result agreements were reached with three guerrillas groups, with the M-19, the FARC, and the ELN. In all cases there were truces, which were supposed to be followed by a National Dialogue. The Dialogue was never very well defined and none ever took place during the Betancur presidency.

After negotiations between the government and FARC in April 1984, the president announced an agreement which included a cease-fire for one year; the creation of a high-level commission to verify compliance with the agreement; the granting of a series of juridical, political, and social guarantees to facilitate the transition of the guerrilla forces back to civilian life; and a rehabilitation program for peasant areas affected by the violence. Similar truces were signed the following month with the M-19 and the EPL. By May 1984 only the ELN had not signed a truce.[25]

By the end of 1985 only the FARC truce continued. Leaders of the other two guerrilla groups accused the government of causing the break, while the government faulted the subversives. Casualties increased, culminating on the morning of November 6, 1985, when the M-19 seized the Palacio de Justicia on the Parque Bolívar in downtown Bogotá.

The FARC truce was still formally in place at the end of the Betancur government. However, hostilities had also resumed between that group and the government, and no national dialogues were begun.

The Barco and Gaviria Attempts

Surprisingly President Virgilio Barco announced no new peace initiative at his inauguration on August 7, 1986, despite continued violence as shown in a ministry of defense report on deaths occurring from the beginning of May 1985 to the end of April: guerrillas, 764; military, 384; and civilians, 670.[26] Indeed it was not until the last two years of the Barco government that changing circumstances led the government and several guerrilla groups to bargain. For the government the context had changed because the growth of paramilitary attacks gave such a negotiation higher priority. Several guerrilla groups also faced different conditions.

This was especially the case of the M-19 which was militarily weak, had less legitimacy after the Palacio de Justicia attack, had never had a coherent revolutionary ideology, and had suffered rapid leadership turnover.[27] In March 1989 the government and the M-19 signed the Declaration of Cauca, expressing their intentions to begin the process of the reintegration of the guerrilla group. Under the Declaration the subversive group would occupy an area in the mountains of Cauca, where they would be protected by the Colombian military. Five hundred soon arrived. "Working tables" would be set up immediately so that the two sides could arrive at agreements to bring the guerrilla group into the political process.[28]

On July 17, 1989, the M-19 and the government signed a pact that would lead to demobilization and disarming of the guerrillas over the following six months, during which time the working tables would continue.[29] Later there was difficulty in the process when the National Congress failed to pass a constitutional reform suggested by President Barco; however, in January 1990 a joint declaration of the government and the guerrilla group indicated that, although the disarmament and pardon would not be on the agreed-upon date, they would look for ways to make the peace formula viable.[30]

During the government of César Gaviria there were negotiations with the FARC and ELN, who had entered a coalition through a *Coordinadora guerrillera Simón Bolívar* (CGSB, Simon Bolivar Guerrilla Coordinator). Gaviria's views of the subversives were that the transformation in Eastern Europe had taken "all viability from guerrilla conflict" and converted many into common criminals.[31] Nonetheless representatives of the Colombian government met with members of the CGSB in Cravo Norte in the department of Arauca in May 1991; in Caracas, Venezuela, from June to November of 1991; and in Tlaxcala, Mexico, in March 1992.

Although in the last year of the Gaviria presidency there were some successes with small guerrilla groups, the peace process with the CGSB was a failure. The peace process, hence, was far from complete when César Gaviria was replaced with Ernesto Samper on August 7, 1994.

In my book on the peace process during the Barco and Gaviria years, I concluded that their peace processes were unsuccessful for five basic reasons:

1. Different ways of conceptualizing peace: while for the government "peace" meant the absence of armed conflict, for the guerrilla groups it meant a change in the basic structure of Colombian capitalism.
2. Belief on the part of some participants on each side that they could still win the war: some individuals on both sides thought there was little or no reason to negotiate since their side could still win militarily.
3. Economic strength of the guerrilla groups: especially in the case of FARC, the income from the cocaine trade made a continuation of the conflict desirable.
4. Lack of viable proposals from both sides: while the government could never convince the guerrillas to accept its peace proposal, the subversives did not seem to have any proposals of their own, only ideological slogans.
5. Lack of unity on both sides: each side had important splits, including between the civilians and the military on the government's side and within the FARC and the ELN.[32]

Rafael Pardo, former minister of defense during the Gaviria government and later a member of the Senate, in a more theoretical fashion analyzed two principal dimensions that the Colombian presidents combined differently in their respective presidencies. The first facet was whether there were preconditions for the bargaining. The second was with what bargaining dealt.

The first question was whether the insurgent groups were to enter a cease-fire as a precondition for other negotiations. Such was the case in the Betancur and Barco governments. It was successful for the demobilization of the M-19 towards the end of the Barco government and for the beginning of the process with the EPL, although that course of action did not end until the early days of the Gaviria administration.

In the Gaviria peace process there was no such precondition. Hence bargaining took place at the same time that armed conflict was going on, with all the difficulties that went along with that combination. Each side, from time to time, took military actions with the goal of increasing their power at the bargaining table. However, this carried the possibility that the side would go too far in such an attempt, leading either to a temporary suspension of the bargaining table (called "freezing" in the Colombian argot), or a definite suspension of the negotiations.

The second issue, Pardo argues, was that there were two different assumptions behind the bargaining—the "volunteerism" or "idealism" of the Betancourt process and the "political power" conceptual framework of Barco and Gaviria. The search of the Betancourt government for peace can been seen as a kind of act of contrition by an establishment that recognizes its errors, at least partially embraces the concerns of the insurgents, and clearly its willingness to make amends. As Pardo states it,

> The peace politics of the Betancur government were guided by good-will, the creation of mutual trust, and demonstration of a capability to agree on substantive issues. The state acknowledged past behaviors and undesirable conditions that fostered violence—such as inequality, injustice, and poverty—and made clear its desire to remedy the situation.[33]

The Barco and Gaviria governments operated from a different conceptual framework. They assumed that the conflict was about power; therefore they believed that the negotiations should be about power and not about the socioeconomic issues that might have caused the conflict.[34] Barco used that framework with the M-19 and the EPL, and Gaviria continued with the same framework during the first two years of the negotiations with the Coordinadora Guerrillera Simón Bolívar (CGSB). However, during the third year in Tlaxcala, Mexico, in 1992 there was an abortive attempt to discuss substantive issues.

Pardo analyzed the consequences of the philosophical differences of the two

Table 1.1: A Theoretical Comparison of Peace Processes in Colombia 1982–1994

| | CONCEPTUAL FRAMEWORK | |
	Idealism	**Power**
Context		
Demobilization	Betancur	Barco
Conflict	Pastrana	Gaviria

approaches. Under the first the government relinquished the defense of a series of beliefs in an attempt to get closer to the guerrillas' posture. Those included the legitimate use of force by the government and this led to more conflict between the president and the armed forces. As Pardo summarizes it,

> The difference between the two approaches is that one is based on demonstrating the government's ability to rectify, and the other is concerned with creating the conditions to negotiate about peace. One implies that is necessary to solve everything—or almost everything—before making peace; the other indicates that negotiation—and especially negotiation about political power—is the only necessary element to arrive at peace.[35]

The positions of the Colombian presidents on these two dimensions are shown in Table 1.1. "Context" indicates whether bargaining could take place with no changes from the guerrilla warfare (conflict) or alternatively if there should be preconditions such as a cease-fire or demobilization. As for the conceptual framework, the idealist position is that since peace can been seen as a kind of act of contrition by an establishment that recognizes its errors, at least partially embraces the concerns of the insurgents, and shows clearly its willingness to make amends, bargaining is to deal with matters of public policy, such as land reform, health care, and the like. The power position, on the other hand, is based on the assumption that the conflict was about power. Therefore, negotiations should be about power and not about the socioeconomic issues that might have caused the conflict.

Although chronological order might be violated, I have placed President Andrés Pastrana in this diagram also. As the table demonstrates, Pastrana was like Betancur in conceptual framework (idealism) but similar to Gaviria in context (conflict). In the chapters that follow, I show that although Pastrana's paradigm was different from those of his three predecessors, his peace process was analogous to theirs in its failure.

Table 1.2: The Themes of Colombian Government Negotiations with Guerrillas

THEME	DESCRIPTION
I	Lack of Unity
	a. Of the civilians in the government
	b. Between the president and the military
	c. Of the guerrillas
	d. Between the national and regional governments
	e. Of the paras
II	Lack of Government Continuity
	a. Elections every 4 years
	b. Change of negotiating team
III	The symbolic imperial presidency
	a. Opposition disloyal
	b. Place in history
	c. Inability to accept responsibility—"It wasn't us"
IV	The "Politician's Dilemma"
V	"The Devil Is in the Details"

Conclusion: Themes Constraining the Pastrana Peace Process

The framework for this study is less theoretical than that presented by Pardo. It is based on more than forty years of observing, visiting Colombia eleven times, and reading all available sources, both published and electronic. To a large degree the themes outlined in Table 1.2 come from the five previous books I have written on Colombian politics. I considered them to be important constraints on bargaining as I began this study, long before the outcomes of the Pastrana peace process were known.

Theme 1: Lack of Unity

In a casual conversation in Bogotá in the early 1980s a U.S. diplomat said to me something along the lines of, "The problem in this country is no one is unified. Not even the guerrillas are united." I place this first because of its importance and because it is one of the themes most often seen in this book. It applies to both the Colombian government and to each of the guerrilla groups and is based to a large degree on the various political archipelagoes that exist in the country.

In the case of the government, while there are differences among the civilians at the highest levels, the most important division has been between the civilian and military leadership groups. While Colombia has not had military coups d'état, officers have at times had strong influence on elected presidents, especially when it comes to matters of national security—including guerrilla groups. Yet as this study will show, the degree of military influence depends on a number of factors, including the prestige and skill of the president and the strength of the insurgent groups. As a Colombian sociologist interviewed for this study said, "During the Samper administration the military opposed a demilitarized zone. Samper was a weak president and needed the support of the military. Pastrana, on the other hand, had promised a demilitarized zone in the campaign and did not give the military time to oppose it."[36]

Between the two guerrilla groups, FARC has always been less unified than the ELN, despite purges in the 1990s to end the disunity and the fact that FARC has had the same leader since 1964. Divisions exist among the different parts of the country and according to the number of years in the guerrilla conflict. One source suggests that the most important difference among the FARC fronts is between those who operate in the previously populated areas and those that operate in the colonization areas.[37] In the latter the guerrilla groups established power before the government and later learned of the money to be made from the drug trade.

In the early 1990s the ELN was divided into three major groups, one of which was dominated by former Spanish priest Manuel Pérez and another that demobilized during the Gaviria presidency. The ELN has always tended to be more democratic than FARC, with meetings required for the organization to take positions.[38] As noted in chapter 2, following the death of Pérez in 1998 there was a leadership struggle that no doubt had effects on the unity of the group.

Finally there are the differences between the national government and the regional ones. Although a centralized country, Colombia introduced the election of mayors in the 1980s and the election of governors in the 1990s. It is at the regional and local level that the political archipelagoes are most evident with politicians from those areas with different power bases than the national president, hence at times likely to oppose (either overtly or covertly) what the chief executive is trying to do.

Theme 2: Lack of Government Continuity

A second theme seen in this book is the lack of government continuity. In one sense this has always affected Colombian governments, with a new president elected every four years. Most new presidents have new peace proposals and new negotiating teams. But the issue is more complex than that—during a given presidential tenure negotiating teams have often changed because of political maneuverings that have nothing to do with the peace process. Other things equal, this detracts from the negotiating power of the government and increases that of the guerrillas.

A related theme is the issue of time. The Pastrana government had a time limit of four years, while both guerrilla groups had existed since the 1960s. Once again, other things equal, this detracts from the power of the government and increases that of the guerrillas.

Theme 3: Symbolism and the Imperial Presidency

The third theme is based on both the centralization of the Colombian constitution of 1991 (although it was less centralized than the 1886 one) and on the symbols of the strong president. Colombia never had dictators with the arrogance of a Rafael Trujillo in the Dominican Republic (who changed the name of the oldest city in the Americas from Santo Domingo to Ciudad Trujillo) or a José Rodríguez de Gaspar of Paraguay, who declared himself the Supreme Dictator of the Republic, or simply "El Supremo"—"the Supreme One."

Nevertheless the elected president of Colombia is the symbolic head of the nation and many times this makes opposition to his policies difficult if not impossible. For example, in a January 2006 interview former National Prosecutor Alfonso Gómez Méndez stated that in Colombia there was little room for criticism of the president because of the personalization of issues. The former head of the judicial system said, "If one questions any policy of the president they say that he or she is an enemy."[39]

As a result a president often sees himself and is seen by his close followers as a messiah and often is concerned with his place in history. Indeed that perception might become overwhelming and lead to foolish or dangerous posturing and bad bargaining decisions. It also means that, no matter how diverse the regions of Colombia might be, negotiations must be centralized in the office of the presidency. Needless to say this leads to regional opposition to the president's policies.

Finally a subtheme applying especially to the president but also going beyond the chief executive is the inability to accept responsibility for failures. In the chapters below we will see numerous cases of what I call "It wasn't us" theme—that the fault must lie with the other side because clearly it was not ours. That subtheme is seen in both the government and each of the guerrilla groups.

Theme 4: The "Politician's Dilemma"

In any democracy, unfortunately, the gains of one's political party (or movement) are often more important than institution-building, including the peace process. In any political process, a chief executive is in a bargaining relationship with other actors, both civilian and military. While this might sound like repetition of Theme 1, how it goes one step farther is captured well by Barbara Geddes, who argues that presidents who face little competition in their parties and can count on party discipline in the legislature are able to use some of their resources to hire experts and build competent agencies, including those to negotiate peace treaties. On the other hand,

> Presidents who lack the weapon of party discipline . . . and who have had to make deals with and promises to rivals in order to secure nomination, may have to exchange most of their appointment resources for the support of political allies that they need to govern effectively. In brief, strong and secure presidents are more likely to pursue appointment strategies that contribute to the development of bureaucratic competence.[40]

There is no doubt that Colombian presidents in general and Samper in particular have lacked the weapon of party discipline and had to spend political capital to gain the support of their own party members.

Theme 5: "The Devil Is in the Details"

Colombian politicians are experts in high-sounding principles and vague documents. Yet a peace process, especially with guerrilla groups who have been fighting for nearly forty years, is a complex matter, both substantively and procedurally.

In the Guatemalan peace process fifteen agreements were signed to end the conflict.[41] This suggests that a lot of fine points must enter into the solution to a long conflict. However, as the chapters below will show, the Colombian peace process included only one substantive agreement—a prisoner exchange between the government and FARC in 2001. All the other agreements were about procedures to be followed in the later attempts to arrive at substantive agreements.

In the Colombian case even those procedural agreements had to be very specific, with details about dates and numbers. It is ironic that, in a country in which bureaucratic nitpicking is a fine art, time and time again even the procedural accords lacked details. This later led to difficulties in interpreting them.

While I considered the above themes to be the constraints on Andrés Pastrana when I began this study in 1998, of course I did not know that he would fail nor how the factors would interact. I sincerely hoped that he would succeed. However, as chapter 2 will show, Colombia came the closest to being a "failed state" during the presidency of Ernesto Samper. Thus, the challenges to Andrés Pastrana came not only from the violent history of his country in general, but from the deterioration of public order during the administration of his predecessor.

The Immediate Context for the Pastrana Negotiations

The Government of Ernesto Samper (1994–1998)

While this book is concerned with the peace process during the presidency of Andrés Pastrana, special note of the events during the previous presidency of Ernesto Samper should be included to make the historical context for the Pastrana peace efforts complete. To that end, in this chapter I will first discuss the Samper efforts (or lack thereof) in the case of peace processes with the FARC and the ELN. In addition, to place the efforts of Pastrana in the changing Colombian context, I will also describe the notable transformations of paramilitary groups between 1994 and 1998 and the FARC modification of strategy.

In addition, I discuss some of the theme introduced in chapter 1 during the Samper years. While I will mention Themes 2 (lack of governmental continuity) and 3 (symbolism and the imperial presidency), I will show that Theme 1 (lack of unity) was most important because of the opposition of the military to the demilitarized zone that both guerrilla groups desired, and which President Samper seemed willing to go along with in the case of the FARC.

The Difficulties of Negotiating during the Samper Years: The Cali Drug Money

Liberal Ernesto Samper won the second round of the presidential elections on June 19, 1994, over Conservative Andrés Pastrana. However, the victory was soon soured by the revelation of cassette recordings in which, during the electoral campaign, Cali drug leaders Gilberto and Miguel Rodríguez Orejuela talked about details of the possible contributions of the drug group to the Samper candidacy. In the tapes the name of Santiago Medina, Samper campaign manager, appeared three times. Samper immediately denied the accusations.[1]

Throughout his four-year presidency Samper governed under the shadow of that accusation. While he constantly denied the allegation and the lower house of Congress refused to impeach him on those grounds, Samper had to spend energy and time to defend himself throughout the four years. That left him less time for the other tasks of governing, including conducting peace negotiations with guerrilla groups. As one interviewee put it, "The Samper government was not able to do anything in the peace process simply because it was so concerned with protecting itself."[2] And a member of the Samper peace process team told me, "Samper spent most of his presidency trying to stay in power after the allegation that he had received drug money during his electoral campaign. There are some indications that efforts to build the state in other ways suffered because of this primary concern."[3]

By turning over original documents, campaign manager Medina demonstrated that the Samper campaign had functioned with two sets of books—one given to the *Consejo Electoral* (Electoral Council), the government body charged with overseeing elections, and another, not sent to the Consejo. This second set of books included contributions in dollars (in both checks and cash). Medina's testimony, the documents he turned over, and additional evidence gathered by the government from the Cali drug group, led many to the conclusion that the cassettes were authentic.[4]

After campaign finance director Fernando Botero Zea testified that he as well as Samper knew that money from the drug dealers was entering the campaign, National Prosecutor Alfonso Valdivieso indicted the president. In the indictment Valdivieso charged that Samper not only knew of the drug money, but also that he personally had verified that the contributions had been received. This was based on testimony from both Medina and Botero, as well as that of a third, anonymous witness.[5]

The president denied all these accusations. On the day that Medina was arrested Samper gave a six-minute speech on television, during which he said that if there had been drug money in his campaign, it was behind his back. "Conclusion: I am not guilty. I never agreed to anything with any cartel and I never knew of money coming from that source to my campaign. . . . I will put up with this as one of the costs that I have to pay while endeavoring to show to the world that we are not a narcodemocracy."[6]

Following the constitutional procedure, the indictment of the national prosecutor went to the lower house of the Congress, which was to decide whether or not to impeach the president. However, according to one source there were as many as 100 members of Congress who had received drug money. In addition, the previous year the Senate had passed a bill that would have had the result that accepting such money was *not* a crime. However, the lower house had not passed this bill and it had not become law.

In the end the lower house of Congress did not impeach Samper. He was able to complete his four-year term, but it was always under a shadow. This was perhaps best summarized by journalist María Jimena Duzán, when she wrote:

> Perhaps the most dramatic effect of the drug business can be seen in the decomposition and uncertainty that it has provoked on all social levels. For the nation's large middle class, including politicians, judges, soldiers, journalists, and police, drug money has inundated economic life with a flood of corruption, wiping out any semblance of a code of ethics or a value system. . . . This is a terrorized political class that has delivered itself to the designs and money of the drug dealers. Those who stand up to the bosses and challenge them have fallen victim, brave politicians such as Luis Carlos Galán, Carlos Pizarro, and Bernardo Jaramillo.[7]

Samper's Failure with FARC

Efforts to establish peace conversations with the FARC began very early in the Samper administration, although in the end there was no notable progress. There were three major reasons for this lack of progress. Most important was the opposition of the Colombian military to one thing that FARC considered a necessary first step: the establishment of a demilitarized zone in which the negotiations would take place especially since many officers believed that FARC could be defeated with arms—if only the civilian government would give the armed forces enough resource. Second, there was the less than completely legitimate nature of the Samper presidency, for the reasons outlined in the opening part of this chapter. Finally there was the importance of symbolism. It was one thing for FARC to control a remote area of Colombia, but quite a different one for the government to give it permission to be in charge of it.

The military's opposition was an absolute. As one interviewee put it, "I am 100 percent certain that the military leaders never wanted the demilitarized zone. I personally knew the top generals during the Samper years (and they were the same ones during the Pastrana government). They were completely, totally against the demilitarized zone."[8] As such, this is an indication of the first theme of lack of unity at the governmental level, mentioned in chapter 1—that the Colombian president negotiates with the military rather than commanding it.

In November 1994 High Commissioner for Peace Carlos Holmes Trujillo announced the parameters for the peace process with any guerrilla group. First, the government was prepared to negotiate without prior cease-fires. Second, it was going to be a more centralized process: only the president and the high commissioner would be coordinators of the process. Finally there would be time limits for the negotiations.[9] With respect to the FARC, Holmes said that he had found "an approximation to a proposal for a useful dialogue that might lead to a process of negotiation that should end in a peace treaty."[10]

The next news of possible peace talks with the FARC came in February 1995 when the press reported that the two sides were exchanging letters. The letters indicated that the process would take place within Colombia and would include people at the very highest levels.[11] The two sides were studying conditions, places, and optimal guarantees for the process. They had agreed to keep everything confidential, an agreement that FARC broke late in the month when it released three of these letters, a break of protocol that was questioned by the high commissioner. The first letter released was a letter from the government dated February 21, in which three sites for the first meeting were proposed.[12] Later news came from the high commissioner himself, first when he announced in the first week of April that the first meeting would be in La Uribe, Meta, center of FARC military operations until 1990[13] and second when he announced that there would be demilitarization of that municipality, as FARC had proposed.[14] However, the government soon added at that only the rural area of La Uribe would be demilitarized, as troops would remain in the municipal seat.[15]

After not hearing back from the FARC about this proposal for over a month, on June 22 the government gave the guerrilla group two weeks to accept the demilitarization of the rural parts of La Uribe. In its open letter to the FARC leaders, the government added "If the real desire for reconciliation of the ones in arms exists, let them show it in ways other than declarations so that the process can go forward. If not the immediate viability of the political solution to the armed conflict—that has cost so much blood to the country—is being put in doubt."[16]

However, if FARC was having difficulties in accepting this proposal, the government soon had their own in making it. The problems were of the Theme 1 (lack of unity) nature—the military did not agree with the idea of a demilitarized zone. In early July in a memorandum the high command of the armed forces (carefully not ignoring the prerogative of the president to lead a peace process) analyzed the risks of demilitarizing 7,000 square kilometers of national territory in "the hypothetical order of demilitarization of the territorial area of the municipality of La Uribe, Meta, and the concentration of troops in the municipal seat." Among other things the military leaders pointed out that the small extension of the municipal seat, with only eighty houses, as well as its location within an "extension zone of mountains," makes it an "easy target." Also mentioned were logistical problems of the troops, who would be isolated in an area surrounded by guerrilla troops.[17]

The following day, in a speech at a celebration of the sixtieth anniversary of the Naval School in Cartagena, President Samper replied to the memorandum: first by praising the armed forces, second by saying that he would not cede "even a centimeter to the violent ones," and third by underlining that, "Here, I give the commands."[18] In the following days it was emphasized that the memorandum in question was only a routine internal one, the kind the military prepared quite often.[19] Minister of Defense Fernando Botero Zea insisted that there never was a crisis with the military and that the memorandum only expressed "legitimate and valid anxieties" of the armed forces.[20]

However, this incident shows one key reason that Samper was not more successful in his peace process initiatives. In addition to the lack of time and psychological energy the president had available to dedicate to the peace process (because of his need to defend himself against charges of accepting money from the Cali drug group), he had to be concerned about the military more than other Colombian presidents. While it certainly was not tradition for the Colombian military to overthrow elected presidents (the only case in the twentieth century was the 1953 toppling of Laureano Gómez during La Violencia), the officers were under unusual pressure because of the drug allegations. Indeed in a casual conversation in April 1997, one major reported to me, "Every time I get on a bus, someone says to me: 'And you officers, when?' "[21] In this context it seems reasonable to accept the interpretation of the La Uribe request made by an official interviewed in the executive branch: "The President was inclined to grant the La Uribe demilitarization, but the military vetoed it."[22] A historian added, "The military didn't like Ernesto Samper because he would criticize them publicly. He would have been much better off if he had criticized the military privately and publicly praised them."[23]

The peace process suffered another setback in July 1995 when the high commissioner of peace was elected to be a member of the National Directory of the Liberal Party. Since he could not constitutionally hold both jobs at the same time, Holmes resigned as commissioner.[24] This is another indication of the relatively low priority of the peace process for the Samper government, as well as an indication of the issue raised in Theme 2: the lack of continuity of governmental negotiators.

The communiqués exchanged between government and FARC leaders continued about La Uribe, with the guerrilla group in August 1995 calling for the demilitarization of the entire municipality. This possibility, however, seemed even more unlikely, as the level of FARC violence was increasing in the country.[25]

Indeed nothing happened during the rest of 1995, making it necessary for the Samper government to use creative semantics at the beginning of the New Year when they stated that the peace plan was not closed but still in place. Despite the FARC military actions, Minister of Interior Horacio Serpa stated that "the interest of the executive branch is to insist in a policy of citizen conciliation."[26]

In March 1996 Costa Rica offered to be the place for FARC-Government dialogues, an offer that was accepted by both parties. However, those conversations never took place. In the months that followed, there was discussion of possibly having regional peace processes, possibly in the southern Nariño department, but the Samper government stated that this would be to have "dialogues" rather than negotiations.[27]

Nothing happened about possible negotiations until November 1997, when FARC proposed an even larger demilitarized zone, made up of five municipalities in the Meta and Caquetá departments (the ones later to be demobilized by President Pastrana). FARC proposed that the zone last 120 days so that the guerrilla group could meet with representatives of the three branches of government and with civil society.[28] Samper had received military resistance to the earlier idea of one of these municipalities, and he received the same—or even more—resistance for this request for five municipalities.[29]

In June 1998 the National Committee of Peace called on President Samper to demilitarize one of the municipalities to get the peace process going.[30] Although Samper indicated his willingness to set up such a zone "any where in the country" if FARC would agree to a "real dialogue," the military remained firmly opposed. Manuel José Bonnet, the commander of the armed forces, said that although he respected the decisions of the president about demilitarization, "The military has not been notified about this matter."[31] Retired General José Joaquín Matallana pointed out that these five municipalities—La Uribe, Mesetas, Vista Hermosa, La Macarena, and San Vicente del Caguán—had been the epicenter of intense fighting between FARC and the armed forces. However, "The presence of the state and of the armed forces has been minimal and has been limited to military bases in municipal seats." On the contrary, the general continued, FARC "knows this region well and the presence practically is theirs and not of the state and the armed forces."[32]

One might ask, then, if the presence of the military in the region had been so slight, why was there so much opposition to changing a de facto situation to a de jure one. I would suggest that there were three reasons—the same reasons mentioned before that explain why Samper made no progress with FARC: the feeling within the military that FARC could be defeated with arms; the less than completely legitimate nature of the Samper presidency; and that it was one thing for FARC to control a remote area of Colombia, but quite a different one for the government to give it permission to be in charge of it. This last showed the importance of symbolism (Theme III). It was one thing not to control an area of the country, but much more serious to admit it.

The Beginning of Talks with the ELN

From very early in its existence, it was clear that the Army of National Liberation considered "peace" to be much more than the end of the armed conflict. As in liberation theology, peace included ending the institutional violence of capitalism by ending hunger, illiteracy, lack of health care, absence of education, and dearth of job opportunities. ELN leader Manuel Pérez stated this clearly, when in 1996 the newspaper *El Tiempo* asked him what the goals of the guerrilla organization were. He replied, "To construct a more just, humane, and egalitarian society, in which there is no hunger and there is education, health, housing, work, and wellbeing for all. Capitalism does not give solutions for the majority."[33]

This position was shown in February 1995 when the *Comando Central* (COCE, Central Command) of the insurgent group sent a message to High Commissioner Carlos Holmes Trujillo, in which it rejected disarmament ("the revolutionary principle is that the arms are in the hands of the people") and called for a dialogue on six themes—unemployment, violation of human rights, oppression, lack of democracy, the concentration of wealth in a few hands, and "the exploitation of the workforce by an insensitive and insatiable minority with money and power."[34] Following a model the ELN had set up for a peace process in 1993, the COCE stated that for each theme the same process would be followed. First the guerrilla group would adopt a position. Then "each round of the negotiations would give the diverse social sectors associated with the theme would participate in the discussion."[35]

In May 1995 ELN leader Pérez rejected a Samper peace proposal, arguing that it decreased the possibility of dialogue and increased significantly that of war. This, Pérez argued, was because the military had become an autonomous agency. Although the president might have the willingness to negotiate, "Does he have the power to do so?"[36]

By mid-1995 the Samper government had received the ELN demand for a demilitarized zone, including a video in which Pérez called for "some areas of national territory" in which they would have "control that allows sustained and coordinated military operations."[37] The clear rejection of this demand was seen when Minister of Government Horacio Serpa stated that "It is impossible to demilitarize any economic region of the country and no region can exist to which the army and the police cannot go."[38] No doubt the military reaction to a zone for the ELN was similar to what it had been in the case of the FARC.

In 1996 the Colombian Catholic Church, in cooperation with the Church of Germany, began trying to get the ELN and the government to talk.[39] For its part, as early as February 1996 the ELN proposed a "National Convention." Writing from the "mountains of Colombia," the leadership of the rebel group began by mentioning the conditions that made such a convention necessary and went on to discuss what form the conference should take. The conditions were a political regime in as bad a shape as the bridges of the country and one that was destroying the country.

Accordingly, the ELN leadership called for five general characteristics of the convention. First, it would have to be an effort by all honest Colombians to find a real solution to the ridiculous situation of traditional politics. Second, it would be an end to a situation in which the powerful were subject to a different legal system than everyone else. Third, there had to be participation by "the true actors of the life of our mistreated Colombia," instead of the governing classes who have always made false promises and been subject to North American interference. Fourth, the governing class had lost its legitimacy through the violation of laws and hence a different solution was called for. Finally, "Accordingly, a solution not arranged by the traditional political structure [must be sought]."[40]

Turning even more specifically to the way for that solution, the ELN leaders proposed that the convention be set up to search for a credible solution to the political crisis, by defining new procedures leading to "the construction of a new government with ample participation." The principal task of the convention would be the establishment of a new legitimacy, "with democracy, social justice, and development." Represented in the convention would be all sectors of national opinion—social organizations, political groups, economic interest groups, the Church, intellectuals, the left, democrats, and patriots. This convention could be "in any place in our national territory" and would establish the framework for a new government "that would make a solution to the conflict possible." What remained, then, was the setting up of the mechanisms of communication among "all the sectors interested in resolving the current crisis of the country . . ."[41]

The ELN leadership had decided that it should not negotiate with the government, as it was too untrustworthy and corrupt. This was made clear by its commander Manuel Pérez in December 1997 when he wrote to a "First Days for Peace and Human Rights" meeting that was being held in Madrid, Spain. In that message he again proposed a National Convention. He first argued that violence was becoming worse in his country, "the conflict so frequent that almost daily one hears of massacres, peasant exoduses, with more than a million and a half affected . . ." And to him the cause was clear: "We do not believe that any of this violence is outside of the state, and for that reason was talk of terrorism of the state in Colombia, not only as a cause of the problems in which the country lives but also as a participant in the huge massacres by being united to paramilitarism, by being tied to drug trafficking . . ."[42]

For the ELN the last straw on the camel's back came when the courts approved the government-sponsored CONVIVIR (see below) and "recognized paramilitary groups legalized now by the government . . ." Therefore it was important for the participants in the meeting to realize "that we are not in favor of war, that we have not chosen war to defend ourselves from injustice: war was imposed on us as the only existing way to defend our rights." The ELN was for peace, but "a just peace, a peace that defends democracy and that defends personal rights."[43]

For that reason leader Pérez called for ". . . . a National Convention in Colombia, a great encounter of all Colombians, of all those who represent different social, economic, and political sectors." This convention would be directed towards the election of a constituent assembly. But unlike most such meetings that are chosen exclusively to write new constitutions, this one would also elect a new government. This was necessary because "the current one is completely corrupt, has alliances with the drug trade, and is sold to and kneels down to North Americans. We believe that a government like this has no authority or legitimacy, and for that reason the framework of the constituent assembly should be to elect a new government." But in addition to this, "A constituent assembly like this can be the scenario through which Colombians might find concord, coexistence, and a climate of social justice and of equal opportunities for all Colombians." The ELN leader continued to suggest other paths towards peace—a "humanization" of the war, approval of international humanitarian law, and respect for civilians.[44]

In February 1998 the government and the ELN signed the "Preagreement of Viana," named for the palace in Spain in which the meeting took place. In its first point the preagreement called for the convocation of "A National Convention for Peace, Democracy, and Social Justice." A preparatory meeting would be held in June 1998, in which both the government and the ELN would have three delegates, as would the *Comisión de Conciliación Nacional* (CCN, National Conciliation Commission). The Comisión was founded by the Bishops' Conference in August 1995 and had as its fundamental objective "to find a negotiated political solution to the armed conflict in Colombia."[45]

At this preparatory meeting the basic elements of the National Convention would be determined, including the following:

1. The definition of the bases for the transformation of the social and political structures through a coordinated action that takes into account, among other things, the full exercise of human rights, social and economic justice, the definition of the role of the armed forces in a peaceful country, and sovereignty, integration, and internationalization.
2. The definition of the membership of the National Convention, to be no more than 100 members representative of economic, political, and social forces.
3. Date and location of the National Convention, which should be after the second round of the 1998 presidential election.

Spain, Mexico, Costa Rica, and Venezuela would be the accompanying nations.[46]

In March 1998 a meeting took place between the Samper government and ELN leaders jailed in Itagüí, near Medellín. The National Government responded to a communiqué sent by ELN in which they reaffirmed their support for the Pre-Agreement for Peace Document signed in the Viana Palace. The government communiqué, signed by Presidential Commissioner for Peace José Noé Ríos and High Commissioner for Peace Daniel García-Peña,[47] indicated that throughout the talks, topics such as demobilization and disarmament for the so-called reincorporation processes were not discussed at all. The government stated that the difficulties inherent to complex processes such as this should not hinder the normal development of the Pre-Agreement Document, in whose full compliance the government reiterated its political commitment. From the jail in Itagüí, the ELN spokesperson Francisco Galán read a letter from the organization's Central Command in which they indicated that "the proposed National Convention will allow Colombians to make a new 'social contract.'" Likewise, the organization's letter highlighted that "within what was discussed, diverse mechanisms for dialogue between the insurgency and the Nation were analyzed . . . from which a working document remains, proposing a preparatory meeting for the National Convention." The guerrilla organization also added that "topics like demobilization and disarmament for the so-called reincorporation processes were never discussed, as has been affirmed by some media." Finally, the ELN letter indicated that misrepresentations by the press regarding the previous point, made the normal course of discussion, up to the moment in the Pre-Agreement, rather difficult.[48]

At about the same time the Central Committee of the ELN issued a public communiqué, announcing their breaking of the Viana preagreement. While maintaining that the insurgent group still favored a peace process along the lines of the preagreement (which had been confidential so that it would not be used for political gain), they declared, "Today the steps taken in Spain are being used for political advantages and the ELN cannot lend itself to the electoral proselytism of all the presidential candidates." The communiqué ended with a declaration that the guerrilla leadership remained committed to the idea of a national convention.[49]

Although this first attempt had ended quickly, this process with the ELN was so different from the FARC ones during the Samper years (and were to continue to be so during the Pastrana ones) that analysis at this point is justified. The first contrast was that the bilateral talks that began in July 1998 were between the ELN and "civil society" (never clearly defined).

The second contrast was that the talks were not initiated by the president directly. Rather it was facilitated by the National Council of Peace. The Council had been established in 1998 and was set up so that "all the organs of the state and the forms of organization, action, and expression of civil society could collaborate in a coordinated and harmonious [way], in a way that transcends presidential terms and expresses the national complexity." It was composed of government members, including the president, the high commissioner for peace, the ministers of interior, national defense, justice, and treasury, the director of the national planning office, three representatives of each house of congress, the general procurator, the defender of the people, and others who might be added for particular meetings. It also had members of civil society including one chosen by the Roman Catholic Bishops' Conference, one elected by other religions, two chosen by labor federations, two from commerce, two from industrial businesses, two from peasant organizations; one from indigenous organizations, one from black organizations, one from retired military officers, one from women's groups; two from peace NGOs, two from human rights NGOs, two from universities, one from demobilized guerrilla organizations, one from organizations of displaced people, one from organizations protecting children, and one from the solidarity sector of the economy. However, other members could be added "when it seems wise." The law said that the Council should meet at least every two months, although the president could convoke it more frequently.[50] In fact the Council did not meet this frequently during the Samper presidency; further, as is often the case in Colombia, Pastrana called its meetings even less often because it was an organization identified with his predecessor.[51]

The ELN had decided on a peace process that would have a national convention, "a dialogue with diverse sectors of society on structuring a more permanent and coherent policy that might find solutions to the country's crisis." The insurgent group believed that the country's structural problems came from "the unjust and antidemocratic economic, social, and political organization, made graver by the terrible disorder generated by the bad governments throughout the entire history of the country." For these reasons, they believed that the very foundations of the society needed to be restructured, including foundations such as social justice, democracy, equality before the law, equal opportunities, liberty, solidarity, and tolerance.[52]

For that purpose the ELN proposed a National Convention, "a deciding stage that will allow all Colombians to think about the seriousness of the crisis in which Colombia lives and based on that thought to understand what the structural problems are from which the country suffers." The Convention would have to listen "above all to the national majorities that historically have been excluded from great decisions." However, it was not intended that the National Convention arrive at agreements on how to change Colombia but "rather it is to get us to agree on what are the structural problems that have caused the national crisis, and also to identify what transformations have to be made to make possible the Colombia we want." The conclusions reached in the National Convention would be important considerations in the eventual dialogues that the ELN and the government had, but it would demand that the ELN change. However, it would identify how "we all should change."[53]

The National Convention then would reach a "National Agreement" that would allow the country to find ways to change in the desired way. The Agreement would also convoke a National Constituent Assembly, as well as defining its objectives, membership, and way that the nation would participate in it.[54]

Several conclusions from this ELN paradigm should be made. First, there was little reference to the government, as it was seen as corrupt and serving the economic elite. Hence, second, it was necessary that the Colombian state be represented in some other way, although the document constructed several years after the process began by the Central Command says nothing about this mechanism.

Given all of the above, it is not surprising that the second agreement in the process was not between the guerrilla group and the government but between the ELN and "civil society." This agreement was a procedural one called the "Agreement of the Heaven's Gate" signed in Mainz, Germany. In this agreement the two sides agreed to start a peace process, to investigate and propose themes that seek "structural or partial" changes in the life of the nation; and "to endeavor that Civil Society facilitate and encounter spaces with the Government in order to demand the fulfillment of the political guarantees and citizen liberties guaranteed by the Constitution in any part of the country." On its part the ELN agreed to stop depriving people of their liberty for economic gains (to the extent that other methods of financing the group were found); to demand that violations of international humanitarian law—such as massacres, genocides, tortures, and disappearances—be punished; and to follow the guidelines that Amnesty International had established to humanize the conflict.[55]

Both sides agreed to support the National Convention. In it they would discuss the problem of national sovereignty over natural resources, including petroleum, in order to propose changes; would seek social transformations, with the goal of democratizing the state and society; and would consider structural changes that were needed, including the possibility of a constituent assembly. This National Convention would begin by October 12, 1998, and would be held in Colombia "in an area in which there is a bilateral cease-fire and in which the necessary guarantees would be given to all the participants."[56]

The signers of this document included politicians, clergy, representatives of NGOs, university professors, and business leaders, among others. There was no clear indication of how these "civil society" representatives were chosen. The diverse backgrounds of the Heaven's Gate signers could be summarized as follows: peace organizations (7), business groups (6), political party representatives (5), universities (5), government representatives (4), newspapers (4), ELN (3), the Church (2), labor (2), demobilized guerrilla (1). Who decided which kinds of organizations should be represented in what proportions and who the individuals should be is not clear. Two interviewees agreed that the ELN made this decision, although one thought that perhaps the Church assisted also.[57]

While all this was going on, the leadership of the ELN was keeping a secret: on February 14 leader Manuel Pérez Martínez had died from hepatitis. Born in Spain, Pérez had been the political leader of the ELN since 1973 and had played a key role in the organization's development. Known as "*el Cura* Pérez," ("Father Pérez" or "Pérez the priest") he had come to Colombia in the 1960s after becoming inspired by Castro's revolution in Cuba. Under his leadership the ELN grew from about 100 fighters to over 5,000.[58] Nicolás Rodríguez Bautista ("Gabino") became head of the insurgent group.[59] With the death of its longtime leader, this group, which valued participation (even when Pérez was still living, all decisions had to be debated and voted on), entered a period of uncertainty. The Samper government reached no additional agreements with the ELN.

The Paramilitary Groups

While perhaps there had been progress during the presidency of César Gaviria (1990–94) in demobilizing paramilitary groups, not all were demobilized and not all the weapons were turned in. Perhaps most important, the conditions that led to paramilitary groups (most notably the inability of the government to protect people from the guerrillas) had not changed. Yet matters were to become more complicated during the Samper presidency for two reasons. First, the Colombian government again began backing private groups, albeit with the hope that they would be more under the government's control than they had been in the previous period of legality. Secondly the private paramilitary groups, especially those led by Carlos Castaño, formed a national organization.

The Government Direct Role through CONVIVIR

The role of paramilitary groups was somewhat legitimized on December 13, 1994, when President Ernesto Samper initiated a new program called *Cooperativas Comunitarias de Vigilancia Rural* (Communitarian Cooperatives of Rural Vigilance, CONVIVIR). This program allowed civilians to set up CONVIVIR units with the intention of providing government troops with intelligence in their regions.[60] Horacio Serpa, the minister of the interior, stated to the national senate that the government had established CONVIVIR "so that citizens can cooperate with the armed forces, with the goal of offering Colombians greater margins of security, especially in rural areas." The stated objective was "informing the army about suspicious people and giving the authorities an invaluable source in an opportune manner about situations of public order."[61]

Some human rights organizations were to argue that CONVIVIR turned out to be quite different. Although the national CONVIVIR president stated that "CONVIVIR units are usually unarmed and armed in exceptional cases," human rights groups concluded that the opposite was more likely the case.[62] Among the accusations made were the following: that CONVIVIR units worked with illegal paramilitary groups; that they were given sophisticated weapons, such as machine guns; that they were given a role that only the government had legitimately—the use of force; and that there were cases of "private justice" carried out by CONVIVIR.[63]

Whether intentionally or not, the model on which CONVIVIR was based was the *Autodefensas Campesinas de Córdoba y Urabá* (Peasant Self-Defense Groups of Córdoba and Urabá), led by Carlos Castaño, in which 950 ranches were in permanent contact through a communications network. According to one Colombian scholar, this was the model through which the military wanted to construct a national network in order to carry out a "total war" against subversive groups.[64]

By November 1997 there were 414 CONVIVIR units in the country. At that time the Samper government dropped the name, dividing the units into "Special Services" and "Communal Services," 210 falling into the former category and 204 into the latter.[65] One reason for this reorganization was that the Constitutional Court was considering the constitutionality of the CONVIVIR organization. The Court later ruled that the organization could continue to exist, but that it would have to return sophisticated weapons to the government, keeping only "personal defense weapons," such as pistols.[66] Later in the same month newspapers reported that groups from all over Colombia were turning in weapons such as submachine and machine guns.

In July 1998, the month before Andrés Pastrana became president, the head of CONVIVIR Carlos Alberto Díaz announced that the number of organizations would be reduced by 70 percent, with the dismantling of 289 of the 414 associations. As CONVIVIR Díaz stated, "With this decision we are saying to the government of Andrés Pastrana that he can count on our help, with our unconditional support. We are notifying him that he can count on us to construct spaces of peace."[67]

Carlos Castaño and Paramilitary Groups

The second major change in paramilitary groups during the Samper presidency came when *Autodefensas Unidas de Colombia* (AUC, United Self-Defense Groups of Colombia) were organized nationally for the first time. To understand this properly, one needs to depart from chronological order and consider the biography of Carlos Castaño.

Although there were some variations, the story of Carlos Castaño began in a way not unlike that of many Colombians. He was the high-school-dropout son of farmer Jesús Castaño, and was reared on a 440-acre area of wild farmland in rural Antioquia. Jesús struggled to feed his family of twelve children, but in 1981 he was kidnapped by the FARC, who asked for a ransom of US $7,500. Led by the eldest son, Fidel, the family raised half of that amount by mortgaging the farm. However, FARC did not release Jesús after receiving that amount, instead leaving his body chained to a tree. Fidel and Carlos turned to the Colombian military for help. At that time the military was training paramilitary groups, and they trained the brothers. As Carlos was later to state it, "We invoked justice, we trusted justice, but it did not respond; we felt that we could take justice in our own hands. I'm not ashamed to say that it was for vengeance."[68]

Soon thereafter Fidel formed a group called "Los Tangueros" (named for a local bird), which was to become one of the most notorious death squads in that part of Colombia, being charged with 150 murders in the late 1980s and the early 1990s. The brothers developed ties with Pablo Escobar and the Medellín cartel in the early 1990s, and Carlos received military training from foreign mercenaries hired by the drug lords.[69] In 1994 Fidel disappeared and, although his body was never recovered, he apparently was killed while on an arms-purchasing mission. At about the same time Castaño changed the name of the paramilitary group to *Autodefensas Campesinas de Córdoba y Urabá* (ACCU, Peasant Self-Defense Forces of Córdoba and Urabá). It became the largest of the paramilitary groups.[70]

Hernán Gómez, an AUC leader, discussed the founding of the AUC in an interview in the Castaño book, stating that until 1997, "small armies" of self-defense groups existed throughout Colombia, including in Córdoba and Urabá (the Castaño brothers), in Puerto Boyacá in the Medio Magdalena, the Eastern Plains, Santander, Valle de Cauca, Cundinamarca, Guajira, Antioquia, Putumayo, and Caquetá. According to Gómez, "All these armed groups were outside of the law and were anti-subversive, but their forces were directed only to the defense of their interests. Put another way, they were security guards for farmers and merchants."[71]

In 1995 Carlos Castaño began the work of convincing each one of these solitary units of the necessity of a union, with one commander, one insignia, one uniform, and one policy. At the beginning the acceptance of one policy was not essential. The Santander group, for example, accepted all but the policy, but committed abuses that were against the guidelines. As Gómez stated simply, "Castaño did not think twice. He killed the Santander leader and appointed another one."[72]

In this way the ACCU of Castaño became the model in both political and military structure. It began with about 3,000 troops, but soon was to grow. According to Gómez, it was the first time in the history of the Americas that a nationwide organization was built, an antiguerrilla organization, in which neither the government, nor the upper class, nor the multinationals participated. Castaño debated over the name to be given the group, finally deciding on Autodefensas Unidas de Colombia (United Self-Defense Groups of Colombia). He said, "What I want to know of each one of the self-defense groups is whether they are really anti-subversive. If a group is not, it isn't. Let no bandit say that he has a self-defense group. No sir! In Colombia there is only one anti-subversive, civilian self-defense group—the AUC."[73]

While Castaño had begun his efforts in 1995, the AUC was founded on April 18, 1997. It was to prove that it was not a paramilitary group organized by the government, but rather an independent group. It was based on success, as in the fighting in Córdoba and Urabá among the ACCU, the guerrillas (both ELN and FARC), and the Colombian Armed Forces. More people died in this struggle than in all the Central American civil wars.[74]

Later Castaño had to make a difficult decision about whether the AUC would participate in the drug trade. Although he was not inclined to at first, he finally decided if the AUC did not control the drug-producing and trade areas, it would not win the war.[75]

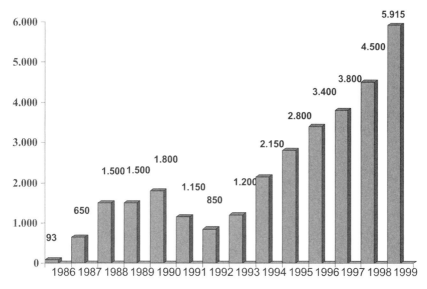

Figure 2.1. Growth of Paramilitary Membership, 1986–1999. Dirección de Inteligencia E.J.C. (Folleto Evolución y Composición Grupos Terroristas), June 2000.

Figure 2.1 shows the growth of the paramilitary groups, according to the Colombian ministry of defense. It indicates that the total number of paramilitary troops increased from 2,150 to 4,500 during the Samper years. While one might doubt the accuracy of these figures, the suggestion that the paramilitary armies doubled in size in those four years appears to be justified.

The Final Samper Challenge: The FARC Change of Strategy

The final difficulty of the presidency of Ernesto Samper came about because FARC decided to change its strategy. No longer would it follow the "prolonged war" guerrilla strategy of ambushes, economic sabotage, and kidnapping. Rather it decided to begin a "guerra de movimientos" ("war of movements"), a tactic that included attacks on medium-sized towns and military bases. Che Guevara defined it as: "After a point of equilibrium, where both enemies respect among themselves, the guerrilla acquires new characteristics in the course of its development. The concept of maneuver; big columns that attack strong areas; war of movements with translation of forces and means of attack of relative potency."[76]

At its Eighth National Conference in 1993 FARC decided to construct a guerrilla army capable of defeating the armed forces in places of clear, strategic

Table 2-1: Colombian military casualties from "The New Way to Operate" of FARC, 1996–1998

Date	Place	Casualties
April 15, 1996	Puerres, Nariño	Deaths, 31
August 30–September 1, 1996	Las Delicias	Deaths, 54 wounded, 17 captured, 60
July 9, 1996	La Carpa en San José de Guaviare	Deaths, 30
December 21, 1997	Pastascoy, Nariño	Deaths, 8 captured, 18
March 3, 1998	El Billar, Caquetá	Deaths, 62 captured, 43
August 5, 1998	Miraflores, Guaviare	Deaths, 30 captured, 100 wounded, 50
November 1998	Mitú, Vaupés	Attack on departmental capital

Fuente: Fuerzas militares para la guerra: La agenda pendiente de la reforma militar (Bogotá: Fundación Seguridad y Democracia, 2003, pp. 21–25).

value. To that end, "blocks" of FARC fronts were created and regional commands were strengthened. Likewise, FARC repeated its goal of urbanizing the conflict through its "Bolivarian militias"; finally FARC announced a platform of ten social and political reforms that would have to be taken to form a "government of national reconciliation and reconstruction."[77]

This change of FARC strategy became dramatically apparent by 1996. The major attacks from April 1996 to November 1998 are shown in Table 2.1. The defeats of the Colombian military were more dramatic than the numbers indicate. The El Billar attack was important because it was against an elite group of soldiers with counterinsurgency training. The army was not capable of detecting or preventing the mobilization of nearly 800 guerrilla fighters. The Miraflores attack was only four days before the inauguration of Andrés Pastrana and came after he had begun discussions with FARC leaders about peace talks. The Mitú attack showed that FARC was even capable of capturing a departmental capital, even if it was one of the smallest and most remote.[78] Clearly the Samper years, with FARC at its zenith and the Colombian military at its all-time low, was hardly a promising time for negotiations.

Yet in retrospect, this "war of movements" might have been a mistake on the part of FARC. As a Colombian sociologist who had talked to FARC leaders told me, "FARC people tell me that the 1996 decision to begin attacks on military bases was a mistake. To do this they had to mobilize members of their urban militias. That left a vacuum that was filled by the paramilitary groups."[79]

Conclusions: Colombia at the End of the Samper Presidency

There are three conclusions of this chapter. The first is that there was no progress during the Samper presidency in negotiating peace with the guerrilla groups. The second is that, largely because of the paramilitary growth in both numbers and organization, Colombia was in worse shape in 1998 than it had been in 1994. The final conclusion is that FARC was at its strongest point.

As for the lack of progress, in addition to the shadow of drug money, a Colombian historian added the following:

> In the Samper presidency there was utter confusion. Things were simply not attended to. Initiatives that had been begun under Gaviria (and were proving to be beneficial) were simply dropped. For example, it took the government over four months to name a new peace commissioner for Medellín and when he was named, he seemed more interested in honoraria, bodyguards, and number of cars at his disposal than in bringing peace to the city.[80]

The question of the Colombian military must be added to the causes of the multifaceted Samper failure—no progress in negotiations with the guerrillas, growth of paramilitary groups, and the new FARC military strategy. Never before or after did the military, most often covertly but occasionally openly, oppose the decisions of their commander in chief. As suggested above, Samper was constantly defending himself against the charges that he had knowingly accepted drug money for his campaign. As a result there was a greater threat of a military coup d'état than there had been since the most recent one in 1953. The military officers were opposed to a demilitarized zone for FARC, but that was one of the preconditions that the guerrilla group had for negotiations. So if Samper had agreed to a demilitarized zone, that would have increased the probability that he would have been overthrown by the military.

As for the conditions in Colombia, the situation that Andrés Pastrana inherited when he became president on August 7, 1998 can be summarized by two analyses of the country at that time. The first was from Danielle Mitterrand, widow of French president Francois Mitterrand. The second was by Juan Manuel Santos, member of the most recent generation of a family who held high posts in the Liberal Party and the Colombian government, as well as being owners of the leading newspaper, *El Tiempo*.

The French observer saw many problems for the new president. After arguing that the system of law had disappeared in Colombia, being replaced with systematic threats, massacres, the "faceless justice system," military power, and assaults on civil society, she continued that it was fundamental to reconstruct the state. This was necessary to stop the abuses and to make progress in any process to negotiate a peaceful solution to the oldest and most violent armed conflict in Latin America.[81]

Santos described the Colombia that President Pastrana would govern in the following way:

> Few times in this century has a president seen himself confronted with such complex problems and challenges. He receives a destroyed country that is going to need a lot of aid to begin its reconstruction, in the material and spiritual as well as the institutional. The most recent proof of the complexity of the crisis in which we find ourselves was the interview of General Bonnet in the daily *El País* of Madrid. He said—no more or less— that the Colombian state is not capable of guaranteeing the security of its citizens. The really extraordinary thing is that such a statement made by the Commander General of the military has been practically unnoticed by Colombians.[82]

The government of Andrés Pastrana spent the next four years in an unsuccessful attempt to end the guerrilla violence. The subject of the next six chapters is how and why the peace president failed.

PART TWO

The Negotiations between the Government and the Guerrilla Groups

In the next six chapters I turn to the negotiations between the government of Andrés Pastrana and the guerrilla groups. Chapters 3 through 6 deal with the FARC case, while 7 and 8 have to do with the ELN. In addition to descriptions, the chapters include low-level generalizations and references to the five themes introduced in chapter 1. Higher level generalizations are reserved for chapter 9.

The FARC Negotiations

From January 1999 until February 2002 the Armed Forces of the Colombian Revolution and the government of Andrés Pastrana held a series of meetings. The government did not insist that FARC enter into a cease-fire before the process began; instead the cease-fire was one of the matters to be negotiated. To encourage FARC negotiations, the Pastrana government granted a demilitarized zone to the guerrilla group, an area of 16,000 square miles and pledged that the insurgents would have complete control of the area during the dialogues. That promise was honored.

In chapters 3 through 6, I analyze this most dramatic peace process of any Colombian president. Chapter 3 considers the initiation of conversations before Andrés Pastrana became president and ends with the beginning of dialogues in January 1999. Chapter 4 deals with the first phase of the negotiations, from January 1999 to January 2001. The chapter ends at that point because there was the first real possibility of the talks ending. Chapter 5 considers the rest of 2001, during which there were many agreements on process but few on substance, while chapter 6 is the "final agony" of the peace process between the Pastrana government and FARC. It includes another possibility that the talks will end, the intervention of the United Nations to keep them going, and the final abandonment of the process.

Chapters 7 and 8 turn to the case of the ELN, with chapter 7 presenting the early promising stage ending in the Geneva agreement of July 2000. Chapter 8 describes how the ELN process finally ended in failure, just as the FARC one had.

In each chapter the analysis begins with a recounting of the major steps and blunders in the process and concludes with a series of conclusions about the period in question. All chapters include charts showing the accomplishments of the process, as well as the occurrences that were negative to the course of action. Likewise all chapters have analyses of the peace dialogue with the guerrilla groups, including how the themes introduced in chapter 1 reappear, albeit at times in modified forms. The analysis also considers why the two negotiations were failures (as most think), as well as presenting the ideas of those who feel that, while the process did not bring peace, it did lead to a stronger government, better able to deal with the guerrilla groups and paramilitary squads.

3

The FARC Negotiations Begin

June 1998–January 1999

In this chapter I describe and analyze the beginning of negotiations between the government of Andrés Pastrana and the Armed Forces of the Colombian Revolution (FARC). As I will show, Pastrana made negotiations with FARC part of his election platform. His victory allowed him to demilitarize parts of Colombia, as FARC had demanded before, but it did not mean that he would have bargaining success with the insurgent group. Throughout the chapter the themes introduced in the first chapter will be shown again, although at times in modified forms. These include Theme II (the lack of continuity of the governmental negotiation team), Theme IV (the priority of political gains of the government over the negotiations), and Theme V (the negative effects of not working out specific details). Interestingly, however, the period shows one important departure from the general themes—that newly elected President Pastrana was able to do one thing that the military had opposed constantly—the establishment of a demilitarized zone (Theme I).

The Agreement to Have Talks

After Pastrana trailed his Liberal opponent Horacio Serpa by 33,729 votes in the first round of the presidential election,[1] former Conservative minister Álvaro Leyva Durán suggested that a strong peace platform would help him in the second round. Leyva gave Pastrana a twenty-point document arguing for a peace process with the FARC. This document was the product of conversations that Liberals, Conservatives, representatives of the United Nations, and FARC leader Raúl Reyes had begun the previous February in Mexico City.[2] Before that point Pastrana had showed little interest in the question of peace during his campaign. He read the document and the suggested speech, adding only one phrase to it: "If one has to go to the mountains to make peace, I am ready to do it."[3] The peace process began as a tactic to win the presidential election.

On June 10 Conservative congressional member Jairo Rojas, a personal friend of Leyva, met with FARC leader Manuel Marulanda and his chief lieutenant, Jorge Suárez Briceño (better known by his nom de guerre, "El Mono Jojoy"). After the three watched a televised Pastrana-Serpa debate, Jojoy said "That man could be the counterpart that we would like to see seated face-to-face with us." Marulanda asked if Pastrana would agree to come to meet with him, and when Rojas replied affirmatively, suggested that the Pastrana campaign could send someone to discuss those possibilities.[4]

On June 15 Andrés Pastrana sent Víctor G. Ricardo, his campaign manager and later the head of his peace process. Ricardo met with Marulanda with the two agreeing that talks would be held between the government and FARC, beginning January 7, 1999, should Pastrana be elected. The following day Pastrana announced that, if he were elected, one of his first decisions would be to pull government troops out of five municipalities of southern Colombia—Vistahermosa, La Macarena, Uribe, and Mesetas in Meta department, and San Vicente del Caguán in Caquetá department. This area comprised 42,138 square kilometers and had some 90,000 inhabitants.[5] The official position of FARC after November 1997 had been that it would have conversations with any of the candidates who might be elected president if he or she met two demands: that these five municipalities be demilitarized and that the paramilitary groups be ended.[6] As shown in chapter 2, they had unsuccessfully made these same demands during the Samper government.

The presidential election of 1998 showed a clear political interaction between the peace process and electoral politics, the fourth theme suggested in the first chapter. In this case it was the FARC and the Conservative candidate on one side and the ELN and the Liberal candidate on the other. As Mauricio Romero argues, "On one side the Conservative Party accepted a tacit alliance with FARC in the presidential elections of 1998, not only to give an image of a real possibility of peace, but also to balance the visible alliance between the Liberal candidate and the ELN, and the proposal of an eventual peace process between that guerrilla group and a Liberal Party in the presidency." The latter had practically been agreed upon in the Mainz meeting in July 1998, making it seem that the

Liberal candidate Horacio Serpa had a more developed plan for peace than the Conservative candidate.[7]

On June 21, 1998, Pastrana was elected. Some suggest that Ricardo's trip and Pastrana's announcement of a demilitarized zone were the key differences in a very close race. A Colombian political scientist also suggested that it revealed a national characteristic: "Colombians have a tendency to look for messiahs. Andrés Pastrana was seen as one when he promised peace. Then four years later Álvaro Uribe was one when he promised to be stronger."[8]

On July 9 the president-elect met with the FARC leader. This was the first of several conversations between two Colombians of very different backgrounds. Andrés Pastrana was the son of a former president (Misaél Pastrana, 1970–74) and was from what radicals call "the oligarchy," meaning the small economic group that dominates the country in social, economic, and political terms. The other was from "the people," the poor who lack education, health care, and, in many cases, stable employment.

While a young man during his father's presidency, Andrés Pastrana finished high school at the prestigious Colegio San Carlos in Bogotá, followed by university studies leading to a law degree at the Colegio Mayor Nuestra Señora de Rosario, also in the capital. He then studied for a master's degree in Public Law at Harvard, returning to Bogotá to begin a career in journalism. He began his political career when he was elected to the city council as a Conservative candidate in 1982, while continuing his journalistic career. In January 1988 he was kidnapped for a week by the Medellín drug group, as a way for that group to pressure President Virgilio Barco. In March of the same year he was elected mayor of Bogotá, and in 1990 he was elected to the national senate as a candidate of the New Democratic Force, an electoral coalition made up of individuals from both parties. It was during his four years as senator that he made his first move to be president, resigning his senate seat to be a presidential candidate in 1994.[9] As pointed out in chapter 2, he lost that election to Ernesto Samper. After three years in Key Biscayne, Florida, Pastrana returned to Colombia, reactivated his New Democratic Force, presenting himself as the reformist candidate of that party.[10]

The background of the FARC leader was dramatically different. "Tirofijo" or "Manuel Marulanda Vélez" are the two noms de guerre of Pedro Antonio Marín, a poor man living in the countryside. He was born in Quindío in 1930 and while little is known of the early life of this man who made his living through cutting wood, he probably received very little education. The political history of this member of the Liberal Party began shortly after the assassination of Liberal leader Jorge Eliécer Gaitán on April 9, 1948, when Marín joined a Liberal self-defense group. By 1964 "Tirofijo" had appeared as a communist guerrilla leader. Escaping the offensive of Colombian troops against the group's stronghold in Marquetalia in 1964, Marulanda was one of 350 guerrillas that attended the founding meeting of FARC in 1966. Later when leader Jacobo Arenas died, Marín (known as Marulanda or Tirofijo) became the head of FARC.[11]

Pastrana and Marín continued discussions about a FARC proposal to pull all security forces out of the municipalities in southern Colombia, creating a temporary "clearance zone" for the holding of peace talks. But there were no explicit agreements about how the guerrillas would use this territory. Nor was there a clear definition of the role of the government in the region.[12]

This was the first of many cases of vague agreements, later to cause problems because of the lack of specificity. As such it begins a recurrent Theme V—"The devil is in the details." One of the later problems that came with lack of specificity proved to be the *Cazadores* (Hunters) Infantry Battalion, which had their headquarters in San Vicente del Caguán. The guerrillas' understanding of the demobilization plan required that the Battalion vacate their headquarters. The government, however, insisted that the 130 troops stationed there were to be allowed to remain.

Pastrana and Marulanda also agreed on four topics that were to be the beginning of the agenda of the dialogue—the struggle against paramilitarism, decriminalization of social protest, a pilot plan of crop substitution for illicit drugs, and the end of public announcements of rewards for the FARC leaders.[13] The lack of specificity in these aspects of the agreements was also later to cause problems in the negotiations.

On August 7, 1998, in his inaugural speech Pastrana began poetically, "As the very wise Spanish collection of proverbs said, 'Without peace there is no bread.' For that reason, above all, I want peace that is peace and bread."[14] The search for peace would be the most urgent task of his administration. He stated, "As president of the republic I assume the . . . leadership to build peace. . . . From this moment, I call on all Colombians to follow and work within the agenda for peace that I am going to direct."[15] In other words the place of the government of Andrés Pastrana in history would be determined by his peace efforts—perhaps a noble sentiment but one that was to weaken his bargaining power, as shown below (Theme III).

During the three years of negotiations, in keeping with Theme II (lack of continuity on the part of the government), Pastrana named four negotiating teams. Typical of his style (and in keeping with Theme IV), they were made up of his close friends ("clientelism") and he gave representation to the Liberal Party and the Church only when he thought public opinion showed that the process should be broader.[16]

The first negotiating team was composed of four members—María Emma

Mejía, Liberal candidate for vice president in the 1998 elections and as such the representative of the opposition party; Nicanor Restrepo Santamaría, head of the powerful Antioquian interest groups, as representative of the private sector; Fabio Valencia Cossio, as representative of the National Congress and of the Great Alliance for Change, as Pastrana's winning coalition had been called; and Rodolfo Espinosa Meola, governor of the department of Atlántico and good friend of Vice President Gustavo Bell Lemus.[17] Valencia Cossio, according to one interviewee, had directed the team that came up with the government's proposal for the agenda and saw his participation as a way to become president in 2002.[18] He had been president of the Senate at the end of the 1990s and was the first to insist that the Conservative Party was more advanced, modern, and concerned with social issues.[19]

As is obvious, all four were chosen because they met certain political criteria rather than for any expertise in bargaining. This was to be a constant theme in all four negotiating teams. About the first group, the daily *El Tiempo* opined, "In the composition of the negotiating commission one sees a political equilibrium game that promises to lead to good results."[20] Others were less favorable in their evaluations. In an interview a political scientist said, "The commissioners were not trained, not suited for the job. They were chosen for reasons of political connections, not for abilities to negotiate. And there was a rotation of negotiating teams in the peace process, disrupting things in the negotiation."[21] One sociologist was even more negative, when he stated (in keeping with Theme III): "The other thing was the oligarchic way of arranging things—the president and his friends. If other people disagreed, it was because they were outside of the center of the oligarchy."[22]

While in the United States in late September the Colombian president stated, "The peace process is moving on."[23] In fact it began slowly, with a number of problems disturbing it. One was that members of the Liberal Party had objected to peace process methods, some even suggesting that they would oppose it. Another problem came when National Prosecutor Alfonso Gómez alleged constitutional irregularities.

In the case of the Liberal Party, at an early September "Forum on Public Order in Colombia," leaders Horacio Serpa, Juan Manuel Santos, Carlos Lemos Simmonds, and Germán Vargas Lleras all stated that the peace process was taking a mistaken path and that it was becoming a theme of opposition for their party. Each leader varied the focus of his critique—Serpa on the lack of a governmental strategy, Lemos on the alleged FARC demand for the retirement of certain generals, and Vargas on the actions that were weakening the armed forces.[24]

At about the same time Prosecutor Gómez wrote the president, asking for his position in the case of Álvaro Leyva Durán. Leyva, who was being investigated by the national prosecutor's office for involvement in the drug trade and who was in exile in Costa Rica, had apparently been mentioned by FARC as one of its possible spokespersons in the negotiations. On August 29 Commissioner Ricardo had met with Leyva in Costa Rica to talk about the viability of the peace process.[25] Gómez, who had learned of the Leyva possibility through an interview that Marulanda had with a publication of the Argentine Communist Party,[26] stated that "peace cannot lead to impunity," nor to ignoring the legitimate rights of the judicial branch of government.

President Pastrana replied to the Prosecutor Gómez in no uncertain terms: "In conformity with the Colombian constitution and laws, it does not correspond to the national prosecutor's office to exercise any political control over the process that is being carried out to achieve peace." However, the president assured the prosecutor that the executive branch would apply the law, agreeing with him that "the price of peace cannot be impunity, or the ignorance of the autonomy of the judicial branch, nor the demolition of judicial power."[27]

On October 15 Pastrana officially announced a demilitarized zone for ninety days, recognized the political status of FARC, and suspended arrest warrants for the three FARC leaders designated as its negotiators. On November 7, 1998, the Switzerland-sized demilitarized zone was established.[28] This was a clear departure from the first theme introduced in chapter 1—a divided government with much power in the hands of the military. During the Samper years, the armed forces had constantly resisted a demilitarized zone. The only way to explain this about-face is that the military could not resist a decision made by a president elected with the establishment of such a zone as a central part of his electoral platform. As one Colombian expert stated, "Samper was a weak president and needed military support. Pastrana, on the other hand, established the demilitarized zone at the beginning of his term and had promised it during the campaign. He didn't give the military time to oppose it."[29] Yet the armed forces remained skeptical and resistant to the demilitarized zone.

This resistance emerged almost immediately—and did so again and again, a recurring problem that had to be resolved before negotiations could begin. The matter was the question of 130 government troops within that zone. While Pastrana stated that all conditions had been met for the beginning of the process, FARC demanded the withdrawal of the unarmed soldiers of the Cazadores Battalion.[30] The FARC spokespersons wrote to President Pastrana on December 3 that he had changed the agreement made with Marulanda in two ways. First, Pastrana had agreed to the complete demilitarization of the municipalities "without any conditions." Secondly, Pastrana had agreed that the guerrilla forces would carry out the verification in the zone, but now wanted it done by an outside group. The letter ended in an arrogant tone that should have fore-warned the government:

> Finally you cannot demand anything of us because we still have not sat down at the table, for the common agreement, to establish the mechanisms that will regulate the conversations. In other words, to this moment there is no agreement between the two sides, except that you would order the demilitarization and that at the [negotiation] table we will deal with everything else. In addition the country still does not know who the spokespersons of the government for the negotiations are, unless you plan to do it yourself.

> Mr. President, if we Colombians do encounter obstacles on the road to reconciliation through this historical opportunity, the responsibility for this huge frustration will be yours alone. And that is what history will record, so that present generations and future generations will judge it.

FARC would continue, the statement continued, to struggle to bring reconciliation and national reconstruction, to lay the foundations of a lasting peace with social justice, an indispensable condition to achieve progress and the well-being of the Colombian family.[31]

The second recurrent problem of the negotiations is seen in the FARC statement—that history would judge President Pastrana for the success or failure of the negotiations. But that was just a repetition of what the president had said in his inauguration and, as suggested above, was to lead the president to make unwise decisions. Finally the statement demonstrates a common theme in Colombian negotiations, from all sides, to stake the claim that if the negotiations failed it would be the other party's fault, not theirs (Theme III again).

President Pastrana finally gave the order for the Cazadores Battalion to leave the area in mid-December, and the dialogues were then scheduled to begin on January 7, 1999.[32] As Luis Giraldo, who for fourteen months was one of the negotiators of the government, pointed out: "The demilitarized zone, for example, was presented as a means to give security to the FARC negotiators and to make the conversations swifter. It was warned, however, that the zone could be used as an untouchable rearguard for the FARC war."[33] Yet that was an empty threat, as the government had no way to monitor what FARC was doing in the zone.

On December 19, 1998, in an action that later was to have effect on the peace process, President Pastrana announced his "Plan Colombia." Based on the principle that peace in Colombia would have to go beyond a political solution to the armed conflict, this plan was described as one that would bring investment and development to those areas most affected by violence. Coordinated by Commissioner Ricardo, the plan would be financed through resources of the state, the private sector, and the international community. It would attend especially to the people who had been displaced by the violence through giving legal title to lands and through projects intended to make the lands more productive.

As Pastrana portrayed it (and as it was to garner support from the government of the United States), Plan Colombia would also assist small farmers in the substitution of illicit crops. In the field of eradication of coca and heroin poppy production, the president insisted that guerrilla groups should contribute to the plan "in the interest of a true reconciliation and in order to guarantee the success of a fundamental peace process." Pastrana also stated that he "invites the insurgent groups to be present in the preparation, formation, and execution of the programs and projects of Plan Colombia." Finally the president reiterated his desire for peace and his readiness to work, after January 7, in the negotiation with FARC. "My government has clearly shown the consistency of its purposes, and has accepted that we have to agree on a substantive agenda of peace with the insurgency, of open doors and windows, and that only can be achieved if there are compromises by the two sides."[34] As reported by a Colombian political scientist, "Pastrana first thought of Plan Colombia as a sort of Marshall Plan for Colombia—with lots of money going into social programs and education. However, when the U.S. government got to it, it became primarily a military program."[35]

By the end of 1998 two FARC positions were known. The first was that a cease-fire was something to be negotiated later, rather than earlier, in the process. That was in direct conflict with the position of the government and was to cause difficulties later, as we will see. The second had to do with the ten points (the FARC Decalogue) that the insurgent group wanted to negotiate. These points, listed below, had been first stated by FARC in 1993 and were to reappear as a formal agenda proposal:

1. A political solution to the grave conflict in which the country is living.
2. A reform of the national military, reducing it to a size adequate to defend national borders and sovereignty.
3. Political reform through strengthening democratic participation.
4. Development and social justice, with private investment allowed in vital sectors such as energy, communications, public services, roads, ports, and the production of natural resources, but that the State should remain as the principal owner.

5. Social well-being, with 50 percent of the national budget dedicated to welfare, job creation, education, heath, and housing.
6. Income redistribution, through the value-added tax being applied only to luxury goods and services and with people with higher income paying higher income taxes.
7. An agrarian policy based on the elimination of large landholdings.
8. Renegotiation of national resource exploration contracts with the multi-national corporations, but not nationalization.
9. A change of foreign relations through a ten-year moratorium on foreign debt payments and a revision of military agreements.
10. The solution to the production and marketing of narcotics with the financial support of the international community.[36]

As one interviewee stated, "Marulanda stated what FARC wanted to negotiate, in a September or October 1998 open letter published in *El Espectador*. This was ignored by the government between the time of the common agenda until the Notables made their recommendation. I saw this from the beginning and did not think that the peace process would work."[37]

In late 1998, before the dialogues began there was some posturing on the part of the president and Manuel Marulanda, showing that the president was not the only one who was concerned about his place in history. On December 23 FARC announced that Tirofijo would not attend the opening meeting. President Pastrana stated "If Marulanda doesn't go, neither will the president."[38] Forty-eight hours later Marulanda replied that he would attend the meeting in San Vicente de Caguán on January 7, 1999, although he would be present for only a very few minutes. He was to speak first, followed by the president.[39]

Despite this adolescent-like posturing and the impertinence of Tirofijo proclaiming that he would speak before the president did, there was a spirit of optimism and euphoria as the New Year arrived. As one interviewee put it, "All had hope—or wanted to have hope—when Pastrana became president. After all, the Samper government, for political reasons, had done very little in the peace process. There were a few things towards the end of the Samper years, such as recognizing international law. But really very little."[40] Yet other observers expressed the opposite view. Retired General Alvaro Valencia Tovar, in an op-ed article in *El Tiempo* was much more cautious.

President Pastrana has risked everything to get the opening of negotiations. He has given more than was advisable in face of the unknowns that come from the ambiguous conduct of the other side and the long history of frustrated dialogues, which really never have been carried out with a sincere will for peace. This is especially the case if one keeps in mind that written guerrilla documents signal clearly that negotiations are no more than a strategic revolutionary stage for the seizure of power through arms.[41]

One interviewee stated, "A retired general I know advised Pastrana that for FARC negotiations were no more than a method for the seizure of power. His family was friends with the president's family and the general had worked with Misaél Pastrana. Andrés Pastrana replied that he would consider the general's advice, but nothing ever came of it."[42]

In a speech right before the January 7 meeting, Pastrana asked that the Colombian people have faith and much patience. He stated that he did not believe that the guerrilla forces were winning the war, but that they wanted to search for a new stage in democratic life. "May we wake up in peace in 2000," he concluded.[43]

The Talks Begin

The talks began badly on January 7, 1999, when Manuel Marulanda Vélez did not appear at the meeting in San Vicente. Some observers interpreted his absence as a sign that the 15,000-member FARC, the Western Hemisphere's oldest and most powerful left-wing rebel force, had already lost interest in discussing peace with the Pastrana administration at a time when the rebels had been gaining strength.[44] Tirofijo, however, stated that he was nearby during the meeting and his colleague Raúl Reyes stated that security conditions were not sufficient for the leader to appear in public. Two members of the FARC National Political Commission stated that the organization had detained two men who had violated security measures and who were ready to attack Tirofijo. The leaders refused to give additional details or to confirm that they had been sent by paramilitary leader Carlos Castaño in retaliation for attacks on AUC headquarters.[45] This last possibility seems unlikely since FARC had exercised de facto control of the demilitarized area for years. Rather this seems to have been a negotiating tactic by the FARC leader, in effect saying "You might have been elected President of Colombia with six and a half million votes, but I am the one who controls this part of the country."

Despite this slap in the face, President Pastrana said that he had come to carry out his word. He stated,

The absence of Manuel Marulanda Vélez is no reason not to proceed with the installation of the dialogue table, to decide upon an agenda of conversations that we should conduct towards peace. The national government, under my leadership, comes to the beginning of the dialogue table with an open agenda, without intentions to veto or to impose topics. We are prepared to discuss, we are prepared to disagree, we are prepared to propose, to evaluate, but over all, to construct. This is the very essence of a democracy. . . . I know where we are headed, I know that the journey will be difficult, I know that we are facing a road that is long and trying. On it we shall find surprises and opportunities.[46]

The following day Marulanda sought out government officials and foreign dignitaries in Caguán, saying that he was committed to seeing talks progress to end the civil war. He said he was absent from a ceremony to start the effort the previous day because of death threats from by right-wing paramilitary death squads.[47] Both Marulanda and the FARC leaders made it clear why they were participating in the dialogue although they were the victims, not the cause, of the conflict. In the previous forty-five years five wars had been carried out against them: one after 1948; another, beginning in 1954; another, beginning in 1962; another, after May 18, 1964; and the current one since December 1990, "when Dictator Gaviria and the upper military leaders began an operation of extermination against the FARC Secretariat in Casa Verde and of militaristic aggression against the popular movement in the entire government." Despite all this FARC was convinced that peace could be achieved if the directing class had the political will.[48]

For his part, Tirofijo added, "The beginning of the bargaining table for ninety days, beginning with the demilitarized zone, has awakened great expectations in the entire country and the world, in order to find a solution with social justice and sovereignty to the armed social conflict that has been bleeding the country for more than four decades." FARC, he added, was a revolutionary movement fighting for changes; it would propose a platform of ten points, for the study of all, "the political parties, intellectuals, industrialists, ranchers, farmers, merchants, professors, students, workers, peasants, communal juntas, the unemployed, those displaced by violence, the insurgence and other organizations, for fundamental debate about the political solution and the radical transformation of the old structures of the state." It would lead to a constituent assembly with direct representation of the different elements of Colombian society, in order that peace might be reached in Colombia at last.[49]

On the second day the meetings turned to procedural matters, attempting to decide on mechanisms that would be used during the meetings, as well as their frequency and location. In what turned out to be one of the most important accords, it was agreed that a prisoner exchange would be the subject of a parallel table, to begin on January 20. Although no agenda was agreed upon, the two sides did agree on three initial points—the desire for peace; agreement on joint communiqués as the only way of informing the public and asking the media to accept that as the only information; and setting up the next meeting.[50]

These agreements made on the second day were the first of many agreements on procedures, while those of substance were lacking. The joint communiqué agreement made the ensuing process more secretive than the ones had been in the Gaviria years, a characteristic that experts on bargaining consider favorable to its success.

Also immediately after the abortive Pastrana-Tirofijo opening day, it became obvious that FARC wanted the peace process to be more than a cease-fire negotiated between the government and the guerrilla group; rather FARC wanted civil society to participate in the elaboration of the agreements. The guerrilla group would propose that the government "accept putting the entire country in discussions" that would lead to agreements that would be submitted for the approval of a constituent assembly. FARC representative "Bernardo" stated that once the government accepted its proposal of including the organized parts of society in the elaboration of an agreement, through a mechanism not yet agreed upon, "We want all of society to elect its representatives in a democratic fashion, so that they can contribute to the discussion." He explained that, for example, black communities, indigenous people, students, and other social groups would designate its delegates for this discussion, in order to contribute to the agreements.[51] It took until October to reach an agreement about the "National Thematic Committee" that would conduct those consultations.

At the negotiating table, the question then turned to the agenda for the meetings. The government included in its ideas that of a cease-fire, so that negotiation could occur without armed conflict, although indications were that the guerrillas saw this as a theme that would come up much later in the discussions.[52] Even before the negotiations had begun, FARC had stated that the cease-fire would come only when 90 percent of the issues had been solved. It was already known that FARC would present ten points at the table.[53] In the second week of January the Pastrana government proposed an agenda, also of ten points. They included protection of the environment and ending paramilitary groups.[54]

Colombian experts began analyzing the two agendas immediately, even though officially the agendas were secret. Journalist Juan José Ramírez suggested that a prompt agreement about a cease-fire was unlikely given continual FARC public pronouncements that an end to hostilities would not be possible until at least 90 percent of its agenda (also a public document for years) was resolved. Ramírez also pointed out that FARC thought it simple for the state to end paramilitary groups since it had created them.[55] Rubén Darío Ramírez, former presidential assessor on kidnapping, suggested that it would not be easy for the guerrillas to stop kidnapping since they received COL$100 billion from that activity each year.[56]

The national comptroller, Carlos Ossa Escobar, pointed to the difficulties in the ending of drug production and trade. The previous year the Colombian government had eradicated 60,000 hectares of coca only to see the amount of production increase in the following year. To that point no viable crop substitution program had been devised. The former minister of the environment underlined that, when the government mentioned the protection of the environment, it meant ending both the bombing of pipelines and the growing and refining of drugs. Two million barrels of petroleum had polluted 2,500 kilometers of the water system through the former, while the latter had led to the deforestation of one million hectares of jungle and the dumping of 600,000 liters of chemicals.[57]

In a very perceptive argument, Armando Borrero, former presidential counselor for National Security, stated

> The only thing that bothers me about the agenda presented by the government are some of its first points, especially all that has to do with the respect for international humanitarian rights. A guerrilla group that respects international humanitarian and human rights is a guerrilla group that has already made peace. That is the nature of an irregular war like that in which the country lives. If the guerrilla group accepts international humanitarian rights it would remain without a way to finance itself and for that reason it's going to be difficult to carry out this objective of the agenda.

Borrero also stated that the agrarian reform issue should be addressed after peace was achieved, since "this cannot be treated as it was fifty years ago when the ownership of the land was talked about. Today it's much more; it's the development of it."[58]

All did not go in a friendly fashion at the dialogue table during the first days. On January 11 Jorge Briceño threatened that FARC would begin kidnapping politicians if the government did not accept its prisoner-exchange proposal. Later Marulanda added that, without the approval of a law that would make exchanges permanent, there would be no exchange. The Congress replied that it would not approve such a law.[59]

Nevertheless the first week ended with a public pronouncement of the two sides which declared the "irrevocable will of the government and FARC to construct a country with sustainable peace, with equity, and with social justice." The document also invited the participation of the entire country in the cause of peace, in effect an invitation for the participation of civil society in the process.[60]

During the second week the talks turned to purely mechanical matters. The goal was to develop an agenda by February 7 that would allow true negotiation to begin.[61] Both sides presented their proposed agendas and agreed that discussions of them would begin on January 24.

The First Freezing

If, after the Marulanda absence on the first day, the Pastrana peace process had begun without euphoria, hope and excitement diminished even more when it was delayed on the evening of January 19, by Comandante Raúl Reyes's announcement of the "freezing" of dialogues between FARC and the government, ending rumors that had been going on since midday that this was to happen. This was the first of five times—four by FARC and one by the government—that the negotiations were "frozen," that is to say, suspended but not ended. The FARC was to freeze the negotiations between January 19 and April 20, 1999, July 18 and October 24, 1999, November 14, 2000, and February 9, 2001, and between October 17, 2001, and January 9, 2002; the government froze them from May 16 to July 3, 2000.

Although this first freezing had not been foreseen by the government, during the entire week the rebel commanders had been talking strongly against the massacres being carried out by the paramilitary squads. In an offensive during the previous two weeks, paramilitary massacres had cost the lives of 130 Colombians. This offensive apparently had a double objective—to sabotage the negotiations between the government and FARC and to obtain for the AUC the same political status as FARC had. On January 20 the leaders of FARC wrote an open letter to Andrés Pastrana, in which they stated that on January 8, the day after the negotiations had begun, the country woke "drowning in blood in the massacres of unarmed civilians carried out in the entire country by the coordinated action of military and paramilitary members leading in four days to more than 200 innocent victims."[62]

Indeed the fifth point of the communiqué read by Reyes signaled that FARC declared the negotiations frozen until they saw satisfactory results in the government's policy against the paramilitary groups. That, Reyes added, did not mean a definitive break of the conversations. Rather it meant that FARC "will wait until there are results in the fight against paramilitaries, until we can see results of this struggle." Answering the question of whether the result might be the capture of Carlos Castaño, Reyes replied that a "serious policy against these organizations" would be more important.[63]

Demanding actions of the government and announcing the "freezing" of the dialogue, the FARC leaders stated, "Sensible people of the national and international community do not understand why FARC maintains dialogues in search of coexistence with a State that, arguing the incapacity of its public forces, does not give convincing evidence of dismantling or giving exemplary punishment to the promoters and organizations which indiscriminately assassinate in the name of the very State."[64] This demonstrates that in this negotiation with FARC, as in the earlier ones during the Gaviria presidency, the unwillingness or inability of the government to control the paramilitary groups prevented agreements with FARC.[65] Later it was to show the difficulty in negotiations when the criteria lack operational definitions. There was no clear indication of what FARC thought "satisfactory results" would be.

Analysts in Bogotá immediately stressed this problem. Former minister Fernando Cepeda Ulloa stated that some reacted to the FARC decision with surprise and confusion, while others stated that it was neither surprising nor unexpected. The reading of FARC documents, he continued, indicated that the dialogues would progress to the extent that there was verification of satisfactory results—that is, ones that are headed in the right direction with credibility. He showed the meaning of "freezing" when he continued, "We are seeing the first case: if they [FARC] do not see satisfactory results in the policy against the paramilitary groups, then they freeze the dialogue. They do not suspend it. They do not throw out the things about which there have been talks. Simply they freeze it, which is a way to preserve the process in the publicly established provisions and it seems the ones that have been accepted."[66]

Emphasizing procedural questions, Alfredo Rangel Suárez, former presidential peace advisor, stated:

This demand for "satisfactory results" in the fight against paramilitarism puts matters in a very difficult perspective. According to this, the continuation of the dialogues depends on the unilateral evaluation that FARC makes, on the basis of whether or not they are satisfied. On the other hand, the act of freezing until results are reached leaves the process stopped in an indefinite way since concrete results cannot be accomplished in two weeks.[67]

Former presidential security advisor Armando Borrero emphasized the substantive nature of the problem when he argued that pretending that the government could end paramilitary groups was disingenuous. "As long as there are guerrilla groups it will be difficult for the State to have the forces to fight on other fronts. In addition, they [the FARC] start from the mistaken idea that the paras are not an autonomous force but a simple appendix of the state."[68]

Commissioner Ricardo wrote to Marulanda, arguing that the Pastrana government was already fighting against the paramilitary forces. He pointed to Presidential Directive No. 3 of October 15, 1998, through which the president had established the government's policy against paramilitary groups (and included a copy in case it had not arrived to FARC headquarters). In addition, to prove that this was more than rhetoric for the Pastrana government, Ricardo stated that during it 370 members of paramilitary groups had been captured, 82 members of the military and police had been arrested for paramilitary activities, as well as numerous indictments, arrests, and convictions.[69]

The following week FARC presented a nineteen-page "dossier of paramilitarism," insisting that in addition to Carlos Castaño they were thinking of ten generals, some twenty other military officers, three former governors, and a former government minister. In addition FARC listed twenty radio frequencies used for coordination between the paramilitary groups and the armed forces and furnished a list of a hundred financiers of the groups, many of whom they also accused of being drug dealers.[70]

The last week of January there was an unsuccessful attempt to unfreeze the dialogues. During a three-day meeting the principal theme was the paramilitary groups, although other themes included the prisoner exchange, the extension of the time limit for the demilitarized zone, and the possibility of moving the dialogues outside of Colombia. In the question of paramilitary groups FARC was expected to argue that Carlos Castaño, head of the AUC, was no more than a proxy of the government, a "fuse" who would be burned when they wanted and replaced with another. The FARC spokespersons were expected to argue that, in addition to the demobilization of the paramilitary groups, the government should plan for the trial of its members, a profound change of the structure of the armed forces, and the end of the military jurisdiction in trials of officers.[71]

Conclusions: The Beginning of the FARC Process

The first seven months of the Pastrana peace process with the FARC included the first appearance of phenomena that were to have an effect on the entire bargaining process. As shown in Figure 3.1, there were both positive aspects (those to the left of the line) and negative ones (those to the right).

The process did begin in a positive way, with an advisor suggesting peace talks as a campaign strategy, meetings of a representative with the FARC leader, and later a meeting between him and the president-elect. Yet negative happenings appeared soon as well. They came from both inside the government and from the guerrillas. The opposition of the Liberal Party is not surprising since

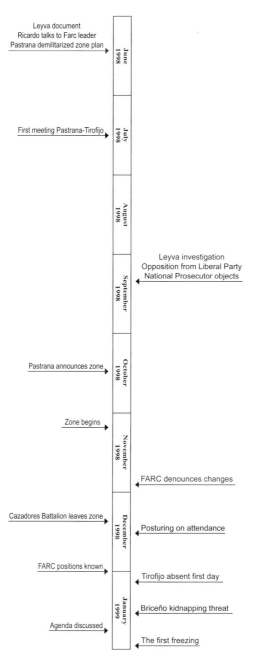

Figure 3.1. Beginning of FARC negotiations, June
1998–1999.

Pastrana had used the peace process as a campaign issue. Nor was it as important as the disunity within the executive branch (Theme I) when, first, the alleged drug connections of Álvaro Leyva interfered or, second, when the national procurator and the president disagreed on which of the two had what constitutional rights in the peace process.

Of at least equal importance were the harmful activities of FARC. Negative effects came from the lack of specificity in the details of the Pastrana-Tirofijo agreement (Theme V). Of much greater severity was the posturing about whether or not Tirofijo would come to the opening ceremony (Theme III) and his ultimate decision not to be there. This was an incredible lack of respect for the newly elected president. If Andrés Pastrana had ended the negotiations at that point, many Colombians would have applauded him. No doubt some would have used the sexist metaphor that he had "put on his pants." Or if Pastrana had used this affront as a way to show hard-nosed bargaining, perhaps even more Colombians would have cheered him. He might have let Tirofijo know, in no uncertain terms, that if the guerrilla leader did not appear for a meeting in a set time the demilitarized zone would end. The other two unconstructive FARC actions were the threat of additional kidnapping and the "freezing" of the talks.

Perhaps the most optimistic things that can be said of the talks during the first seven months are that they did begin and that they were "frozen" instead of ended. Indeed one might be surprised that the negotiations were still alive after the first month.

However, President Pastrana did not end the process at the end of the first month. Perhaps he hoped that matters would improve (unlikely as that might have seemed)—or perhaps he was still concerned with his place in history (Theme IIIb).

4

The First Agreements of
the FARC Negotiations

January 1999–January 2001

At the end of the first month of negotiations with FARC there seemed to be little reason for optimism: Manuel Marulanda had not appeared for the opening ceremony; FARC later "froze" the negotiations because of paramilitary activities. However, neither side wanted the negotiations to end.

In this chapter I turn to the two years between the end of January 1999 and January 2001. The process was one that went from accomplishments at the table to failures on the field and at the table, because of actions of one side or the other in the continuing war. Almost all of the themes introduced in chapter 1 that militate against bargaining emerged time and again. Even when considering the few agreements that were reached during this period, all were about the process to be followed in the negotiations. None concerned substantive matters. The period ended with the real possibility that the Pastrana peace process with FARC would come to an end.

The Second Series of Conversations and the First Agreement

Despite the frozen status of the negotiations, by the first week of February the minister of defense and the highest levels of the military were concerned from the signals they were receiving from the civilians in the executive branch, that

Pastrana would extend the period of the demobilization.[1] As pointed out in chapter 3, the military had agreed on a demilitarized zone only when a president was elected with that promise. In this continuation of Theme IIIb, some officers clearly thought that the original ninety days would not be extended; others, both military and civilians, no doubt thought that extensions would be conditioned on a certain amount of progress; yet others must have believed that extensions would be negotiated, with FARC making concessions for the continuation of the demilitarized zone.

On February 5 the zone was extended; all three of the groups mentioned were wrong—the government did it unilaterally without FARC concessions. Perhaps the only way to interpret this extension is as a way that the Pastrana government thought it could increase goodwill with FARC. Experts on bargaining say that this is a good idea. If that was the motivation of the Pastrana negotiators, it was the first of many attempts to increase goodwill.

Besides the extension of the demilitarized zone, very little happened from the last week of January until April 18 when President Pastrana threatened FARC with the end of the zone if negotiations did not begin soon. As commissioner Ricardo said several weeks later, "There is no book that teaches you how to deal with the guerrillas. You can't ask Colombia to achieve a peace agreement overnight just from a series of work sessions." The process would take time, "But the important thing is that we are near to having a common agenda that would permit us to move on to the next phase, that of negotiations."[2] According to commentator and former ELN member León Valencia, it was Ricardo who was able to end this "freezing" by promising that the government would confront the paramilitary problem and would be especially tough on connections between the *paras* and the military.[3]

During any of the four times that FARC froze the peace process, the government could have ended the peace process definitively with dignity. As one interviewee stated, "The peace process could have been called off a number of times over more than three years."[4] Another agreed and added along the lines of Theme IIIb, "It is a wonder that the peace process with FARC didn't end before it did. One reason was that Pastrana was determined to make it succeed to guarantee his place in history. He was eager for it to work—perhaps too eager."[5] This was the second time that one of my interviewees mentioned the place of Andrés Pastrana in history.

This is also perhaps the reason that each time the government agreed to extend the dialogue, it did so without demanding that FARC do something in exchange. Along the lines of the Theme II, a Colombian sociologist interviewed saw this as part of a more general problem in the Pastrana government's negotiations with FARC: "The government lacked a bargaining strategy. This was shown when they made unilateral concessions and when they extended the demilitarized zone without FARC giving anything in return."[6]

Clearly the government thought that it was, to borrow a medical metaphor, too soon to take the peace process off life support. The dialogue resumed on April 20 and within a few days the government and FARC made progress in the study and design of a common agenda for the negotiation stage of the process, that is to say, an agenda to which the two sides would have agreed. A joint communiqué also announced that the two sides had decided to create three subcommissions: one to work on the common agenda; a second to develop the design of the procedures for the negotiation, including the manner through which civil society would be consulted; and a third to concentrate on crop substitution for illicit products, including areas for trials and methodology.[7] It was agreed that the government would deliver a document describing its policy against paramilitary groups, while FARC would submit a second list of individuals involved in paramilitary activities. Finally the two sides would meet again on April 24 to talk about differences and a common agenda, the government's document on paramilitary policy, the analysis of a plan to substitute illicit products, and work on the development of a study of the environment and protection of natural resources.[8]

The dialogue table met again on April 25 and April 29–30. In the first meeting, using a methodology that was approved at the beginning of the session, the two sides considered a common agenda for negotiation; the search for a common procedure for the discussion of the themes that might be included in the agenda; and the design of an experimental plan for the substitution of illicit crops.[9] In the second get-together the two sides reported that they had finished 80 percent of their proposal to agree on a common agenda, a methodology, and a process for citizen participation through public hearings.[10]

On May 2 the two sides signed the "Acuerdo de Caquetania"[11] in which, after pointing out that the government-established timetable for the demilitarized zone ran out on May 5, the two sides agreed to begin on May 6 the "initiation of the period of negotiation and dialogue" on an agreed upon common agenda. In addition, for this purpose they would agree "by common accord, to an international accompanying commission, that might serve as a verifier in order to overcome any obstacles that might happen."[12]

This was the first of many times that an agreement—always about process—was signed as the time period for the demilitarized zone was about to run out. Indeed nine agreements about process were approved during the FARC negotiations, but little was agreed to about the substance of the peace process. While some might see procedural agreements as being a necessary first step, and they would state that making agreements about procedure is better than not making any accords at all, others see it as more Machiavellian. A Colombian sociologist said that "I have an unusual hypothesis—that FARC tried to keep the government at the table, as in a card game, with the house letting the player have small wins to set up a big win for the house."[13] A similar way to interpret it would be to argue that the continuation of the demilitarized zone was a "win" for each side. For FARC it allowed the guerrilla group to continue resting troops, training recruits, growing coca, and hiding kidnapped people in an area of Colombia where the government could not bother them.

Along the same lines one might argue that the Colombian military was the group that wanted the zone to continue. The Samper years had shown that they were not capable of winning against FARC. Hence they were the ones that wanted a demilitarized zone—to keep many of the FARC troops out of battle while the military became stronger through Plan Colombia. This second hypothesis was argued by another Colombian sociologist when he stated:

> As much as they might have verbalized against it, the military wanted the demilitarized zone. It would remove a substantial number of FARC troops from battles. The military knew, as the Samper years had shown, that FARC could win battles in which they deployed all their troops. For that reason the military wanted time to build their forces, and, although they might have objected publicly to the demilitarized zone, they were really in favor of it.[14]

This hypothesis is far from the common interpretations of the military's attitudes and statements during the Pastrana peace process and should be kept in mind in the following analysis. And many experts would disagree with it. Another Colombian, who had been in the Samper administration, replied as follows when I presented the second hypothesis to him and asked if he agreed with it: "Absolutely not. I am 100 percent certain that the military leaders never wanted the demilitarized zone. I personally knew the top generals during the Samper years, and they were the same ones during the Pastrana government. They were completely, totally against the demilitarized zone."[15]

The Acuerdo of Caquetania was also the second time that an agreement, which seemed good in principle, later turned out to be a problem because it lacked specificity (Theme V). In the first instance, it was the vague status of the Cazadores Infantry Battalion, discussed in chapter 3 that became a problem. In this case, it was the vagueness surrounding the international commission that was to be a problem.

On May 6 the two sides agreed on a common agenda, an important procedural agreement. While the agenda officially had twelve "large" points, according to one source it contained forty-six themes,[16] while several others stated that it was more than one hundred.[17] Analyst Alfredo Rangel stated that the government proposal had 101 points and as such it was a bad strategy since it showed all the government's "cards" at the beginning of the game. Apparently, Rangel argued, the government thought that this would cause FARC to continue the dialogue, without realizing that a long dialogue was exactly what the guerrilla group wanted, so that they could use the demilitarized zone for rest, regrouping, and retraining of its forces. Rangel concluded, "If from today one point a month is considered, the negotiation would last about ten years—a major error after granting a demilitarized zone in such a hurried way, without conditions or clear rules of the game."[18] A Colombian sociologist added, "The Valencia Cossio agenda would have given FARC everything that they wanted. The government would give things to FARC without receiving anything from them. It was so long that it would have taken years to go over each of the points."[19]

Table 4.1 shows a number of interesting points about the common agenda. Each side proposed items that did not make it into the common agenda. In addition to the eight topics listed in column 2 of Table 4.1, FARC had included development and social justice—allowing private investment in vital sectors such as energy, communications, public services, roads, ports, and natural resources, but making it clear that the state should be in the principal owner of them—as well as social well-being, with 50 percent of the budget in social programs, employment generation, education, health, and housing.[20] In addition to their eight topics in Table 4.1, the government agenda had included the protection of the environment and ending paramilitary groups.[21] The last is especially interesting since that had been a FARC demand before.

Further, there were matters in the common agenda that were not in the agendas of one or the other proponents. FARC had mentioned nothing about the protection of human rights or the justice system. Neither did they propose any ways for the formalization of the agreements. Likewise the government had not brought up explicitly a political solution, although it was clearly implied. Nor had the government mentioned natural resources or military reform. In addition, there was more specificity in the FARC items about agrarian reform, natural resources, economic and social structure, drugs, military reform, and foreign relations, while the government's proposal was more specific in human rights, the social and economic structure, political reform, and formalization of the agreement.

In short the "common agenda" represented a compromise between the two sides and indeed is one of the most notable cases of such compromise during

Table 4.1: Comparison of 1999 FARC and Government Proposals to the Compromise Common Agenda

FARC Proposal	Government Proposal	Common Agenda
Political solution to grave conflict		Negotiated political solution
	Unconditional protection for human rights and International Humanitarian Law	Protection of human rights
Agrarian policy centered around elimination of latifundios	Agrarian reform	Agrarian reform
Natural resources, including renegotiation of contracts but not nationalization		Exploitation and conservation of natural resources
Redistribution of income, with those highest paying the highest taxes	Social and economic structure, concentrating on the objective causes of violence —poverty and inequitable distribution of income	Economic and social structure
	Strengthening the justice system	Reform of justice system
Elimination of the production and marketing of drugs, with the financial backing of the international community	Fight against corruption; alternative development and crop substitution	Struggle against corruption and drug trade
Political reform, with democratic participation in decision making	Political reform of the state, to deepen democracy and the construction of a new State of Law, guaranteeing among other things separation of powers, independent control mechanisms, electoral rules, decentralization, minority rights, and guarantees for ethnic minorities	Political reform to increase democracy and reforms to the state
Military reform—with a resulting military that is		

FARC Proposal	Government Proposal	Common Agenda
of the size necessary to defend the nation's border and defend its sovereignty		
Foreign relations, based on moratorium of ten years of paying foreign debt and revision of military agreements	Assistance of the international community in the process	International relations
	Vitalization of the instructions for peace, through a democratic process with the participation of the totality of the Colombian people in the ratification of the agreement, leading to "a new constitutional and legal regimen that puts an end to violence and allows the country to become one of peace, equity, and social justice"	Formalization of the agreements

SOURCES: FARC proposal, "Los diez puntos que llevan las Farc a la mesa de diálogo," *El Tiempo,* December 19, 1998; government proposal, "En diez puntos está condensada su agenda para la paz, que ayer comenzó a ser discutida," *El Tiempo,* January 12, 1999; Common Agenda, "Las pláticas de paz en Colombia se realizarán aun con 'percances graves', señala senador," *La Cronica de hoy,* May 7, 1999.

the three years of conversations. Of course since it was only an agenda it was completely a procedural matter. Yet bargaining theorists would see this as a good first step and hence was similar to the Framework Agreement for the Resumption of the Negotiating Process between the Government of Guatemala and the UNIDAD Revolucionaria Nacional Guatemalteca. Signed in 1994 the Guatemalan document began with a common agenda that had been agreed to earlier, but went farther in calling on the United Nations to be a mediator, setting up a way for civil society to be consulted, and naming foreign countries to be the verifiers of the process.[22] The first Guatemalan procedural agreement was to be followed by numerous other agreements with some about matters of substance such as human rights and agrarian reform.[23] That the same did not happen in the Colombian case is one of the comparative matters considered in the final chapter.

The Colombian common agenda also was one of the many documents signed by the two sides which made the progress made seem greater than it really was. Both governmental and FARC leaders later pointed to it as a sign that progress towards peace was being made. In fact the official agenda was a painless compromise and was meant to show that something had been accomplished in four months. To increase this impression even more, President Pastrana met with Marulanda on May 2, 1999.[24]

The next difficulty in the negotiation came from opposition to it from within the Colombian government (Theme Ib). On May 26, several weeks after two generals were forced to retire because of alleged connection to paramilitary groups,[25] Minister of Defense Rodrigo Lloreda abruptly resigned, citing disagreements over the peace process with the FARC. Lloreda also protested statements made on May 21 by government Peace Commissioner Víctor G. Ricardo that had indicated that the demilitarized zone might be extended indefinitely. The defense minister also cited Pastrana's failure to return a phone call inquiring about Ricardo's statements. At a news conference in which he outlined his reasons for leaving the post, Lloreda added, "Too many concessions have been made by the government to the rebels and that's the perception of the overwhelming majority of Colombians."[26] Two interviewees agreed that Lloreda, in their opinion the best defense minister in years, was in conflict with the peace commissioner, Ricardo.[27] Lloreda was instrumental in the development of Plan Colombia which, as argued in the conclusions, was probably the greatest contribution of the Pastrana government to peace.

Lloreda's resignation was accompanied by the resignations of at least fifty other high-ranking officers, including eighteen generals. Apparently many had been convinced, through a reading in a course in the military academy, that the only acceptable way for an officer to disagree with an order of the president was to resign.[28] While President Pastrana accepted Lloreda's resignation, he refused to accept the others. The head of the armed forces, General Fernando Tapias, offered a public show of support for Pastrana. Indeed Téllez, Montes, and Lemus called this "the worst military crisis in the recent history of Colombia" because Lloreda had become a symbol of the military dissatisfaction with the Pastrana government's handling of the FARC negotiations.[29]

Two days later, after the Bogotá daily *El Tiempo* stated that the head of the national police had taken actions to avoid a military coup d'état, President Pastrana met with the remaining generals. At that meeting General Rafael Hernández stated, "Mr. President, with all respect I would like to say to you that this is the first time that you have met with all the generals, while you have met twice with the head of FARC, Manuel Marulanda."[30]

All the above notwithstanding, on June 6 the commissioner of peace announced that the demilitarized zone had been extended for another six months. Clearly neither the resignations nor other military discontent had affected Pastrana. But it was not at all certain how it had affected the negotiations. In an op-ed piece in *El Tiempo* National University professor Alejo Vargas Velásquez suggested that there were three possible scenarios. The optimistic scenario was that the crisis would strengthen the negotiating process because FARC would think that maintaining an uncompromising position would strengthen the national opinion that was against the process and FARC would therefore be more flexible. At the same time the government would try to construct a climate of confidence, insisting on partial agreements in the short run.

The pessimistic scenario was that the confidence between the two sides would decrease and there would be a hardening of their respective positions. FARC assumed that the government had conceded a lot to the military in order to resolve the crisis. The government, for its part, considered its priority to be to rectify its errors and apparent unilateral concessions and would harden its positions, especially in the prisoner exchange.

The third scenario, suggested by international observers more than Colombian ones, was that the negotiation with FARC really had only one really important point in its agenda—the substitution for illicit drug crops—and that all the other points were only an exercise in academic rhetoric.[31]

The following months demonstrated that a fourth scenario was really the one that applied: some talks, some procedural agreements, and some "freezing" of the process. The suspension of the talks came when even the Acuerdo de Caquetania—an agreement on process—led to two different interpretations. On July 18 FARC "froze" the negotiations for the second time, with the suspension of the conversations lasting until October 24. This was another demonstration of Theme V, primarily by a disagreement on what a "verifying commission" was supposed to do and when it should be established.[32]

In mid-July President Pastrana had urged the formation of that verifying commission, in order to investigate the accusations of FARC crimes committed both in the country and in the demilitarized zone. The former were the use of unconventional weapons against civilians, including cylinders filled with gas, while the latter included accusations made to the national prosecutor's office about activities within the demilitarized zone.[33] Raúl Reyes, for the FARC, insisted that the negotiation table begin, leaving the theme of the verifying commission to later.[34] As the Bogotá daily *El Tiempo* pointed out, "Now, three months later, the agreement [of Caquetania] is the principal obstacle so long as FARC maintains that, with the impossibility of forming the verifying commission by common agreement, negotiations can begin without it. The government insists that not convoking it [the verifying commission] would be not carrying out the agreement."[35]

In early August President Pastrana tried a different tactic to get the conversations started again. He suggested that, if the two sides could not agree on the verifying commission, they could enter into a "humanitarian agreement" that would establish the basic rules for the demilitarized zone. That agreement would include no recruitment of minors, no assignment of logistical tasks to the civilian population, no kidnapping within the zone, no humiliating corporal punishment, and respect for religious and cultural beliefs.[36] FARC, however, never accepted this proposal. Instead in late August the guerrilla group stated that, while ready to reinitiate conversations, they would not accept conditions like the approval of international humanitarian law. "The president," FARC leader Felipe Rincón added, "should accept that dialogue was imposed on us in the middle of war and we have our own norms, for example, in the case of kidnapping."[37]

On September 18 in a violation of the confidential agreement to the negotiations, FARC sent an "Open Letter to Public Opinion" through its website. In it, by listing eight points, the insurgent group made it clear that it was the government's fault (Theme IIIc) that negotiations were frozen:

1. The government insisted on the international verification commission for the continuation of the dialogues, and this was unacceptable to FARC.
2. The government had not made satisfactory progress against the paramilitary groups.
3. The alliance of Pastrana with the United States in order to increase the war against FARC, with the sophism of fighting drug trafficking together, made it doubtful that the president really wanted peace.
4. The pressures of the Colombian and U.S. governments to limit the political activities of FARC did not contribute to reconciliation.
5. The social problems of poor people—like jobs, health, housing, and security—remained without solutions.
6. There had been little progress on prisoner exchange. Rather the government was using artificial classifications, like "terrorists" and "kidnappers" when all were political crimes.
7. The elements mentioned here were for FARC not clear demonstrations of compromise for a lasting and definitive peace, but rather war-like attitudes that could lead to a civil war of unforeseeable consequences.

8. "In contrast to the state policy, on our part we ratify before Colombians and the international community, our invariable policy of searching for peace with social justice, and independence and sovereignty for Colombia and its people."[38]

By late September *El Tiempo* suggested why the impasse had occurred and why Pastrana was compromising. The initial insistence on the verifying commission was because this was an agreement with leaders of the military after the Lloreda resignation (Theme Ib). The military officers were concerned about the lack of clear rules for the demilitarized zone. However, as time passed other voices were heard for a compromise—from ex-presidents, the Congress, the National Council of Peace, and from the opposition Liberal Party.[39]

On September 25 FARC leader Raúl Reyes, after a meeting with Commissioner Ricardo, said that the two sides would meet soon to talk about when to restart the conversations. This was possible, according to Reyes, since the government had dropped its insistence on a verifying commission.[40] Several days later in a news conference Commissioner Ricardo stated that the decision from the meeting with Reyes had been that a subcommission of the negotiators would receive any complaints about the conditions in the demilitarized zone. However, the details of the composition of this subcommission had been left for a future meeting.[41] Indeed the idea of the subcommission disappeared, and by mid-October the crisis seemed to have been resolved in another way—FARC recognized the constitutional authority of the elected mayors to receive complaints. However, it was not known if those officials could or would be able to take effective actions on the complaints.[42]

The Third Attempt at Dialogue

The negotiating table was reestablished on October 24 in what *El Tiempo* reporter Juan José Ramírez saw as an "encounter of two Colombias who agree on the essential: that negotiation might lead to peace."[43] Raúl Reyes discussed the economic problems of Colombia and rejected extradition. In his speech of strong recriminations against the government, the state, the governing class, and the political parties, he said "The costs of peace with social justice . . . should be borne by those who have taken Colombia to the worst crisis in its history. Neither the workers, nor the people, or the popular organizations are responsible."[44] Peace Commissioner Victor G. Ricardo gave a conciliatory speech and said that there would be a peace without winners and losers.[45] One source suggests that both sides had compromised. The government decided to postpone an international verifying commission and FARC agreed to study a cease-fire.[46]

In late October the two sides began meeting to discuss the methodology of the "National Thematic Committee." As Ricardo had stated the previous week, the goals were to define the functions of the committee, as well as the manner in which it would work and the mechanisms—Internet, free mail, teleconferences—that Colombians would have at their disposal to present their ideas.[47] Ricardo had been the Conservative Party representative in the similar exercise that took place during the 1989 negotiations with the 19 of April Movement (M-19). The idea might have come from there.[48]

There was agreement on these procedures. The committee was to be an instrument to guarantee citizen participation in the process, but without any decision-making authority. Its function would be to make recommendations to the table based on the discussions of the "public hearings." It would organize the hearings, consolidate the information, develop options, and make recommendations to the National Negotiation Table.[49] However, the procedure became much more clerical. As one member of the committee said in an interview, "The task as given to the committee was to take everything that people had testified and put their verbatim statements into categories. We were to do no synthesis or change any of the testimonies. So the result was a thick document."[50]

In making the decision to consult with FARC about issues of national politics through the National Thematic Committee, the Pastrana government had agreed to something that FARC had long called for—a discussion of substantive topics as part of the bargaining process. But some questioned the wisdom of this procedure. As one interviewee stated, "It was a mistake to talk about substantive issues, just as it was in Tlaxcala in 1992. That gave a certain amount of legitimacy to FARC. It suggested that they represented the people. The government should have maintained that it was the legitimate pathway to make decisions—through the Congress and the executive.[51]

It was decided that the hearings would begin in January 2000 and would be convoked and moderated by the Thematic Committee. The committee would also choose the specific social groups to invite. Anyone else who wanted to make a proposal could do so by air or electronic mail, fax, or by calling a toll-free number.[52] The purpose, according to Néstor Humberto Martínez, the government's coordinator of the Thematic Committee, was "to create a structure for people to persuade the negotiators with strong theses that not only have their own value but also solid scientific and ideological support."[53] FARC leader Iván Ríos, for his part, stated, "The national thematic committee, as a child, as a product of the development of the conversations for peace with social justice at the national dialogue table, has a great purpose and it is that the public hearings would make it possible that the voice, after experiencing the worries, the proposals for solutions to the grave social, economic and political crisis in which our country lived, be heard, arrive at the national table for peace dialogues."[54] Raúl Reyes added, "The moment has arrived when each Colombian can come to this place, in different ways, in order to participate in the great task that we all have to carry out to find solutions to the great problems that affect us . . ."[55]

Others questioned how the process turned out and how representative it was. One former government member of the committee stated,

> FARC wanted certain people at the hearings, so they chose the groups who would come on buses. FARC leaders would call, for example, labor unions and tell them to send people. Then the ones chosen would make a trip of twenty or more hours by bus. When the buses arrived for the hearings, FARC members would meet the people and take them to their tents. A little later FARC would have a political meeting for them, and then that evening a party with food and drink. So sometimes the individuals were very tired when the hearings began.[56]

People who went to the demilitarized zone numbered 23,795, where 1,069 presentations were made, presumably all in the hope that this would lead to changes.[57]

As 1999 neared its end, the two sides issued a progress report to the Colombian people. After promising to continue working together to find the political solution that would lead to a new Colombia, they listed the six accomplishments of the talks in 1999. First, the two sides had begun a dialogue within the demilitarized zone in an "atmosphere of confidence, respect and tolerance" (perhaps disingenuous since that dialogue had been frozen). Second, as analyzed above, a common agenda had been approved and, third, the negotiation stage, in which they were making progress (although no specifics were given, perhaps because there were none), had begun. Fourth, the National Thematic Committee had been put into action, with the goal of gathering the opinions of Colombians (albeit the ones chosen by FARC). Fifth, communication mechanisms had been developed to allow all Colombians to know how the process was proceeding (although it was not clear what this referred to). Finally the two sides had agreed to a methodology for the negotiation and mechanisms to allow the participation of Colombians.[58]

On December 20 FARC announced a unilateral cease-fire that would last until January 10. This did not mean that FARC did not have the right to respond to aggression from the "security forces of the state and para-state," and it was to show FARC's "unquestionable political will to contribute to the search for peace with social justice."[59]

By this time the Pastrana government—either in an effort to win the counterinsurgency war militarily or to increase its bargaining power at the tables—had developed "Plan Colombia" further. While the plan originally talked about strengthening the economy and making the country more democratic, it also stressed combating the narcotics industry and promoting the peace process, perhaps because the Clinton administration insisted on that focus.[60] Since the narcotics industry to a large degree was being run by FARC, Plan Colombia from its beginning had at least an implicit antiguerrilla theme, as noted by FARC at the negotiating table.

Plan Colombia was planned to be a US$7.5 billion program. President Pastrana pledged US$4 billion of Colombian resources and called on the international community to provide the remaining US$3.5 billion to assist this effort. In response to Plan Colombia, and in consultation with the Colombian government, President Clinton proposed a US$1.6 billion package of assistance to Colombia. Adding to previously approved U.S. assistance to Colombia of over US$330 million, the new initiative requested US$954 million as an emergency supplemental for FY 2000 and US$318 million in additional funding for FY 2001. The proposed U.S. assistance package was to help Colombia address the breadth of the challenges it faced—its efforts to fight the illicit drug trade, to increase the rule of law, to protect human rights, to expand economic development, to institute judicial reform, and to foster peace.[61]

In that context, the national negotiating table met again in mid-January 2000. Despite the surprise presence of Manuel Marulanda nothing was accomplished. The delegates of the government suggested that human rights and international humanitarian law be discussed first, while FARC delegates suggested that "social matters," such as agrarian reform, employment, and the economic model have priority.[62]

On January 28, 2000, the two sides agreed on an agenda of three blocks—the economic and social model; human rights, international humanitarian law, and international policy; and political reform. It was agreed to take them in that order, with the time needed for the first one calculated to be six months. It was also estimated that the three blocks could be discussed in eighteen months and during that time other themes, such as a cease-fire, could be raised. It was also agreed that, should irresolvable disagreements be reached, the topic would be left with both sides leaving a written statement of their positions. The opinions of international experts would be sought.[63] It should be noted that the first priority of the government (a cease-fire) was not in the agenda; rather these were matters that FARC wanted to discuss before a cease-fire was discussed.

The next day FARC leaders made it even clearer what the priorities of the insurgent group were. Anticipating the first theme of the agenda, Manuel Marulanda wrote an open letter to President Pastrana, stating unequivocally that Colombian businesses were going bankrupt "because of unfair competition, product of the neoliberal policies of previous governments, which has to be modified by President Andrés Pastrana." For this purpose, "We of the FARC-EP will be present until a short- and long-term policy is found to end unemployment in its many manifestations, demanding that the state and the industrialists make large investments in new jobs, with the understanding that it is more profitable to invest in peace, that war is the policy of the state, to defend its class interests and to submit workers to starvation salaries of exploitation." Yet Tirofijo did not limit himself to economic themes. Plan Colombia was also criticized; finally he disparaged "the paramilitarism of the state has been and continues to be one of the great obstacles to peace and national reconciliation."[64]

The same day, at a meeting in San Vicente, Raúl Reyes first reported on the accomplishments of FARC within the demilitarized zone and then also hammered on the economic theme. In one year, according to Reyes, FARC had constructed more than 250 kilometers of new roads and had repaired another 250 kilometers for the benefit of the inhabitants of the demilitarized zone, while constructing twenty bridges, paved sixty-four streets, and had vaccinated more than 20,000 people. Meanwhile crime had gone down in the five municipalities. Given their results and their identification with the Colombian people, Reyes called on the government to do likewise:

> We insist in the immediate necessity that the government find solutions for the more than three million Colombians who are unemployed who cannot buy housing, clothing, education, health, or security for their families; for the more than 1,500,000 peasant families without land who could work it, who wait for an immediate solution to their problem from the government. The workers on the countryside continue waiting for the reactivation of the agricultural sector with resources of the State and the private sector, guaranteeing the marketing of their products at prices that correspond to the high prices of production, to make the right to work a reality once again.

Reyes concluded that the solution to the grave economic crisis that affected Colombia could not be found in the sale of state enterprises or "in mortgaging the patrimony of the country to the International Monetary Fund or the World Bank."[65]

On January 31, 2000, the permanent site of the peace dialogues was inaugurated in the Los Pozos area of Caquetá and symbolically called "Villa Nueva

Colombia." Time would demonstrate that no real progress was made on the three-block agenda that had been set up several days before.

On February 3, 2000, a new tactic to jump-start negotiations was attempted: a FARC-government group took off on a four-week tour of Europe. The trip meant a dramatic change of climate—from the rain forest of the demilitarized zone where temperatures were over 40° Celsius (104° Fahrenheit) to Stockholm, with temperatures that were below 10° Celsius (14° Fahrenheit). Peace Commissioner Victor G. Ricardo and a delegation of FARC negotiators traveled to Sweden, Norway, Switzerland, Italy, France, and Spain on a "tour" facilitated by Jan Egeland, the special representative for Colombia of UN Secretary-General Kofi Annan. The trip's primary purpose was to enrich the negotiations' discussion of Colombia's economic model by familiarizing participants with the mixed economies of Scandinavia and Western Europe. An unstated secondary goal of the visit was to increase exposure of FARC to a changing world and the international community's expectations. A likely third goal was so that the participants from the two sides would learn to know each other as individuals, far from the conflict that had separated them for nearly forty years.

The Colombian group held meetings with leaders of the parliaments of France, Norway, Italy, and Spain and with representatives of the International Red Cross and the Vatican. Without doubt the two groups learned to know each other better, and at the final cocktail party Raúl Reyes stated, as he raised his glass, "We Colombians cannot continue killing each other." They returned to Colombia on February 26, and the respective delegations were to meet with leaderships of their groups in order to elaborate a document summarizing the accomplishments of the trip.[66]

That document was issued in March. In it the following accomplishments were mentioned:

- There are no taboo topics.
- There is more confidence and more respect within the two teams.
- They agreed that human rights and international humanitarian law were of great importance.
- They had a wider viewpoint and agreed that the economies of all countries should be placed within the global world.
- They realized that the negotiation had international support.
- They agreed that, although the Colombian conflict should be resolved in its own way, negotiation was the right way to solve it.
- The foreign trip made it clearer that social reform was necessary for peace with social justice.

In conclusion, "The trip to Europe is, without doubt, another proof that we are taking the correct path in a negotiated political settlement. The negotiation process is underway. We still have much to do and much work remains for Colombians to achieve peace. We are continuing with a good wind and in calm seas."[67] While goodwill among the bargainers might have increased, time was to demonstrate that that spirit did not lead to specific achievements.

On March 10 the two sides agreed on a methodology for the public hearings on the first theme—"The model of economic and social development which has as its objectives the generation of jobs, the growth of the economy, the distribution of income, and social development." In keeping with that, the National Dialogue Table and the National Thematic Committee would begin their study of economic growth and employment that day, including the subthemes of stimuli to small, medium, and large private businesses; assistance to cooperatives; stimuli to foreign investment that benefits the nation; investments in social well-being, education, and scientific investigations; national resources and their distribution; substitution of illicit crops and alternative development; and democratization of credit, technical assistance, and marketing.[68]

Although the public hearings began on April 9, little else was accomplished during 2000. The government continued developing Plan Colombia. FARC began increasing its attacks on towns, kidnappings, and extortion while two notable events took place in March and April 2000. In March FARC announced the establishment of a clandestine political party—the *Movimiento Bolivariano por la Nueva Colombia.* Manuel Marulanda, in an interview, announced that the Bolivarian Movement was a wide popular movement, within which there was room for people of different political and religious matrices, who agreed on their repugnance for the directing class and its corrupt and excluding way of governing and had sympathy towards FARC. He said, "The Bolivarian Movement is one similar to the Unión Patriótica, with the difference that the former will be clandestine, so that its members will not be assassinated like those of the UP."[69]

The Manifesto del Movimiento began with Theme IIIc ("It wasn't us."): "The revolutionary guerrilla war exists in Colombia by the exclusive responsibility of the oligarchy. The revolutionary guerrilla war does not exist in our country because someone invented it, or through transplanting the experiences of other people of the world, or for any order given from the centers of the old Socialist camp." The rapacity and terrorist violence of the class in power, the manifest continued, "OBLIGED the people to develop its unquenchable creativity to protect itself and later, in the transpiring of the struggle, to become conscious that it was insufficient to resist and the important thing was to liquidate the roots of the cause that made possible its own existence."[70] Nothing resulted from this bombastic statement.

Then on April 25 FARC demonstrated that it rejected the authority of the Colombian government when its military head, Jorge Briceño Suárez, announced that any person whose net worth exceeded US$1 million would be "taxed" by the FARC. Briceño stated that despite the peace process, the State continued to strengthen both its legal and illegal armed forces. The latter was no doubt a reference to the paramilitary groups. He continued that the government of the United States also continued intervening, most recently under the pretext of fighting against illicit drugs through Plan Colombia. In addition multinational corporations continued exploiting the riches and work of the peace of Colombia.

Since funds were needed for the objective of a new Colombia and since to that point FARC had not been able to reach agreement with the government at the negotiating table, FARC had resolved that those people whose net worth exceeded US$1 million would be charged the tax for peace. All those who fulfilled that criterion should come forward and make their payment. A second call would mean an increase in the amount of the tax. Those who did not pay would be detained, and their liberation would depend on the prompt payment of an amount that would be determined on a case-by-case basis.[71]

At the same time the government was stepping up its military actions. Thanks to the aid of the United States through Plan Colombia, the Colombian military became larger, better equipped, and more adequately trained. This made it possible to attack FARC troop concentrations and prevent the continuation of the insurgent group's transition to a war of movements.[72]

On April 26, demonstrating Theme IIb (the lack of governmental continuity), High Commissioner for Peace Ricardo announced his resignation. While he said that he was leaving because the peace process had reached "a point of no return," many observers speculated that frequent death threats influenced his decision. Camilo Gómez, the president's private secretary and a member of the government negotiating team, replaced Ricardo as high commissioner. Since Ricardo had developed a certain level of confidence with FARC leaders never to be attained by Gómez, this change damaged the negotiation process.

Nevertheless, on May 11 FARC proposed a bilateral cease-fire to the national negotiation table. FARC would be one side, while "the public forces and the other security forces of the state" would be the other.[73] Yet nothing was to come of this in the short run, as on May 16 the government froze the process because of the death of Elvira Cortés, a peasant woman, a day after FARC rebels allegedly killed her by rigging a bomb around her neck in a bungled extortion attempt.

It was the first time in the 18-month-old peace process that the government called off talks with the FARC. A rebel spokesman, however, denied the FARC was responsible for the so-called "necklace bomb" attack in central Boyacá province. He described Pastrana's decision as a "bad sign" but said the rebels would not walk away from the peace table.[74] FARC issued a communiqué in which they "repudiated and condemned" the "cruelty of the assassination" as well as "the yellow journalistic treatment given to it by some sectors of the press, evidence of the grave moral infirmities that are sinking Colombia in an ignoble quagmire."[75] Later evidence led to the governmental conclusion that FARC was not responsible for this action, although one military official interviewed suggested that FARC was the only group in Colombia with the expertise to rig this bomb.[76]

On July 3 the two sides exchanged cease-fire proposals. Although they were in sealed envelopes and were supposed to be confidential, FARC leaked theirs. Their proposal called for a bilateral cease-fire for a limited time, but would also be renewable. It also stated that there should be a discussion of a presidential decision to mandate that all military forces accept the cease-fire "in order to prevent the army, as has happened to past processes, from invoking constitutional reasons to continue its operations and patrols." In addition there should be discussion at the negotiation table of "the government's policy about paramilitarism, since that was a great obstacle to peace and national reconciliation." It was also necessary to purify the armed forces of officers and enlisted men who were involved in the dirty war.

The FARC proposal continued that there also had to be an end to the violence against workers in the city and countryside for the sole reason of mobilizing and reclaiming their political, economic, and social rights and better conditions of life for their families. In addition there needed to be an "end of the neoliberal policies responsible for hunger, unemployment, misery and the armed conflict among Colombians because some have everything and some have nothing, not even the means to survive." Finally there had to be an exchange of prisoners of war. With all of the above resolved at the table, it would be necessary to name a national committee of verification, made of the two sides and whose members would be elected in a method commonly agreed upon.[77]

If the public release of the FARC proposal went against the rules of formal negotiations, bargaining in general was affected on September 8 when a FARC guerrilla named Arnubio Ramos hijacked a commuter airliner and forced it to land in San Vicente del Caguán in the FARC demilitarized zone. Government officials insisted that the guerrillas turn Ramos over as an indication of their commitment to the peace process. The guerrillas refused to surrender him, arguing that Ramos hijacked the plane on his own account and "the FARC bears no responsibility."[78] Indeed one source states that the FARC guerrillas panicked when the plane landed, took defensive positions, and were ready to attack the plane because they had no idea who had hijacked it.[79]

This is the first indication of Theme Ic—lack of unity on the part of the guerrilla groups. In the case of the FARC, the question is to what extent are the leaders (Tirofijo, Raúl Reyes and the central committee) responsible for the activities of the various FARC fronts and individual guerrillas. According to analysis published by a Bogotá think tank, collegial decisions of the organization's secretariat were supposed to be followed by all levels of the organization, although they might not be. Especially since the 1993 Conference, when the Fronts were created, FARC had become a decentralized organization. Members of the Secretariat were sent to be coordinators of each front, which they directed along with the respective military commander. Hence the leaders did not need to travel to or make contact with the central leadership.[80] While this decentralization protected the organization, it might also have led to local decisions that did not closely follow the directives of the central leadership.

Two leading Colombian experts on violence and negotiations offered similar analyses. When I asked them to read the think tank's conclusions, one replied, "I think FARC has strategic centralization and tactical decentralization. That is to say, the fronts have their own initiatives, within a framework of action decided by the Secretariat in a very centralized way. For example, I do not believe that the airplane hijacking was consulted and approved by the Secretariat."[81] The other expert reached the same conclusions, but for different reasons:

> Recently guerrilla forces have great communication difficulties because of the improvements of the technical intelligence of the armed forces. The relationships between central commands and fronts are very complex and I have the impression that central control has been relaxed. The central command no longer distributes resources to equilibrate rich and poor fronts; rather now each front finances itself however it can and that can generate tendencies that in the future can be "centrifugal," leading to the decomposition of the apparatus.[82]

All this notwithstanding, this hijacking negatively affected the negotiations, with matters worsening even more when on September 24 FARC called an "armed strike" in the southern department of Putumayo, where the U.S.-funded antidrug offensive was taking place. Demanding an end to the Plan Colombia's military component, the guerrillas prohibited all vehicle traffic on the roads, resulting in isolated towns and hamlets suffering severe shortages of food, gasoline, and drinking water. The strike lasted until early December, when the FARC unilaterally lifted it.

At this time, Luis Guillermo Giraldo, a Liberal who had been named a member of the third negotiating team, stated that the negotiating process had become one of three parallel tracks that never made contact. The first was private discussion between Commissioner Gómez and Marulanda or with special negotiators of FARC. These discussions had to do with the humanitarian exchange, the causes of the conflict, and the cease-fire. The second track was the formal negotiating table, which Gómez never attended, where the common agenda was discussed. Neither the representatives of the government or those of FARC had any power and the former received no instructions from the president or the high commissioner. The third track consisted of the public hearings and the meetings of the Thematic Committee.[83]

This, a continuation of Theme IIb (frequent changes of negotiating team members), showed the chaotic condition of the government's negotiation. One interviewee put it this way: "The Pastrana team worked in a very disjointed, unorganized way. This was seen from the beginning. For example, the problem of the Cazadores in Caguán should have never happened."[84] As mentioned in chapter 3, the process came close to not beginning because the lack of specificity in the demobilization agreement led one side (FARC) to believe that all army troops would leave the demilitarized zone, while the other (the government) did not think that the withdrawal applied to the Cazadores troops (Theme V, "devil's in the details").

In October elections were held for both municipal and departmental posts. Officials said that aside from isolated fighting between members of the FARC and army troops in the outlying provinces, voting was carried out with no major disruptions. Meanwhile at the negotiating table the two sides agreed to create a two-person commission, composed of one member named by each side, to "determine the solution to an impasse within one month and inform the table of such a solution."[85]

Nevertheless, on November 15 FARC declared a unilateral "freeze" on the peace process, saying that they were suspending the talks until the government took firmer measures against paramilitary groups. FARC leader Andrés París said, "We think that until the president of the republic and his government make their position on paramilitary terrorism clear to the country and to the world and develop policies to liquidate it [paramilitary terrorism], the current dialogues should be frozen." Since there were only a few days left until the time for the demilitarized zone to run out, the military let the president know that they were ready to retake the zone.[86]

On December 1 peace negotiator Camilo Gómez met FARC leader Manuel Marulanda although the talks remained officially "frozen." On December 6, President Pastrana announced that the guerrillas' demilitarized zone would be extended until January 31, 2001, even though the FARC still was maintaining its freeze on the talks.

The year 2000 ended with two negative notes for the peace process. On December 12, clearly demonstrating Theme Ib, Colombian army chief, General Jorge Mora, declared that the army was prepared to reclaim the FARC demilitarized zone whenever it might be called upon to do so. Then on December 29, Diego Turbay, a Colombian legislator who headed a congressional peace committee, was assassinated along with his mother and five other people on a highway in southern Caquetá department, not far from the FARC demilitarized zone. The assassination was widely attributed to the FARC, casting further doubt on the future of peace talks.

Conclusion: Accomplishments During 2000

As 2000 ended, there were more reasons to be pessimistic about the Pastrana peace process than to be optimistic. This chapter has shown that, with the exception of Theme IV, all of the themes that were negative to successful negotiations had occurred. This overall pattern of the period is shown graphically in Figure 4–1. While the guerrilla group was responsible for more of these contretemps than the government was, both sides were responsible. In addition one negative government contribution (the Lloreda resignation and the military crisis) shows a very important characteristic of the process—that the government side was not monolithic. However the same could be concluded from the hijacking of the airplane. This was no doubt an incident that did not have the prior approval of Marulanda and the FARC leaders but rather something initiated by a single guerrilla fighter. The same might be said about the Turbay assassination; while it seems clear that it was done by a FARC group, that is not to say that it had been approved by higher-ups.

Nevertheless, there are some more favorable aspects of the negotiations in this period. First, the trip to Europe no doubt did lead to a closer relationship among the bargainers (albeit one that had no apparent subsequent results). That the two sides agreed on a common agenda and exchanged cease-fire proposals are positive features, also, as was the Acuerdo de Caquetania.

Yet at the end of January 2001 it was not clear if peace negotiation cup was half full or half empty. The following year was to be another of ups and downs in the negotiating process, as we discuss in chapter 5.

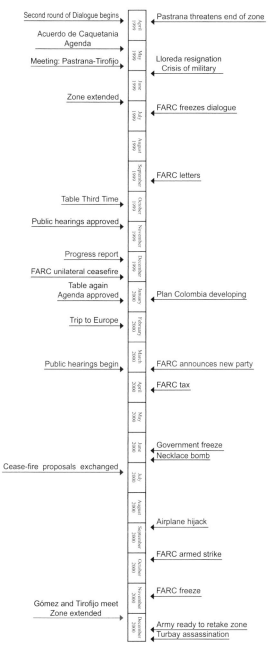

Figure 4.1. First phase of FARC negotiations, April 1999–January 2001.

5

The Negotiations in 2001

Agreements on Process but Not on Substance

The two-year anniversary of the FARC peace talks passed on January 7, 2001, with pessimism, the dialogues having been frozen since mid-November. The year was to be similar to the previous one, with both gains and losses. Among the positive characteristics were important agreements on the process to be followed. A prisoner exchange took place. Negative things happened as well, both at the table and in the continuing war. At the table FARC broke the rules, leaking proposals that were supposed to be confidential. In the war there were foreign agents in the demilitarized zone, kidnappings, and interruptions of electoral campaigns. Although an occasional detail was included in a one or another document, in general Theme V (lack of specificity) was in full play. Other themes were manifested frequently during the year as well: the apparent disunity of FARC (Theme Ic); opposition to Pastrana being considered disloyal (Theme IIIa); and blaming the other side (Theme IIIc). By the end of the year the momentum was clearly against peace.

Bargaining about Restarting Negotiations

In the last two weeks of January the two sides demonstrated that they were interested enough in negotiations to suggest how they might begin anew—or at least not end definitively. On January 19 Marulanda made public a letter that he had sent to the president and peace commissioner two days earlier, in which the FARC leader had eleven points, including that the president extend the demilitarized zone until the end of his presidency; that certain generals come to the zone to talk with him; that an agreement be signed as soon as possible for a prisoner exchange; that a ten-person committee be set up—five to be named by the government and five by FARC—to establish if the government had the ability to stop the paramilitary groups; and that Pastrana and Marulanda meet again.[1]

However, the memorandum contained threats and denials. The Negotiating Table was unilaterally frozen by FARC and would be so until the government showed its policy and concrete results in the fight against paramilitarism. Further, in response to a threat from Commissioner Gómez on January 4 (that the government would make no agreements for prisoner exchange until FARC explained the deaths of Turbay and the kidnapping of Araújo and Villegas), FARC responded, "In these conditions we consider the dialogue about prisoner exchange to be closed." In addition, this was the third freezing of the dialogues by the government, "without considering that there is dialogue and negotiation amidst armed conflict and since the two sides have not arrived at agreements on a ceasefire, neither of the two can complain about events like the ones mentioned." Marulanda was incorrect how many times the government had frozen the process. He was no doubt participating in Theme IIIc behavior. Although most of the "freezings" had been declared by FARC, it still was the fault of the government since it had not done something that the subversive group wanted or had done something not desired.

Marulanda then suggested ways out of the impasse. There could be another international trip by both sides, "to see if we can achieve new dynamism." An additional possibility was a ten-person "commission of personalities," to investigate the government actions against the paramilitary groups. A third option was a meeting of representatives of the political parties in the demilitarized zone, to evaluate the effect of the end of the demilitarized zone on the upcoming elections. Further, that "friendly meeting" could consider the effects of drug fumigation on the department of Putumayo, an area dominated by FARC where much coca was grown, "as well as the death of 1269 peasants there at the hand of members of the military, dressed as paramilitary troops."[2]

A few days after the Marulanda letter, the government offered a proposal to restart the talks, which FARC rejected on January 23. The proposal had included a call for an end to kidnappings and the guerrillas' use of bombs made by filling empty propane cylinders with explosives. With a January 31 deadline for renewal of the demilitarized zone approaching, the Colombian army announced that 600 counterguerrilla troops had been airlifted to sites near the zone. They also secretly put into effect a "Plan B," designed sometime before, for the military assault of the demilitarized zone. This included other troops and aircraft, all ready should the president decide not to extend the zone.[3]

On the eve of a deadline for the demilitarized zone, the government of Andrés Pastrana participated in some of its most hard-nosed and effective bargaining. This began when the president stated, "If Manuel Marulanda wants an extension of the safe haven, he has to sit at the negotiating table." The president extended the zone for four more days, asking for a face-to-face meeting with FARC leader Marulanda. The FARC leader accepted a meeting on February 8. This was the first time that the Pastrana government insisted on FARC concessions before extending the demilitarized zone. It should be noted that the "concession" was a small one—a meeting between the FARC leader and the president. Yet when the minister of labor asked Pastrana if he knew the risk he was taking, the president replied "I know the risk clearly, but we cannot continue with the demilitarized zone if there are no negotiations."[4]

In addition FARC leaders no doubt knew of the "Plan B" that the Colombian military was considering. Hence if the FARC wanted to continue the demilitarized zone, it might be time to give in on some points.

The Los Pozos Agreement and Another Start

On February 9 President Pastrana and Manuel Marulanda signed the Agreement of Los Pozos. In it the two sides agreed to continue the peace process by beginning the dialogues again. The third point of the agreement stated, "For that purpose the dialogue and negotiation table will create a commission of national personalities that will formulate recommendations on those two matters."[5] But this was not a FARC concession; this "Commission of Notables" had been proposed by FARC. It was to play a central role later in the year, although it ultimately led nowhere.

In addition, the Agreement of Los Pozos stated that the two sides would concentrate on a "humanitarian agreement" that would allow the freedom of ill soldiers and guerrilla fighters. This was to lead to one of the major accomplishments of the dialogues. Further, so that the negotiations were not interrupted again as they had been in the past, the two sides agreed to create an internal committee to study the causes of interruptions of the negotiations and make recommendations to avoid future difficulties.[6] Additional provisions of the agreement of Los Pozos are listed below:

- The Table of Dialogue and Negotiations would set up an internal committee to report periodically about activities in the demilitarized zone.
- A group of friendly countries and international agencies would be invited to an information session on March 8.
- The two sides would discuss the eradication of coca crops, along with the communities involved.
- National organizations would be invited to Los Pozos on February 28, in order to give dynamism to the process.
- The Table of Dialogue and Negotiations might be enlarged and would meet at least three times a week.

It is of note that, in a rare case in which Theme V did not apply, certain details (specific dates by which things should be done) were actually supplied.

On the same day as the Los Pozos agreement President Pastrana and Commander Marulanda held a joint news conference. Notably absent from it was the rancor that each side usually had for the other. For example, when Marulanda was asked if the agreement meant that FARC would not "freeze" the dialogues again, the commander pointed out that there was no such agreement in it. President Pastrana added that point seven of the agreement called for the joint commission to avoid such problems. Marulanda finished the news conference optimistically when he stated, "We cannot continue with the expectation that there will be nothing since we are showing in this meeting that very concrete elements are already produced, which will begin immediately."[7]

The new momentum continued on February 16, when the members of the negotiating table returned to their discussions of substantive matters and of a cease-fire. They also set up a timetable for the rest of the month. On February 21 the talks would be on economic growth and job creation. On February 22–23, each side would explain its cease-fire proposal. On February 28 the two sides would meet with the signatories to the Acuerdo de Caquetanía, and on March 8 they would meet with the countries who were present at the June 2000 International Hearing, to inform them of the state of the process. Finally the two sides announced that they had agreed upon an "Auxiliary Commission of Special Cases," made of one negotiator from each side and with the task of "studying those conjunctional situations that might affect the progress of the process, with the goal that the dialogue and negotiation not be interrupted."[8]

Also in February FARC evaluated the peace process in its journal *Resistencia*. They began by listing the important achievements: the demilitarization of five municipalities for the talks, the signing of the Common Agenda for Change Toward a New Colombia, the formation of the National Issues Commission with representatives from both sides to organize public hearings, a mechanism for democratic participation of all sectors of the country, and the holding of twenty-five public hearings. Theme IIIc (securing a place in history) was alive and well, we see, as FARC implicitly took credit for those accomplishments.

The FARC document then gave a summary of the hearings. The first issue discussed by the National Thematic Committee was "Economic Growth and Job Creation," with the decision that the subject of the debates would be the proposals of Colombians at the public hearings, so the spokespersons would not be conversing in a vacuum. More than 20,000 Colombians came to Villa Nueva Colombia for the hearings which were of two kinds—the "ordinary" ones in which all those registered participated individually, and the "special" hearings, called by sectors. Hearings were held with Afro-Colombians, women, youth, the country's strategic economic sectors, the education sector, the health sector, credit users and the victims of the current housing system, informal workers, community action councils, and peasant producers of illicit crops. The latter participated in the international hearing, convoked by the National Table, so their viewpoint and solutions to the problems could be heard before a delegation of twenty-one invited countries and the Vatican.

The issues committee was to collect and organize all the speeches given at the hearings, and to prepare a report containing the diagnosis as well as the proposals of each participant. To facilitate the discussion at the National Dialogue Table, the committee provided it with this document, with the proposals of Colombians, taking into account the main issues considered.

The FARC document concluded "The process has come this far; now the National Issues Commission must begin discussion of the first issue and present the country with the short-, medium-, and long-term measures to confront unemployment. This would be the true demonstration of the government's will to achieve peace. It would show Colombians that the country's alternative is not war." However, anticipating the possibility of accusing the government of sabotaging the talks, FARC warned that "the quarrelsome and procrastinating attitude of the national government is highly suspicious."[9]

On March 9, the negotiators met with representatives of twenty-six foreign governments to inform them about the process. The United States declined an invitation to attend. In the meeting the government and FARC presented a proposal for "friendly governments" and international organizations to receive bimonthly bulletins about the progress of the peace process. In addition every six months there was to be a meeting of all. It was agreed that the friendly countries would be Germany, Austria, Belgium, Brazil, Italy, Japan, Mexico, Norway, Holland, Panama, Peru, Portugal, the United Kingdom, Sweden, Switzerland, Venezuela, and the Vatican, as well as the special delegate of the Secretary General of the United Nations and the European Community. Of those the facilitating commission would be made up of Canada, Cuba, Spain, France, Italy, Mexico, Norway, Sweden, Switzerland, and Venezuela.[10] This procedural agreement was parallel to one made in Guatemala in 1994.

On April 5 the negotiators met with members of the Commission of Friendly Countries, establishing guidelines for the commission's operation. At the same time the government and the FARC continued to hold negotiations for a possible "humanitarian exchange." As part of this swap the FARC wanted the government to release a group of captive rebels in exchange for some of the 500 military and police officers in its custody.

Both governmental and FARC sources stated that plans for an exchange were in doubt. Earlier Marulanda and Pastrana had agreed to try to arrange a prisoner exchange. The FARC had presented a list of 85 prisoners they hoped to release. The army feared that their freeing in turn some captured guerrilleros, many of whom suffered from relatively mild ailments, would hurt troop morale and encourage soldiers to murder guerrillas who surrender in the future. Further, they feared that the released prisoners might reenter the ranks of the FARC troops.

On May 11, the negotiators established the "Commission of Notables" to recommend ways to do away with paramilitarism. Each side chose two members: Ana Mercedes Gómez Martínez (director of the Medellín daily *El Colombiano*), and Vladimiro Naranjo Mesa (former member of the Constitutional Court) by the government; Carlos Lozano Guillén (director of the Communist party daily *Voz*), and Alberto Pinzón Sánchez (a medical doctor) by FARC.[11] This commission was to have ninety days in which to send its conclusions to the negotiating table. It could not only talk to the two parts to the conflict, but also to any other sectors of Colombian society that it might find useful.[12] The Commission of Notables was an attempt to get past the paralysis of the negotiating table, where no agreement had been reached; hence the idea was to let an outside group come in with recommendations.[13]

On June 2 the two sides signed an accord for the humanitarian exchange of prisoners of war, the major points of which are shown below:

1. The government delivered a list of FARC members in its control whom they deemed ill enough to qualify for humanitarian release.
2. FARC declared that the list of forty-two sick soldiers and policemen delivered to the government are the individuals who will be released for humanitarian reasons.
3. FARC will release Col. Alvaro Leon-Acosta immediately, given his state of health.

4. Once the state of health of the sick soldiers and policemen under FARC control is established, they will be delivered to the International Red Cross committee on the same day that the members of FARC are released.
5. The sick members of FARC that the government has determined to be eligible will be released to the International Red Cross Committee.
6. FARC undertakes to release unilaterally at least 100 soldiers and policemen who are not sick, within 15 days of the delivery of the sick soldiers and police officers.

On June 5, 2001, FARC released Colonel León Acosta and three other officers, the beginning of compliance with a prisoner exchange agreement. On June 16 the prison of Valledupar released eleven sick FARC members, who were transferred to the demilitarized zone by the International Red Cross, while FARC released twenty-nine police and military officers. On June 19 FARC announced the unilateral liberation of 250 police and soldiers. Then on June 28 FARC unilaterally released another 242 soldiers and police officers. However, the group also threatened to increase its kidnappings. FARC leader Jorge Briceño told the prisoners, "We have to grab people from the Senate, from Congress, judges and ministers, from all the three powers (of the Colombian government), and we'll see how they squeal."[14]

It is difficult to understand this Briceño statement right after the first substantive agreement of the peace process. There seem to be three plausible explanations: First the FARC leader did not want the government to think that things were going that well in the negotiation process and that more concessions from FARC should be expected. For the same reasons the Briceño statement can be seen as one for internal FARC consumption. It was not yet time for the troops to relax, even after an exchange that seemed to favor the guerrilla group more than the government.

Finally this statement might have been an indication of Theme Ia—the lack of unity of the guerrilla group. Briceño had been in FARC since he was a teenager. He was acknowledged as a very able military strategist, but also was credited for many FARC hard-line policies. He apparently was skeptical about the talks.

The Briceño statement notwithstanding, things seemed to be going very well in the negotiation process. Then, perhaps for the same reasons mentioned above, the combination of four things listed below changed the direction of the talks.

- a FARC statement that Pastrana should be removed as president
- an increase of high-profile kidnappings by the FARC

- a joint contribution—the publication of the ceasefire agendas of the two sides, showing that there was no progress on that crucial matter
- the discovery of members of the Irish Republican Army in the demilitarized zone

July 2001 began with a bombshell when FARC leader Raúl Reyes, in an interview published in Bogotá daily *El Espectador* on July 2, proposed that President Pastrana be replaced with a "government of reconciliation and reconstruction" composed of five to ten people. This government would be "pluralistic, patriotic, and democratic, made up of various social, economic, and even business sectors that have social sensibility and who understand that solutions can be found for problems through conciliation, understanding, and social investment." The insurgent leader suggested that the government could be chosen by popular vote, but did not dare to suggest the name of the persons who might make it up. He did say, however, that FARC would be part of the government, although it was not certain how that person would be chosen either.

The insurgent leader was very clear: "What we want is to govern; the struggle of FARC is to be the government, to make a new state that guarantees the rights of people." Progressive members of the Liberal and Conservative parties might be included, "if and only if they agree to develop the platform that is approved there, that would be based on the twelve points of the common agenda, approved in the Dialogue Table." Finally Reyes stated that the proposal had not officially been presented to the government at the negotiation table because it was not on the agenda.[15]

In reaction to this FARC proposal, both the high commissioner and the president made public statements. Early in July, Peace Commissioner Camilo Gómez stated publicly that the government had decided to take a more direct role in the negotiations. Privately he criticized the governmental negotiators for lack of ability. As one member of the government said in a confidential interview, "Camilo was always unhappy because the [governmental] negotiators criticized him too much. Although it was true that in a year he had met with the negotiators only three times—one of which was a social occasion—the commissioner maintained that the person who should be in charge of the peace process was he."[16]

In addition the peace commissioner, in an interview in *El Tiempo,* assured the public that there was no secret agreement with FARC. "Colombians can be tranquil because the government is not turning over the country." Rather, he stated, there were some things that were not negotiable—the democratic system, territorial unity, individual liberties, and private property.[17]

The next week President Pastrana stated that Colombians should not fear that FARC would enter into politics, although that might come at the end of the peace process. And he was optimistic: "There are reasons to be optimistic, amidst the difficulties and the challenges that a conflict that has been going on nearly forty years presents."[18] He gave no specific reasons for this hopefulness.

Then in several days two FARC kidnappings were to anger the government and the international community and slow the pace of the peace talks. On July 15 FARC guerrillas in Meta department kidnapped the department's former governor, Alán Jara, while he was traveling in a clearly marked United Nations vehicle. A FARC statement issued later accused Jara of paramilitary ties, criticized the UN for transporting him, and promised to submit the former governor to a "popular tribunal."[19] In addition, on July 16 the FARC kidnapped three German development workers in Cauca department, demanding an end to coca fumigations in the zone (which had started the day before).[20] It is not known to what extent these were actions ordered by the FARC leaders or simply actions of individual guerrillas or fronts (Theme Ic, lack of unity among the guerrillas).

A third negative thing happened in the third week in July when both sides released their cease-fire proposals. The proposals had been exchanged in July 2000 and kept confidential by both sides for the following year. The idea behind confidentiality (supported by the literature on bargaining) was stated clearly in the first Guatemalan agreement of 1994: "Disclosure: the parties agree that the bilateral negotiations will be conducted in the strictest secrecy in order to ensure that they are carried on in an atmosphere of trust and seriousness. They agree that the only public information on their conduct will be that made available by the representative of the Secretary-General of the United Nations."[21]

For this reason, the government expressed its dismay when FARC leaked their proposal on July 22. Commissioner Gómez said, "It should be clear and is to be regretted that FARC decided unilaterally to break the confidentiality agreement that we ratified again just a week ago."[22] The same day the commissioner released the government's proposal. He also reported that, since July 22, 2000, when the proposals were first discussed, there had been "more than ten discussions" of a cease-fire at the negotiating table.

As Table 5.1 shows, the two sides agreed on nothing. FARC included more units in the cease-fire and "all government security agencies," no doubt meaning the paramilitary groups also. Verification would be by international groups for the government and the Commission of Notables for FARC. While the government would have FARC demobilized in one place, the guerrilla group called for seventy places where they claimed to be already located. The government called

Table 5.1: Government and FARC Proposals for Cease-fire, August, 2001

Stipulations	Government	FARC
Units included	Armed Forces and FARC	All governmental security agencies and FARC
Veri cation	International	National personalities
Location of FARC members	All troops in one place	In seventy areas where currently located
Preliminary conditions	All kidnapped people released	Not accepted
Additional demands	An international mediator to facilitate the process	End to extraditions of drug dealers, dismantling of paramilitary groups, and decriminalization of social protests
Additional stipulations	Cessation of all kid-napping, extortion, and attacks of people and economic infrastructure	End of the neoliberal policies

Source: "Revelan propuestas de Gobierno y guerrilla sobre cese de fuego," *El Tiempo*, August 29, 2001

for all kidnapped people to be released as a precondition, while FARC had no such stipulation. Finally as far as additional matters were concerned, the government wanted the termination of all kidnapping, extortion, and attacks on people and economic infrastructure by FARC and an international mediator to facilitate the process. The FARC for its part wanted the end to extraditions of drug dealers, dismantling of paramilitary groups, and decriminalization of social protests as well as the end of the neoliberal policies.[23] Clearly these were first demands in the process of negotiation that should have been kept confidential.

The fourth and final occurrence in the downward spiral came on August 12 when the Army captured three Irish citizens as they left the demilitarized zone. They were later accused of being members of the Irish Republican Army who were training FARC members in urban warfare tactics.

On August 24 the spokespeople of FARC wrote to Peace Commissioner Gómez, referring to the kidnapping of the three German citizens on July 16. The letter pointed out that on August 2 FARC had promised the government to look into the possibility that some Front of the organization had committed the kidnapping. Further, on August 16 Iván Ríos, commander of the Jacobo Arenas Column, publicly admitted that they had kidnapped the three. Yet the spokespeople responded in more general terms. First, "The solution of particular matters not pertinent to the agenda cannot be the concern of the Dialogue and Negotiation Table." The case of the Germans should be a matter for their government and the Jacobo Arenas Column. Finally, in a typical disavowal of responsibility (Theme IIIc), it declared: "This type of thing, which happens every day in this country, is the product of the social and armed conflict in which Colombia lives and the decision to carry out negotiations in midst of the conflict has been a state policy since the Gaviria government and is of the current one." Hence it could not be used as an excuse "to freeze, make conditional, or delay the discussion in the table of such urgent themes as unemployment, paramilitarism, ceasefire, and the hostility of the State against the people."[24]

It was not until the first days of September that the National Dialogue Table met again. As that took place, the leading economic interest groups, headed by the National Association of Industrialists, asked that the demilitarized zone be extended beyond October 8 only if FARC agreed to a cease-fire. According to Sabas Pretelt de la Vega, president of the National Association of Merchants, "It's time to negotiate without war," and for FARC to give something in exchange for the demilitarized zone.[25] The private sector seemed to understand the negotiation process better than the Pastrana government did. Also notable is that this was the first time that anyone outside of the Pastrana government had "participated" in any way in the FARC peace process. Unlike the case of Guatemala, Colombian "civil society," including a number of nongovernmental organizations (NGOs) concerned with peace, played no important role in Colombia.

The Commission of Notables

In August and September the Commission of Notables emerged as key players in the process. In a meeting with President Pastrana, Commissioner Ana Mercedes Gómez Martínez (director of the Medellín daily *El Colombiano,* and one of the two members sympathetic to the government) stated that she did not agree with the draft the group had prepared, especially the part that called for the immediate establishment of a constituent assembly. Her opinion was that such an assembly should come after the demobilization of the guerrilla and paramilitary troops and not immediately, as the draft proposed.[26] Further she thought that it would increase political instability and polarization.[27] As she stated in her letter to President Pastrana, "Some of the solutions that the Commission suggests would mean a jump into a vacuum. . . . The convocation [of a constituent assembly], before first defining some issues so fundamental as guerrilla and paramilitary disarmament, would place society at a great disadvantage in face of the armed proselytism exercised by the illegal violent actors."[28]

On August 27 Ana Mercedes Gómez resigned because of this disagreement, as well as because one of the other members of the commission had implied that she had paramilitary ties. President Pastrana had failed to defend her after that accusation. The three remaining members issued a statement to the press, expressing their dismay that she had resigned and their "great surprise that Doctor Gómez did not express her worries and objections within the Commission . . ."[29]

In this way a commission that was intentionally divided equally between the two sides (two for FARC and two for the government) became one in which the guerrilla group had a majority. On September 19, the FARC-dominated commission issued a report recommending that the government-FARC talks proceed under a six-month cease-fire. The lengthy document included many major points. Most importantly, during the truce, the government would reaffirm its agreement to respect the norms of international humanitarian law, as would FARC. Both sides would abstain from using unconventional weapons such as mines, gas cylinders, dispersion bombs, the recruitment of minors, and the attack on civilian populations. FARC would not carry out attacks against civilians, such as kidnapping, forced collection of contributions, and attacks on the energy and petroleum infrastructure and transportation infrastructure.

The government, along with FARC, would study mechanisms of financing that allowed subsistence to the combatants during the truce. The government would promise to work on crop substitution and manual eradication and both sides agree to the protection of the environment. The negotiating table would study on the basis of the common agenda and arrive at agreements that would include a definite plan of constitutional reform, as well as those points that should be considered by the Congress or implemented by the executive. During the truce period the work of the Table would be intensified, to at least three meetings a week, inviting members of Colombian society who could contribute various points of view. During the period of bilateral truce and, in general during this democratic process, the demilitarized zone would be maintained.

The agreements made at the Table would define the list of specific proposals for constitutional reform for a Constituent Assembly, the convocation of which the government promised to push. That Assembly would be made up of representatives of the different parties and political movements, as well as labor unions, sectors of production, independent sectors of civil society and of FARC and the other insurgent groups that might decide to become part of this process. The membership of that Constituent Assembly, as well as the place of its meetings, agenda, duration, and other aspects related to its functioning would be decided by the two parts during the bilateral truce. As an alternative, the Table would also study the alternative possibility of a popular referendum.

The government, together with the Table, would analyze—in light of the constitution, the laws, and the political circumstances of the country—which of these alternatives (constituent assembly or referendum) was more suitable and expeditious for constitutional reform. The two sides would promise to accept decisions made by a constituent assembly or referendum.

Once the constitutional reform proposals were agreed upon, they would be submitted to an intense process of diffusion to the Colombian people, so that they would have sufficient information about them as a part of the process discussion of the proposals before the referendum, if there would be one. In the case that a Constituent Assembly be convened, its sessions would be a maximum of six months and the time between its convocation and sessions would no more than three months. The Assembly would be chosen through a free and democratic election of its members, without prejudice that other special methods might be adopted for choosing the members of the insurgency who would represent it.

The understanding for the convoking of a Constituent Assembly or referendum would be the culmination of the process of dialogue and negotiation, and that once the process was agreed upon and begun, the FARC would disarm. In the same way, once the peace was agreed upon, the Colombian armed forces would adjust to the parameters agreed to in the constitutional order that established it as the defense of sovereignty, independence, the integrity of the national territory, and of the constitutional order.

By common accord the Table would determine the mechanism that would guarantee the implementation of the promises acquired by the signatories during the truce period and in general for the entire process of the political solution proposed in these recommendations. "We suggest, for example, that the nations of the friendly countries be chosen as observers."[30]

If after the end of six months of truce it were not possible to carry out the agreements of the previous articles, the two sides might extend the truce for a period that they considered prudent. The Ejército de Liberación Nacional would be invited to join this process and to accept the peace treaty, with the same guarantees and commitments.

The political movement that the FARC might found as a consequence of this process would enjoy all the guarantees and rights and would have all the responsibilities that all other political parties had. In the case of the danger of breaking the truce by the failure to carry out the agreements of this proposal by either of the sides, the Dialogue and Negotiations Table would meet immediately, with the presence of the national and international guarantors and of the high officials of the government that it seems pertinent to invite, with the goal of finding a quick solution to the problem.

In reference to the phenomenon of paramilitarism, the Notables made a number of recommendations. The most important were the following six:

1. The national government, through the armed forces and the security mechanisms, would continue carrying out actions directed to combat paramilitarism in its diverse forms.
2. With the changing of pertinent laws the government would carry out activities designed to encourage the surrender to justice by those implicated in paramilitary activities.
3. The sides would implement the recommendations about the Colombian conflict and this particular theme made by the United Nations and the Organization of American States.
4. A government authority would be designated in charge of coordinating the actions against paramilitarism.
5. In conformity to the jurisprudence of the constitutional court, any person—civil or military—who was implicated of collaboration, complicity, of omission in the crimes of paramilitarism would be submitted to ordinary justice.
6. The process would be continued, within the Armed Forces and the Police, of the expulsion of all those individuals who had been involved in paramilitary activities.[31]

The report of the Commission of Notables was for some, a high point of the negotiations—although for others it was the exact opposite. That there was no stalemate—so notable in other parts of the process—was because the two delegates chosen by the FARC were in constant contact with the guerrilla group and that after the Gómez resignation FARC was left with two representatives, while the government had but one.

Marches, Kidnappings, and Assassinations

September ended on a negative note because of the abortive march to the demilitarized zone by Liberal presidential candidate Horacio Serpa and because of the FARC assassination of former minister of culture Consuelo Araújonoguera. Serpa claimed that he, as a presidential candidate, had the right to campaign anywhere in the country—including the demilitarized zone. The Serpa march, which had begun several weeks before, left Neiva on Sunday. The first problem encountered were tacks on the road. Then when the caravan got nearer to the demilitarized zone, marchers heard gun shots and the firing of mortars.

The weekly magazine *Cambio* described the ensuing actions in the following way:

> The silhouettes of dozens of subversives with unfriendly faces, appeared in the mountains. And in the road an armed guerrilla made the convoy stop. Tranquilly Serpa got off the bus and went to talk to the subversive commander. Despite his well-known oratory ability, he encountered a frankly hostile atmosphere, in addition to the promise that the way was completely blocked a few meters ahead. Resigned, he turned to his followers and ordered a return to Neiva, saying that he felt personally responsible for the safety of those accompanying him.[32]

At a news conference called as soon as he knew what had happened, President Pastrana deplored the incident and announced that he would make a trip to the demilitarized zone, along with other government authorities and members of the Frente Común por la Paz, including both Serpa and another presidential candidate, Naomí Sanín. Later that trip proved to be impossible. Further, the news of the death of Consuelo Araújonoguera eclipsed the Serpa failure.[33]

On September 29, the peace talks plunged into a crisis when the army found the body of the former minister (and wife of the attorney general) a week after she had been kidnapped by the FARC. As is almost always the case in Colombia in a situation like this, the two sides made conflicting statements.

FARC issued a communiqué in which they addressed both the Serpa and Araúonoguera cases. As for the Serpa march, the FARC spokespersons stated that it was a provocative action, and that the guerrilla southern block had told Serpa that it could not promise his security. Further the Colombian army had used the march as an excuse to enter the demilitarized zone. This led the southern block to end all vehicular transportation into the zone. Finally they pointed out that Serpa was not talking about any of the "great national themes related to the country's grave crises, such as Plan Colombia, extradition, unemployment, paramilitarism, the neoliberal economic policy, the fiscal deficit, the economic recession." Finishing their Theme IIIc statement, the FARC spokespeople concluded that the march was "an irresponsible attitude that puts the dialogue between the national government and FARC in danger."[34]

As for the death of the former minister, the spokespeople said simply, based on the communiqué of their Caribbean block who had captured her, "it is clear that the responsibility for her death lies with the army. It makes no sense to detain a person for political reasons and then kill her."[35] The FARC statement hence raised two themes that were constants in the negotiation process—first, the question of FARC unity, or lack thereof (Theme Ic) and second, the "it wasn't us" nature of the personalistic basis of Colombian politics (Theme IIIc).

The first was that some front had carried out the action and, while it might have been operating within general FARC policy, that did not mean that the specific action had been approved by the FARC leadership. The second has been seen many times over the years in the Colombian conflict. Kidnapped people are killed when the army or police try to rescue them, not by the kidnappers. Hence the leadership was denying culpability for two reasons—that they had not approved the kidnapping and it was the action of the army—not the kidnappers—that caused Araúonoguera's death.

I have raised the question of FARC unity before, stressing that since 1993 the guerrilla organization had become to some degree decentralized. But whether the central FARC leadership was involved in either the kidnapping or the minister's death, this was considered to be a crucial harmful event in the negotiations of the Pastrana government with the FARC. One former member of the Gaviria cabinet suggested to me that, in fact, these two events were the real end of the peace process, although it appeared to continue for some additional time.[36] Pastrana did cancel a September 30 meeting scheduled with FARC[37] and apparently also thought of completely ending the peace process.[38] Rather than doing so, he announced to the Colombian people that the future of the zone would be decided calmly, searching for the common good and listening to the majority of the population. He condemned the Araújonoguera assassination and concluded "You can be certain that the necessary serenity and reflection in moments of crisis are the guarantees for all Colombians on the part of a state that during my mandate has been strengthened to assure its presence when the most extreme circumstances demand it."[39]

Acuerdo de San Francisco de la Sombra

Yet by the end of the next week the peace process turned completely around. On October 5 the two sides signed another agreement, the Acuerdo de San Francisco de la Sombra. To end the impasse the two sides agreed to immediately undertake a complete study of the document of recommendations presented by the Notables; to invite the presidential candidates and the political movements and parties to discuss the aforementioned subjects, give their contributions to the current process, and exchange ideas about the current political state of the country; to invite different sectors of the national community to make contributions to the process; and to invite the National Council for Peace to carry out an exchange of opinions covering the same topics.

In addition the National Dialogue Table would intensify its work, and at its first meeting would develop a timetable for the analysis of the documents of the Notables. A monthly evaluation would be carried out assessing the advances in the discussion of the topics mentioned and public opinion would be informed in an unbiased manner by the mechanisms of information agreed upon before.

The two sides reiterated that the demilitarized zone had as its sole purpose to promote dialogue and negotiation. Accordingly, the democratically elected mayors and the remaining municipal public servants would exercise the only authority in this zone without interference exercised by the national government. In the same way the FARC ratified its commitment to respect the policy functions of the mayors of the zone, along with the civic police and the police inspectors.

In the demilitarized zone all the candidates, as well as the inhabitants of these five municipalities, could carry out their political and electoral activities. The negotiating table, in conjunction with the mayors of the demilitarized zone, would promote open meetings which would allow the inhabitants of the zone to express their opinions, and to which observers could be invited. Finally FARC stated that kidnappings at roadblocks on the national highways were not part of their policy. The FARC would give instructions to all of its members not to carry out this type of activity.[40] Camilo Gómez said, "We believe that this is an agreement that will change the course of the (peace) process."[41]

This was, at least on paper, one of the most successful bargaining moments for the Pastrana government. For once FARC was conceding something in order to assure the continuation of the demilitarized zone. Most notably the cease-fire and the end of kidnapping were placed ahead of the social issues that the insurgent group wanted to consider first.

This accord gave the Pastrana government yet another opportunity to show the Colombian people that progress was being made. Time would show that the San Francisco de la Sombra agreement was worth no more than the paper on which it was written. However, at the time it did give hope—and did help silence the criticisms of the peace process.

An interesting question is how the San Francisco de la Sombra agreement was possible when so many negative things were occurring in the negotiations. I believe that a possible explanation is as follows: A representative of the government stated something like, "Of course the government would like to extend the demilitarized zone without any conditions, as we've done before. However, we have so much pressure from public opinion in general and the military leaders more specifically that we must show that we are getting something in return. Signing the agreement would do that." This interpretation is supported by two things. First, Pastrana met with the top military commanders before he made the decision to extend the zone. Second, a poll right after the Araújonoguera death reported that 61 percent of the respondents thought the FARC negotiations should end.[42] General Fernando Tapias, general commander of the armed forces, said of the meeting with the president: "We had a frank, cordial, and sincere meeting in which all the commanders of the armed forces expressed our evaluations and reservations to the president and gave him all the information we have about the peace process, with the goal that he might be able to make the best decision for the country, for national security, and for the peace process." He continued that it was clear that the demilitarized zone was a unilateral concession of the government that could be changed or suspended at any time. And the armed forces would follow any decision that the president made.[43]

That things had changed because of the Serpa and the Araújonoguera cases, as well as the subsequent discussion with the military, was shown only two days later when on October 7 President Pastrana announced increased military controls around the demilitarized zone. Specifically there were more rigid rules about entering and leaving the zone, the security circle around the zone was strengthened, roadblocks were increased, the Air Force intensified its control of the zone's air space, and foreigners could enter the zone only with permission of the Department of Administrative Security and the commissioner of peace.[44] Then on October 11 the president issued a decree controlling the presence of foreigners in the demilitarized zone.

Marulanda then decided that he preferred more public negotiating by letter instead of talking with the government at the table. In the first of three letters, on October 16, 2001, he ordered his negotiators to stay away from talks with the government until the military ceased overflights and alleged infiltration of the FARC demilitarized zone. He reported that there was constant aerial surveillance, during the day and at night, over the entire area, as well as "other repressive measures . . . for the penetration of agents disguised as vendors and coca harvesters." For these reasons, he went on to say, "In these conditions we are not disposed to mobilize ourselves to attend meetings at the table, given the risks, while these measures are not completely stopped in the demilitarized zone."[45]

Marulanda also asked his spokespersons to talk with Commissioner Gómez and his advisor Juan Gabriel Uribe, "to demand that the president immediately suspend the measures he had taken in the demilitarized zone, which are certainly very dangerous for the peace process, making it possible for it to end at any minute." Marulanda continued, "By following this anomaly, the government is failing to carry out the agreements made since its beginning, unless this is an excuse to end everything with the single stroke of a pen."[46]

The second FARC letter was to President Pastrana. In it, in addition to repeating the same concerns, Marulanda added, "The historical responsibility [for the future of the peace process] will lie on those who have created uncertainty in the process." This was the third reference tying Pastrana's place in history to the peace process. Marulanda ended his letter by suggesting a "great national effort" so that all sectors would support the negotiations, "without conditions or retributions."[47]

The third letter was from the collective leadership of FARC "to the national government about peace and the future of Colombia." They reported having listened to the presidential speech of October 7 and had many reactions to it. In the first place, they agreed with the president's statement that "we are defining the future of Colombia and the future is between war and peace." Colombia, they continued, was going through the most profound economic, political, and social crisis of its history—caused by the Colombian oligarchy. To meet that crisis there were two schools of thought. The first was through peace with social justice, while the second was one of war, with "a scorched earth policy, echoing the geostrategic interests of other nations."

Reminding the government that the San Francisco de la Sombra accord spoke of "the historic responsibility before the people of Colombia, that in the middle of its difficulties and sacrifices maintains its faith and hope of living in a peaceful country with social justice," repeating its oft-heard litany, the FARC leaders called for an agreement on the following themes:

- the common agenda, the ceasefire, and the recommendations of the commission of notables
- the termination of paramiltarism and the punishment of those responsible for it
- the end of the criminalization of social protest, the physical extermination of popular leaders, massacres, torturing, disappearances, extrajudicial executions, arbitrary arrests, displacements
- the transformation of the neoliberal policy that causes loss of jobs, loss of the right to work, loss of collective bargaining rights, the closing of public schools and colleges and hospitals
- the displacement of peasants, the increase of child labor, privatization of state enterprises, increase of taxes, persecution of informal workers, ruin of the countryside, bankruptcy of small and medium-sized businesses,

concentration of wealth and monopolization of the financial, commercial, agricultural, and mining sectors, unemployment and social inequity

- agreement on a complete agrarian reform that gives titles to the millions of peasants who have little land, no credit, and no markets
- the termination of extradition and the reestablishment of the dignity and sovereignty of the Colombian state
- punishment of corrupt officials who are responsible for the theft and misuse of billions of pesos
- the end of Plan Colombia since it only results in contaminated lands, dead farm animals, damages to the ecosystem, economic ruin, and the displacement of the peasants
- the end to the hostility of the great media concentrations against FARC, the Colombian people and its social and political organizations

The letter admitted that there was very little time for such a large task. It would not be possible to set a time limit on how long it would take. Most importantly it would only work if there was "a firm resolve to change the structures of the state, its political system, and its economic base."[48]

At this juncture there seemed to be a real possibility that the peace process might end, as seen in a statement of governmental representative Juan Gabriel Uribe. While the government wanted FARC to talk about a cease-fire, at the table FARC wanted to talk only about the new controls. Commissioner Gómez stated "If they [FARC] want peace, let them make it concrete through agreements."[49]

The two sides then participated in a Theme IIIc exercise, with each blaming the other. On October 20 Gómez wrote a public letter to Marulanda. After qualifying the FARC letters as "not very responsible," he said the government was keeping its word and hoped that FARC would do likewise. He then accused the guerrilla group of delaying the peace process and added that the controls of the demilitarized zone would continue as long as FARC continued kidnapping, extortion, attacks on civilians, and its other violent actions. Further he stated that the letters were "an excuse not to carry out agreements made."[50]

FARC also evaluated the peace process as being at a "critical" state and blamed that on Pastrana. They accused the government of being more interested in increasing the armed conflict than in negotiating peace. "The conversations are at a very critical moment and it seems that Pastrana is not interested in social and economic changes but in making the war worse." They added that there was thought about canceling the peace process, which would lead to war. For FARC the responsibility for this was clear: "The government, the military, the traditional parties, the bourgeoisie, and the communication media state that it is FARC that is delaying the process by not wanting to agree to a cease-fire, but in reality the government is the one that does not want to consider any kind of change."[51]

By November the process was, as *El Tiempo* op-ed columnist and former ELN member León Valencia put it, "in a knot which no one knows how to untie . . . Neither the government nor FARC likes any of the possible scenarios. It's a strange case, but that's the way it is."[52] Columnist Margarita Vidal continued the metaphor and added, "Confronting the Gordian knot of the FARC peace process, alarm bells are going off, tardy diagnoses are being made all over the country and in the government, by the church, interest groups, the military, politicians, the media, and social clubs." The problem, as she saw it, was that FARC wanted to delay the process.[53]

In the remaining months of 2001 few things changed. Jan Egeland, special peace envoy of the United Nations, suggested that the UN might be a third party to facilitate the process (as it was to be in January 2002). FARC refused this initiative. The guerrilla group had always refused outside mediation, arguing that the conflict was with the Colombian government, not with the United Nations. At the same time they threatened to end the peace process if the new controls over the demilitarized zone were not ended. In mid-December Marulanda stated that Pastrana had not done anything about the controls; nor had it responded to a FARC proposal for a meeting of leaders in the demililitarized zone in mid-January.[54]

Conclusions: Uncertainty at the End of 2001

In this chapter I have shown that, while the two sides were doing better in hammering out details in agreements, the lack of unity in both the Colombian government and FARC was becoming more important. By the end of 2001, the talks between the Pastrana government and the FARC were clearly in a downward spiral.

As Figure 5.1 shows, there were notable accomplishments in the year, both in agreements on process (Los Pozos, establishment of and report from the Notables) and the most important substantive agreement of the process—the prisoner exchange. Yet the negativity at the end of the year came from dramatic events away from the table by FARC—the killing of a former minister, the ending of Serpa's march—followed by equally intense reactions from the government, especially the additional controls to the demilitarized zone. The result was a continuation of the freezing and the refusal to accept UN mediation.

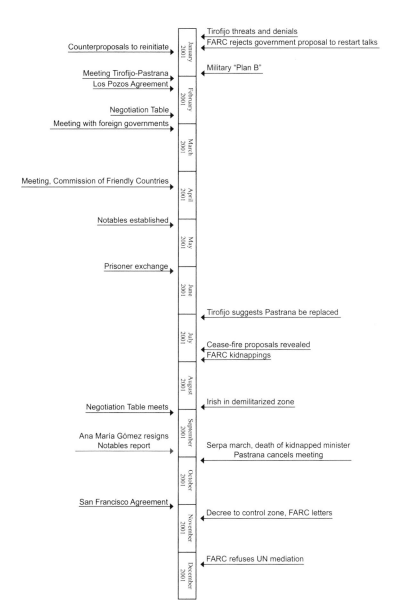

Figure 5.1. Second phase of FARC negotiations in 2001.

6

The FARC Negotiations End

January–February 2002

On February 20, 2002, President Andrés Pastrana ended the FARC demilitarized zone. In this chapter I first describe the final attempts to maintain the dialogue and the failure that led to its end. While some improvement will be shown (such as more detail in agreements, contrary to the typical Theme V vagueness that had blanketed the peace process since its inception), other themes continue, including blaming the other side (Theme IIIc, unwillingness to accept responsibility) and uncertainty if FARC's national directorate was responsible for actions being taking in the field (Theme Ic, lack of unity among the guerrillas).

Based on Colombian opinion I will then present conclusions about why the FARC process was a failure, as well as suggestions from two people who argue that, from a long-term perspective, it could be seen as a success. More general conclusions, however, will be reserved for chapter 9.

The Final Agony in 2002

Two days of meetings in the first week of January were very difficult, with FARC rejecting without discussion the government's proposal to begin talks about a cease-fire, even though they had agreed to do so the previous year. FARC leader Raúl Reyes stated that a cessation of hostilities could be discussed in April and

May, after the preceding months were used to talk about unemployment. But before any of this began, President Pastrana would have to end the controls of the demilitarized zone initiated at the end of the previous year.[1]

FARC issued two public communiqués concerning the two meetings in that first week of January. In the first communiqué, in classic Theme IIIc fashion, they reported that they had arrived "greatly inclined to find formulas to get the process going" and discuss the issues. Instead they had heard the "constant chorus . . . demanding unilateral concessions of the insurgency while keeping quiet about the substantive issues that concern common Colombians." They then gave a list of those issues, repeating much of what they had stated many times before.[2]

In the second communiqué the FARC spokespeople first pointed out that while they had been meeting with government representatives, President Pastrana was meeting with the heads of the military. Then the FARC leaders stated: "To our surprise General Tapias, Commander of the Armed Forces, stated in the press that none of the measures announced by the president on October 7, 2001, were negotiable, thus ending any possibility of finding consensual ways out of the actual paralysis of the National Table of Dialogue and Negotiation." As a result "The possibility of peace with social justice in Colombia will succumb, once again, beneath the weight of real power, enemy of national reconciliation and reconstruction."[3]

Nevertheless, at that point the two sides exchanged proposals. The government proposed a document to be signed by both sides, stating that the demilitarized zone had been set up to facilitate the negotiation and FARC agreed that the necessary guarantees were in place. Further, the negotiating table would be in permanent session until January 20, discussing the diminution of the conflict and unemployment. Finally, the first item of discussion would be the cease-fire as proposed by the Commission of Notables.[4]

After another adjournment FARC returned with a counterproposal, with four major points: that the forces of the government would not enter the zone under the excuse of carrying out the law; that the governmental flights over the demilitarized zone, at any altitude, would be cancelled; that governmental control around the demilitarized zone—even if disguised as paramilitary actions—would be discontinued; and that the government would state publicly that FARC were neither terrorists nor drug traffickers.[5]

At the end of those counterproposals, on January 9, 2002, the high commissioner of peace announced that "the government understands that FARC is not continuing in the process" and as a result the agreed-upon forty-eight hours for the guerrilla group to leave the demilitarized zone had begun.[6] The government's position was not the only alteration. As an interviewee said, "One could really see a change in the public opinion polls about the Pastrana peace process in early 2002. The people seemed fed up with continually extending the demilitarized zone while FARC continued to kidnap, bomb, and attack."[7]

Probably because they saw a real possiblity of the Pastrana government ending the demilitarized zone, on January 8 FARC leaders wrote to James LeMoyne, special advisor of the Secretary General of the United Nations, asking for his assistance in the process. Either disingenuously or with selective recall, they stated, "The connection of this international organization to the search for a political solution to the armed, social conflict in our country is a positive fact that we had mentioned on various opportunities."[8] Several days later, LeMoyne, traveled to the zone to talk with FARC leaders.

Exactly what LeMoyne proposed is not clear, although it did have positive results. On January 11 the insurgent spokespersons publicly stated their appreciation for the assistance of the international community, "especially the efforts carried out in the name of the Secretary-General of the United Nations, Kofi Annan, by James LeMoyne, his special advisor." As a result FARC pledged its continuing efforts to find solutions by negotiating.[9] The next day FARC made a proposal to restart the talks immediately, making reference to the Acuerdo of San Francisco de la Sombra, to the agreement of Los Pozos, and to the Commission of the Notables. More specifically it stated that the two parties would invite Monsignor Alberto Giraldo to be the "Honor Witness" at the table. President Pastrana would reiterate that the peace process was a state policy and the table would be enlarged. The president and the government would guarantee the demilitarized zone, in which a two-person committee would resolve conflicts. A commission would be formed to consider complaints in the areas near the demilitarized zone, and problems that might arise in the process would be submitted to a committee made up of Monsignor Giraldo and FARC commander Andrés París.[10] This proposal was an attempt to add details to the process, which might better have been resolved several years previously (Theme V).

In a televised speech on that same day President Pastrana, not surprisingly, stated that the FARC proposals were not satisfactory and therefore the forty-eight hours were running. Nevertheless two days later the French ambassador read a FARC statement that the guerrilla group publicly recognized that the guarantees for the demilitarized zone were sufficient for the continuation of the dialogues. President Pastrana agreed, but put a condition: by the date that the demilitarized zone ran out (January 20) that the two sides must have agreed to a chronogram of activities that began with the discussion of the cease-fire.[11] This was another attempt to take care of the "devil in the details" problem.

On January 20, after a week of meetings, the Government and FARC signed an accord for a timetable for the future of the peace process. One former member of the Colombian military correctly suggested to me that this was the first time that the Pastrana government had been a tough bargainer, extending the demilitarized zone only if FARC made a concession.[12]

In this last procedural agreement of the peace process, FARC and the Colombian government agreed to a timetable for cease-fire discussions, something the government had wanted from the beginning but FARC had insisted would have to wait. The main issues to be discussed were cease-fire terms, kidnapping, and paramilitarism. Most importantly, the document stated that the National Dialogue Table would immediately undertake the study of the truce with the cessation of hostilities and cease-fire, in accordance with the document of the recommendations of the Notables. In addition they would immediately incorporate the subject of kidnappings as an inseparable component of the proposal presented by the Commission of Notables to the National Dialogue Table, within the discussion of the truce with the cessation of hostilities and cease-fire. Likewise, they would invite the presidential candidates and representatives of political parties and movements and the National Council for Peace to give their contributions to the process and exchange ideas about the actual political moment of the country, as agreed upon in the Accord of San Francisco. This promised to open the peace process with FARC as it had never been.

This new process document then made references to earlier ones. The process seemed to be cumulative for the first time, rather than each meeting starting *de novo*. Accordingly, first the two sides would set up through common agreement an International Commission of Accompaniment to verify the agreements and to surpass any difficulties that might occur, as had been described in the Accord of Caquetanía. Second, in accordance with what was agreed upon in the Accord of San Francisco, the two sides would generate monthly reports that would be presented to the public, outlining major aspects relative to the advances in the dialogue and negotiations. Third, as mentioned in the Accord of San Francisco, FARC pledged once again immediately to send instructions to all of its members not to carry out kidnapping at roadblocks on the national highways. Finally the new agreement stated that the public hearings and round tables about the subjects that the Table of Dialogue and Negotiation agreed upon would be re-initiated and that the negotiating table would have as its goal the signing of a concrete accord about truce with cessation of hostilities and cease-fire by lessening the intensity of the conflict, having as a deadline April 7, 2002.[13]

For this purpose, a precise timetable, shown in Table 6.1, was established, and as a result President Pastrana extended the demilitarized zone until April 10. As the description below will indicate, however, none of this elaborate schedule was followed.

Matters continued in February as if none of these agreements had been

Table 6.1: Accord for a Timetable for the Future of the Peace Process, January 20, 2002

Dates	Activity
January 23–February 8	Discussion of the document of recommendations presented by the Commission of Notables
February 2, 2002	Presentation of the first drafts dealing with the lessening of the conflict
February 6, 2002	Defining a more active participation of international accompaniment
Invitations of the Negotiating Table: February 13	Presidents of the political movements and - parties
February 14	Presidential candidates
February 15	National Council for Peace
Beginning February 20, 2002	Study of the drafts presented by each of the parties about the truce with cessation of hostilities and cease-fire
April 7, 2002	Goal established by the Table for the signature of the first accords on a truce with the cessation of hostilities and cease-fire as of the lessening of the conflict
April 10, 2002	Accord for timetable of other issues
the last Friday of every month, beginning February 2002	Presentation of reports from the Negotiating Table to public opinion
January 23	Definition of methodologies for the discussions
January 24–25	Beginning of discussion of the elements of the document of recommendations presented by the Commission of Notables
January 30–31 and February 1	Session of the Negotiating Table on the issues agreed upon
February 2	Presentation of the first drafts on lessening of the conflict, and the subject of unemployment
February 6	Accord on International Accompaniment
February 7–8	Session of the Negotiating Table on the issues agreed upon

Dates	Activity
February 13	Invitation to the presidents of the political movements and parties
February 14	Invitation to the presidential candidates
February 15	Invitation to the National Council on Peace
February 20–22	
February 27–28 and March 1	Session of the Negotiating Table on the issues agreed upon
March 6–8	
March 13–15	Study of the drafts presented by each of the parties to the truce about lessening of the conflict
March 25–26	Preparation of the final documents on the truce about lessening of the conflict
April 1	Report to public opinion
April 7	Goal established by the Negotiating Table for the signature of the first accords on the truce about lessening of the conflict
April 10	Accord to set a timetable for other subjects

Source: "Accord for a Timetable for the Future of the Peace Process," January 20, 2002, http://www.ciponline.org/colombia/012004.htm.

reached. On February 2 FARC issued another draft proposal to restart the talks. It began with traditional FARC rhetoric, following Theme IIIc—that the armed conflict in Colombia was the consequence of economic, social, and political conflicts of Colombian history that had not been resolved by the bipartisan Liberal-Conservative oligarchy; that the cause of the profound divisions in Colombia was the existence of an antidemocratic and violent political regimen over which an economic system has been constructed with a privileged minority while the great majority of Colombians were deprived of their most elemental rights; and that it is for that reason that the common agenda for the New Colombia had become the fundamental guide in the process of dialogue and negotiation between the Government and FARC. Accordingly, "As we affirmed in the Accord of San Francisco de la Sombra, we realize the historical responsibility before the Colombian people, who in the midst of difficulties and sacrifices maintain the faith and hope of living in a unity in peace with social justice that overcomes the great economic, political, and social differences that keep Colombians in conflict."[14]

Ignoring the earlier common agenda that had been so celebrated by both sides, the document then set forth the agenda below:

- change of the doctrine of national security and of state paramilitarism
- respect for the human, civil, and political rights of Colombians
- change of the neoliberal policies
- freedom for prisoners of war
- end of extradition
- punishment for the corrupt
- end of Plan Colombia and a program of crop substitution
- sanctions for mass media who apologize for paramilitary groups
- unemployment compensation

Notably missing was the question of a cease-fire. FARC criticism of the doctrine of national security, as a U.S. invention, went back to the years of the Cold War. The criticism of neoliberal reforms was not new either, although its intensity was stronger in this document as FARC explicitly criticized the International Monetary Fund and the governments of Barco, Gaviria, Samper, and Pastrana, who had brought "the worse economic crisis in recent years." Criticism of the international context of the Colombian conflict continued with the statement that Plan Colombia was "the aggression of the State against peasants in development of the interventionist policy of the United States, which cannot continue with the excuse that they are growers of coca and poppies." FARC ended with the statement that the mass media had become "one of the principal instigators of the conflict" and that if they "continued their policy of apologizing for the paramilitary groups they should be sanctioned by canceling their licenses."[15]

Also partially ignoring the earlier common agenda, on February 4 the government issued its own draft agenda in response. Entitling it "To avoid the effects of the armed conflict on civilians is the first step towards the reduction of the conflict," the document began by making reference to the Agreement of San Francisco de la Sombra and to the timetable to which the two sides had just agreed. After calling for an agreement that might lessen the conflict and referring to the document of the Notables, the government called for specific steps: first, a cease-fire agreement; once cease-fire was agreed upon, the negotiation of the points of the common agenda; development of mechanisms of popular referendum and the surrender of arms by FARC; and the post-conflict stage.[16] These two agenda proposals show that, after more than three years of talks, the two sides were still far apart about that most basic procedural matter—the subjects that should be considered in the conversations.

On February 5 a FARC offensive began, consisting of sabotages of infrastructure and bombings of urban areas, increasing skepticism about the peace process. Nevertheless, the same day the government proposed a six-month cease-fire and the following day the table met, after which they issued a communiqué stating that they had met as called for in point 11 of the timetable. The progress they reported had to do with making the international accompaniment more specific.[17] This was to be the last joint statement of the peace process.

That notwithstanding, the website of the presidency stated the scheduled meetings for the second week in February. As declared in the timetable, the table would continue its discussion of the diminishing of the conflict and a truce on Wednesday the thirteenth; on Thursday the fourteenth it would meet with presidential candidates and representatives of the political parties; and on Friday the fifteenth it would meet with the members of the National Committee of Peace.[18]

In addition Commissioner Gómez reported to the Colombian people that progress had been made on the cease-fire at the first meeting: "The position of the government was clear: negotiation amidst violence should not continue and that is the route that has been taken in the process and in the document of the Notables." He added that this position reflected the position that Colombians wanted. "We believe that this is the position that reflects the sentiments of Colombians, who do not want more violence or more kidnapping, that the kidnapped be liberated, that there be no more infrastructure bombing."[19]

At its meeting the table also decided on the rules for the presidential candidates. First the government and FARC would have fifteen minutes for presentations. Then each candidate would have ten minutes, followed by another ten minutes for the government and the insurgent group to present its respective conclusions.[20] Three candidates did present their views; Álvaro Uribe chose not to participate in this process.

On February 19 FARC and government representatives met again (and as it turned out, for the last time), once more exchanging cease-fire proposals. The government proposal called for maintaining guerrilla fronts in small zones to keep them separate from the armed forces, a notable change from their earlier position.[21] The FARC statement was a simple repetition of their earlier proposal. In a separate statement Raúl Reyes repeated the oft-stated FARC position: If Colombian social problems were not resolved, the war would continue even if there were an immediate cease-fire.[22]

That same day President Pastrana met with the National Council of Peace, stating the government's position: only with a cease-fire would it be possible to make progress in the peace process. During that cease-fire FARC would be in a single area (different than the "small zones proposed at the table), under the watch of an international verification commission since "it should be avoided that troops leave that territory and that be accidental combats with the national armed forces [occur]." Pastrana also asked the members of the council, when they went to the demilitarized zone on Friday, to demand that the rebels sign a truce "as soon possible."[23]

What might have happened when the council went to the demilitarized zone—and whether a cease-fire would have been agreed to—will never be known. On February 20 individuals apparently from FARC hijacked a domestic airliner, forcing it to land on a stretch of highway in Huila department. All passengers were freed but one—Colombian Senator Jorge Gechem Turbay—the fifth member of Colombia's Congress to be kidnapped by FARC since June 2001. Although the high commissioner said that "this action could not have been carried out without the knowledge of the FARC secretariat," in an interview with a radio network second-in command Raúl Reyes said he had no information. He added, "I know absolutely nothing. On our part . . . we have no information."[24] As suggested above, given the FARC structure after 1993 this argument was possible—and might or might not have been true.

President Pastrana immediately took three actions. First, he asked the Juridical Secretary of the Presidency to prepare the resolution to end the demilitarized zone; secondly, he ended the political status of the FARC negotiators; and third he asked the national prosecutors office to reactivate the arrest warrants for the FARC leaders.[25]

Pastrana in effect was responding to the hijacking by announcing the end of the three-year-old talks with the FARC. Aerial bombardment, the first phase of military operations to retake the demilitarized zone, began at midnight. In his speech to the Colombian people earlier that night, President Pastrana began by recalling that the six and a half million votes he had received in the election of June 1998 were in support of his peace process and "for that reason, since the first day of my administration I have not ceased to work to comply with the mission which you gave me." But, the president continued, terrorist acts had increased in recent months. Then there was the kidnapping of Senator Gechem. In addition there were other examples of FARC malfeasance—construction and enlargement of airstrips for airplanes with illicit goals; increase in coca cultivation; and construction of highways in the middle of the jungle, also with illicit purposes.[26]

The president then, in his version of "It wasn't us" theme, directed himself personally to Manuel Marulanda: "I gave you my word and I always kept it, but you have assaulted me in my good faith, not only to me but also to all Colombians. From the first moment when you left the dialogue seat empty when I was there, guarded by your men ready to talk . . ." Next the president claimed that the legal political regime was unassailable: "May FARC and all other groups who insist in sowing violence and death around it know that any army of 40 million Colombians is invincible! You can never defeat us! Never, even in your dreams, can you get through power with arms, because here power is won through the ballot boxes of democracy." The Roman Catholic president finished addressing the nation saying, "May God bless you. And may God bless me. And may the Archangel Saint Michael protect us."[27]

As he was beginning his speech, the Colombian air force was being ordered to bomb the demilitarized zone.[28] The Pastrana peace process with FARC had ended.

The next day, not to be outdone by the president, the FARC stated their side of the story with their "not our fault" account of events (Theme IIIc). FARC made thirteen major points. The first was that Pastrana had made a unilateral decision to end the discussions while FARC was ready to continue them. They went on to say that it was peasants, unprotected by the government, who cultivated coca, not FARC. Then they argued that a double standard was being shown by the government: "The government expects FARC to show 'good conduct' and 'peace gestures' while it escalates the conflict by strengthening the armed forces and the police, encourages the terrorism of paramilitary groups, and develops Plan Colombia at the insistence of the United States."

FARC activities had no ulterior purposes, the communiqué continued. They constructed highways in the demilitarized zone during its three years because during thirty-six years the state did not do so. More than 1,000 kilometers, with bridges, were built. The repair of landing strips was of ones that existed with the permission of the Aeronautic Agency of the government.

The declaration of the insurgent group continued that the end of the peace talks was a demand of the military, the economic interest groups, the large media, some presidential candidates, and the U.S. embassy, in their haste not to carry out the changes that the current moment demanded. Once again the Colombian oligarchy had impeded the economic, political, social, and military structural changes that needed to be made by dialogue. These problems came from the Liberal and Conservative governments. Further FARC had wanted peace. "During three years we sought solutions by dialogue and negotiation of the grave problems that thirty million Colombians complain of without the government responding to the necessities of the people."

It is clear, FARC stated, that the true objective that moved the government in making the decision to end the process was to hide the fundamental issues of the common agenda that marked the path towards a new Colombia from the people. The statement continued:

> As proof of our desire for peace the people and the proponents of a political solution remain with the common agenda for the change towards a new Colombia and the platform for a government of national reconstruction and reconciliation, proposals that we are prepared to exchange with any future government that might show interest in returning to a path of a political solution to the social and armed conflict.

The Colombian people were encouraged to "continue their struggle and mobilization in an organized way to find the solution of the problems of unemployment and the lack of education, health, housing, and land for the peasant," as well as for political liberties, democracy, and national sovereignty, for a new government that reconstructs and reconciles the nation. And the Colombian people could be assured that "FARC will keep its ideological and political banners raised, those that have characterized its struggle for more than thirty-seven years in the interest of the people, even though our class enemies call us whatever they like.[29]

If Pastrana's speech and the FARC statement were not sufficient to end the peace process, FARC punctuated it two days later when, on February 23, they kidnapped senator and presidential candidate Ingrid Betancourt as she was traveling by land to the former demilitarized zone on a mission to advocate respect for the rights of the zone's residents. The FARC gave the Colombian government one year to negotiate the exchange of Betancourt and five other kidnapped legislators for FARC prisoners in Colombian jails.[30] At this writing more than four years later, Betancourt is still in captivity.

Conclusions: The FARC Negotiations End

Figure 6.1 shows the flow of the final two months of the FARC negotiations. While the information to the left of the vertical line indicates that some progress was made with the assistance of the United Nations, the negotiations ended for two immediate reasons. One was that the cease-fire proposals showed that no progress was being made in this important issue, even after nearly three years of talk. Second, whether known or approved by the insurgent leadership, FARC fronts continued military actions against important political leaders.

If those were the immediate causes, they were not the basic reason that the negotiations failed. The final question of this chapter has to do with more gen-

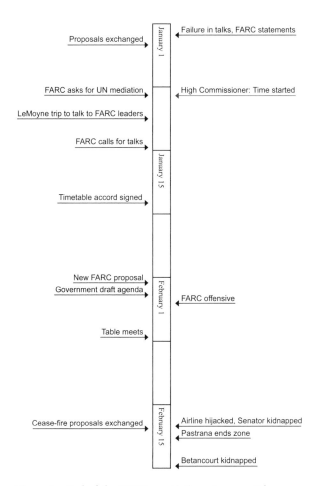

Figure 6.1. End of the FARC negotiations, January–February 2002.

eral reasons that Colombians thought the process was not a success. It is not surprising that individuals interviewed after the failure of the FARC negotiations gave many views of why they did. While matters of a higher level of generality are purposefully left for the final chapter of the book, the following four kinds of specific criticisms were made of the Pastrana process with FARC.

Andrés Pastrana

The first set had to do with President Pastrana himself. Andrés Pastrana had never been that interested in the issue of peace negotiations, but then was in too much of a hurry in suggesting the peace process. This was because he was trailing Horacio Serpa after the first round of the 1998 presidential election and was looking for an issue with which he could win.[31] After Pastrana became president, he was too eager to win peace in order to establish his place in history.[32] This weakened his bargaining power, giving more to the opponent. Finally the entire process was based on the "great man" theory of history—that Pastrana and Marulanda could do it alone, regardless of the complexities of Colombian life.[33]

Government as Bargainer

The second group of reasons has to do with the government as a bargainer. The government policy was not coordinated[34] and lacked a clear bargaining strategy.[35] Good planning was lacking.[36] Further it was a closed process. One interviewee suggested that it was tradition of the Colombian oligarchy and their way of arranging things. It was the president and his friends. If others disagreed, it was because they were outside the center of the oligarchy.[37] Others more simply suggested that the government was too closed and had no networks to talk to people.[38] Another pointed out that anyone who suggested errors in the process were considered to be against peace,[39] while a final interviewee added that the Pastrana government did not consult with experts such as Jesús Bejarano and Rodrigo Pardo, both of whom had experience in negotiating, nor with Alfredo Rangel and Eduardo Pizarro Leongómez, academics who might have proved extremely helpful,[40] nor with retired military officers who might have had invaluable suggestions.[41]

Bad Strategy

The third cluster of explanations had to do with mistakes in strategy on the part of the Pastrana government. One thought that the demilitarized zone was a mistake.[42] Another agreed and suggested the metaphor that "It is like in a game of chess—sometimes you lose on the first move."[43] Another mistake was the short periods for demilitarized zone, causing frequent crises.[44] Another interviewee suggested that the length of the demilitarized zone was less a problem than the fact that the government kept extending it without the FARC giving anything in return.[45] Finally the agenda of the government was too long[46] and also would have given FARC everything they wanted.[47]

Bad Negotiators

A last set of explanations has to do with the individuals whom the Pastrana government chose for the negotiations. The high commissioners not well trained and were chosen for political reasons.[48] Nor were the negotiators well trained.[49] In addition the government negotiators were at a disadvantage when they met their FARC counterparts, who had "a gun, a rifle, and a machete."[50] Further, the government team had little institutional memory.[51] Another individual made the same point, "One gets the impression sometimes that the guerrillas think that every four years a new group is going to arrive, to try the same thing over again."[52]

Given all of the above, the proper question might be "Why did the Pastrana peace process with the FARC last so long?" instead of "Why did it fail?" The answer is because Andrés Pastrana and the Colombian military wanted the process to continue. The president wanted the process to succeed, in order to assure his place in Colombia history. The military wanted the process to continue, at least as long as they perceived they were at a strategic disadvantage with the FARC.[53] Plan Colombia was changing that evaluation, although it is not clear how the military calculation was changing.

Yet there were others who said that, while the Pastrana presidency did not end the guerrilla war with FARC, that did not mean it was a "failure." A Colombian political scientist suggested that the guerrilla group had less legitimacy after the Pastrana years than before for two reasons. One was that they changed their military strategy by staging large attacks on less isolated areas. Secondly, "Pastrana gave them everything, but they still would not make peace."[54] The same argument was made in greater detail by a Colombian economist when he said,

In a certain sense Pastrana did not "lose" in the peace process with FARC. Rather, there were at least three "successes" from the process: First, it gave the government time to build the strength of the armed forces, who had suffered serious defeats during the Samper presidency. Second, FARC lost international prestige. It showed that they were not "Robin Hoods." Finally, FARC lost prestige within Colombia. Everything had been given to them, but they did not negotiate seriously.[55]

I refine many of these conclusions in chapter 9. However, before we can make final conclusions about the failure of the Pastrana peace process we must first look at the other case—that of the *Ejército de Liberación Nacional*.

7

The ELN Discussions through the Declaration of Geneva

September 1998–July 2000

In this chapter I describe and analyze the process between the *Ejército de Liber-ación Nacional* (ELN, National Liberation Army) and the government of Andrés Pastrana from his inauguration in August 1998 until July 2000. The closing date is chosen because of a meeting held in that month in Geneva, Switzerland. There the two sides agreed to the Declaration of Geneva, which called upon "friendly" countries to assist in finding the necessary conditions for a negotiated settlement between the government and the guerrilla group.

In the analysis I show how the process with the ELN was different from that with the FARC in many ways, but similar in others, and with the same themes operating. While some of the early agreements did have the necessary detail, others did not. The most important difference between the two processes was the importance of departmental and municipal officials as well as civil society organizations in Bolívar, all opposing, usually successfully, the wishes and even commands of the president. This aspect of Theme I (let's call it Theme Id) did not occur in the FARC case.

The Meetings Begin, September 1998–March 1999

President Andrés Pastrana gave greater emphasis to the FARC negotiations than those with the ELN. In part this was no doubt because the former was much larger, richer, and more powerful than the latter. In addition, since the Samper government had begun the process with the ELN during his administration (albeit with little success), Pastrana probably felt less likely to establish his place in history with the ELN.

The first push for ELN-government meetings came from the National Council of Peace about a month after Pastrana became president. The council had been established during Samper government. One member reported, "During the Pastrana government the council never met with High Commissioner Victor G. [Ricardo] and [met] with Gómez only two times. It was ceremonial. We would meet. Pastrana would come and give a 45-minute speech and then there was a photo op."[1] Nevertheless in this case the council played a key role.

As described in chapter 2, the ELN had suspended the preparations for the National Convention after some members of the peace council during the Samper government had met with paramilitary leader Carlos Castaño. One month into the Pastrana presidency, on September 7, 1998, the council urged Commissioner Ricardo to make contact with two ELN leaders, "Francisco Galán" and "Felipe Torres," both of whom were imprisoned in Itagüí, Antioquia. Ricardo stated that the government believed that the National Convention, also described in chapter 2, was the best way to carry out peace talks with the ELN.[2] The next week the two imprisoned leaders sent a message to local, departmental, and national leaders, but not to the month-old Pastrana government. It called for a meeting in the penitentiary to talk about kidnapped mayors and the conflict in Antioquia.[3] Ironically, by calling on local officials the ELN leaders were unwittingly bringing a new level of officials into the process, officials of the same level as those who later were to oppose the ELN peace process in another part of the country.

By mid-September, the operating committee of the National Convention produced a draft document, one of the longest and most detailed of the entire futile process. The major item considered was a document prepared by Francisco Galán and Felipe Torres. After a diatribe against paramilitarism, "a counterinsurgency tactic created and directed by the state in the doctrine of national security," the ELN leaders turned to the National Convention, "which has as its central objectives the analysis of profound conflict and crisis, the search for solutions, and the active participation of all sectors of society."

The ELN document went on to present an eight-point agenda, shown below. Many of the points were broad, containing more than one idea.

1. Economic and social system, state, corruption.
2. Democracy and the state, armed forces, clientelism, communications media.

3. The conflict and the insurgency.
4. Human rights, impunity, international humanitarian law.
5. Social problems.
6. Natural resources, sovereignty, energy, ecology.
7. Culture, national identity.
8. The agrarian problem, drug trade.

Next it listed the participants in the convention—social organizations, political movements, interest groups, principal universities, representatives of economic groups, individuals, and the insurgency. A special note was clear: "Representatives of the government will not participate."

Third, it established two committees to carry out the work, the preparatory commission and the operating committee. The preparatory commission was to be composed of forty-two individuals who had signed the Acuerdo de la Puerta del Cielo (Heaven's Gate agreement) discussed in chapter 2, plus Galán and Torres. The commission would become an assembly charged with carrying out the agreement. The operating committee would be made up of eighteen members, fifteen of whom had signed the agreement plus Galán and Torres. Its tasks would be to orient the work, serve as intermediary with the government and other insurgent groups, divide the work between the groups, and assign responsibilities for the National Convention.

Since the committee was large and had many duties, five of its members (plus the two ELN representatives) would form the coordinating team. The team's functions would be to maintain the program, create the budget, determine the international accompanying countries, work out the guarantees with the state, develop and present a list of members of the National Convention to the preparatory commission, coordinate all other work for the National Convention, and define the methodology of the convention.[4]

On September 22 the Central Command (COCE) of the ELN asked that Galán and Torres be given safe-conduct passes so that they could leave their jail and attend a meeting to make plans for the National Convention. Those passes were finally given so that the two leaders could join their colleagues in a meeting with civil society, a meeting that took place on October 11–12, in Valle del Río Verde, Antioquia. It was also preceded by a meeting with Commissioner Ricardo, the first meeting between the Pastrana government and the guerrilla group. ELN leader, Antonio García, summarized it as "of an exploratory nature, so that the government might know our willingness to talk and so that we could know the willingness of the government, and to look at the possibilities of our continuing to talk because up until now we have not had a formal process with this government."[5]

In the following days the commissioner announced the membership of the negotiating group for the government. He also sent a letter to the ELN central committee in which he stated "The carrying out of a national convention, as a forum of analysis of the national problems, constitutes an initiative that will bear important fruit in the search for peace." Accordingly he announced the formal beginning of the dialogue between the government and the ELN.[6]

The Río Verde meeting led to an agreement on the agenda, the methodology, the timetable, and the participants. There was also an agreement about how the location of the National Convention would be chosen. The place, as will be shown below, turned out to be the true problem in the process.

The agenda had five major parts, once again wide-reaching, making the complete agenda longer. The first part was international humanitarian law, human rights, impunity, justice, insurgence, and conflict. The second (echoing an ELN concern that had begun many years before) was natural resources and energy policy. The more general third one had to do with democracy, the state, the armed forces, and corruption. Fourth was the economy and social problems, while the final one was almost a residual category—culture and identity, nation, region, territorial arrangement, the agrarian problem, and drug trafficking.

The methodology was of five points. After the formal installation of the National Convention, there would a subdivision along the five themes. Each theme would have a coordinating group made up of those who subscribed to the Heaven's Gate agreement. Then there would be a session for synthesis in which the conclusions of the five groups were presented, and the conclusions would then be adopted by consensus.

The participants were enumerated in a vague way. In addition to the participants of the Heaven's Gate agreement, "200 additional persons will be invited to participate, representatives of social groups, economic interest groups and economic sectors; the Catholic and other churches; political parties and social movements; representatives of the three branches of the government; and other personalities of the country." There was no clear indication of who would invite these people.

The timetable, on the other hand, was very detailed. Installation would be on February 13, 1999. Discussion of the first theme would be on April 13, with the second theme on June 13 and each following theme beginning on the 13th of the subsequent months. Sessions of synthesis, context, and conclusions would begin on October 12. Mass media would be asked to publish verbatim documents that had been approved, and the government would be asked to participate in the convention.[7]

These detailed documents seemed to indicate that Theme V (lack of specificity) would be absent in the ELN case. However, whether any of the four matters described really would have worked that way was not to be known, as the item listed third in the agreement—places of deliberation and development— was to prove to be the stumbling block of the process. The statement was clear enough: "The sites for sessions and the development of the process of the national convention will be agreed upon by the national government and the ELN taking into consideration that they should be places inside the national territory that have the basic conditions of security and the necessary infrastructure."[8] Those conditions proved to be impossible.

Another reason for the failure to hold the ELN convention was a military action by the ELN on October 18, 1998. On that date, just after midnight, militants bombed a pipeline near Machuca, Antioquia. According to official investigations, the oil and gases released by the destruction of the pipeline took six minutes to descend a slope, cross a river, and reach the town on the opposite bank. Many residents there depended on open flames for light and cooking. The mixture ignited, engulfing sixty-four dwellings and the sleeping families inside them. Seventy-three people, among them thirty-six children, ultimately perished.[9]

Nevertheless, during the rest of 1998 there were other meetings of the operating committee and commission in Itagüí, and various documents were written by Galán and Torres. Some decisions were made (the members of the National Convention would be chosen democratically by the civil society groups which were invited, but without stating who would invite them) and others were delegated to other, new organizations (a "technical team" would organize procedures and obtain the necessary financial resources).[10] Of special note was the consideration of the "Santa Methodology" necessary to set up the meeting to prepare the National Convention. A Galán-Torres document spelled out the roles of the ELN and the military for such a meeting.[11]

A new element was added in January 1999, in a meeting of the operating committee with the two ELN leaders in the Itagüí jail. After reiterating that the convention would be within Colombia, they added that a meeting of President Pastrana with the ELN central command (no doubt to give the ELN the same status that FARC had after Pastrana met with Marulanda) needed to take place before the convention. Finally it added that "everyone would fit in the convention." Although names and numbers were not given, the convention would include fourteen groups, including labor, peasants, interest groups, universities, research organizations, the church, and the state, as well as representatives of the ELN and international observers.[12]

In February 1999 Antonio García met with Commissioner Ricardo in Caracas. At that meeting the insurgent group expressed its desire for the demilitarized zone to be in the department of Norte de Santander and their hope that the president would be able to meet with the central command. Ricardo was also expected to give the president a list of the 250 participants that the ELN had chosen for the convention.[13] At the meeting the ELN also stated that the insurgent group and the government would begin bilateral talks (in addition to the Convention) with the goal of ending the fighting.[14]

Problems began almost immediately. The first was a variation on Theme IIIc, not the usual "it's their fault," but rather, who should take a positive step first. The ELN asked for the demilitarized zone; the government replied that a cease-fire would have to occur before that.

Second, there was no agreement on the meeting between ELN leaders and President Pastrana, or about the date or place for the National Convention, or the demilitarized zone. The only agreement was on the date for the next meeting in Caracas.[15]

The place for the National Convention took center stage in the days that followed, a position that it was to retain for most of the rest of the conversations. The ELN suggested that, if not Norte de Santander the southern part of the Bolívar department would do. Some believed that this change represented an alteration of the agreements of Heaven's Gate and Río Verde. Then it was suggested that the National Convention might have to be outside of Colombia, a possibility that was received negatively by some of the participants. Francisco Santos, one of the Heaven's Gate signers, replied to this prospect:

> The ELN cannot play with the good will of those of us who have participated in this process and who have felt the criticism and threats that we've had for participating in it. . . . I feel deceived because I think the ELN is playing a double game and is using the so-called civil society to obtain goals that are closer to war than a negotiated solution to the conflict.[16]

By the end of the February 11 meeting it was clear that the demilitarized zone was an unsurmountable problem. The government gave a categorical "no" to the ELN demand for four municipalities in the southern part of Bolívar—Simití, Morales, Santa Rosa, and San Pablo. ELN leader "Gabino" was equally uncompromising when he replied, "The demilitarization of the four municipalities is the basic security guarantee for the convention participants. If there is no demilitarization there is no dialogue."[17]

The ELN in this case was trying to use the peace process to restore its control in an area of Colombia where it had been displaced by the paramilitary squads. The southern part of Bolívar had been the cradle of the insurgent movement but the paramlitary groups had forced them to retreat to the mountains. Further, as compared to the FARC demilitarized zone, southern Bolívar was more strategically located. The municipality of San Pablo was only half an hour by road from Puerto Wilches and forty-five minutes from Barrancabermeja. The former was a center of agricultural production while the latter was the location of the largest petroleum refinery in the country. Finally the proposed demilitarized zone included the major highway between the Atlantic Coast and the major cities of Bogotá and Medellín. If the insurgents were to control that highway they could paralyze commerce.[18]

Both sides presented different versions of what had been happening, as usual, in their statements after the February 11th meeting. The government reported that they had offered a situation for the national convention that would be a lot like the three-day Río Verde meeting of the previous October. The ELN said the problem was one of security for the convention participants and that they would continue in their efforts to find a region in Colombia—or even in a foreign country—so that the convention could be held.[19] Yet a day later Gabino stated that the meeting had been a failure and announced that the process was "frozen." However, after civil society participants in the agreements of Heaven's Gate and Río Verde pointed out that there was nothing in either that promised a demilitarized zone, Antonio García stated in a radio interview that the Caracas meeting had not been a failure and that the ELN awaited the reinitiating of the talks with the government.[20] These contradictory statements from ELN leaders, the first indication of Theme Ic (lack of unity on the part of the guerrillas) in their case, suggest that the crisis caused by the death of leader Pérez had still not been resolved.

When on March 10, 1999, the mayors of twelve municipalities of southern Bolívar threatened to resign if the government approved a demilitarized zone in their region, Theme Id entered into the peace process. This was but the beginning of the problems with setting up the zone there, problems that were to prove insurmountable.

The Second Attempt after Kidnappings

The ELN process came to a halt in May 1999 after two kidnapping events. The first was when the insurgent group hijacked a commercial airplane flight with forty-six passengers, keeping at least twenty-five as hostages. The following week thirty ELN members kidnapped the worshippers at La María Catholic Church in Cali. By the end of the month the ELN held eighty-five hostages and the government announced that there would be no talks until all were released.[21] An impasse followed, with civil society intervening in early August by suggesting that both sides take simultaneous actions to reinitiate the talks. The ELN should release all hostages, while the government should "begin the process of the national convention, including a demilitarized area acceptable to both sides."[22] Later in the month a commission from civil society once again made contacts with the ELN leaders jailed in Itagüí. They issued a very general communiqué, but nothing happened until mid-September when a group of Colombian politicians, businessmen, and academics met with ELN leaders in Caracas.[23] Although the meetings lasted several days, there was no progress. In October government officials met with ELN leaders in Cuba.

In early November ELN COCE member Pablo Beltrán (the nom de guerre of Israel Ramírez Pineda) announced that there would be a National Convention in Colombia since the Pastrana government had agreed to demilitarize an undesignated zone in northern Colombia, and stated, "We are already talking about where it is going to be." In that area there would be "cogovernment," with the guerrillas as the armed forces but with all the civilian authorities of the state. Beltrán stated that the ELN would speed up the liberation of the hostages.[24] By early December the facilitating commission of civil society decided to pressure both the Pastrana government and the ELN so that the National Convention would be held in the first three months of 2000.[25]

Although there was no agreement about where or when by the end of 1999, because of the existence of the FARC demilitarized zone there was agreement on what the similar zone for the ELN would be. First, it would be a "coexistence zone" rather than a "demilitarized" one. Second, all the civilian officials of the Colombian state would still be there; only the military would leave. Third, it would be no more than 5,000 square kilometers (as compared to 42,000 for the FARC zone). Fourth an international verification commission would be announced as soon as the convention began.[26] Commissioner Ricardo traveled to Bolívar where he met with Beltrán, afterwards reporting that there was progress but no specific agreement about the place and date for the convention. Members of civil society, who had contacts with ELN leaders, also stated that the only thing lacking was where the zone would be. Once that was decided, "the process could definitively start."[27]

Events in the first week of January 2000 showed that the "only thing" was not a simple matter. First, ten thousand Bolívar residents marched in protest to the idea that the zone might be in the area where they lived. They planned to end their protest with sending a message to President Pastrana, stating their support for Colombian peace as well as their opposition to having the zone "in their back yard." Who these people were, and who organized them, is considered at length below. Second, the governor of Bolívar, Miguel Raad Hernández, stated his opposition to the zone being in his department, which led President Pastrana to calling Raad an "enemy of peace." After stating that the governor "is the only one who opposes peace in Colombia," the president added, "Here there can be no municipality that is banned for a peace dialogue."[28] This was another case of Theme Id. President Pastrana and local officials simply did not agree on many matters.

Table 7.1 shows the conflicts over the demilitarized zone in southern Bolívar over the next year and a half. The period began with the mayor of Santa Rosa del Sur stating, "If the government decides to demilitarize the municipality for a dialogue with the ELN the population is ready to defend its land however it can. If the army and police leave, this area will remain without God or law, no person will have any guarantee." He went on to say that the population feared murders, kidnapping, and extortion.[29] Some inhabitants of the area were willing to allow it to be used for a demilitarized zone, but as is usually the case, those who were willing to take to the streets were noticed more than those who simply wrote letters of support to the president.

The issue became more intense in early February when ELN leader Beltrán said that he would not attend another meeting with government representatives until municipalities in southern Bolívar were demilitarized. Although Beltrán did not insist on specific municipalities in his letter to Commissioner Ricardo, he did say that demilitarization of southern Bolívar would allow a discussion of three topics all having to do with the paramilitary groups: the construction of private armies to increase the privileges of the elites; the financing of those bands through the drug trade; and the alliance of the ultraright to annihilate opposition to the system.[30] "Francisco Galán," from his prison in Itagüí, gave the official line of why southern Bolívar was optimal for the national conference:

> Our goal is not dirty politics with a language of peace; we are interested in constructing a process in which everyone fits and through which we can begin to solve our own crisis as a nation. For that reason, when we proposed southern Bolívar as the place for the encounter, we did it thinking of Colombia. That region is a clear replica of the convergence of all the problems in which our society lives and it is over that reality that we wish to act.

For that same reason the ELN was not interested in other areas within Colombia or in a foreign location. "Those could serve as spaces for preparations, but not for a National Convention of permanent character and a dialogue continuing with the national government."[31]

By February 8, 2000, Bolívar inhabitants were taking actions to stop transportation as a protest to the possible demilitarization. Some 7,000 people blocked the highway between Bogotá and the Atlantic coast in two places while others

Table 7.1: Attempts to Set Up the ELN Zone in Southern Bolívar, 2000–2001

	2000
January 5	March in southern part of Bolívar against possible demilitarized zone; Pastrana states that Bolívar's governor is "enemy of peace" because he opposes zone in his department.
January 6	Mayor of Santa Rosa states, "If the government demilitarizes the municipality the people are ready to defend their territory however it may be."
February 2	ELN leader Pedro Beltrán rejects idea of meeting outside of Colombia; states he will not meet with government again until zone is established in Bolívar.
February 8	Blockade of roads in southern Bolívar; lasted ten days with 15,000 people involved; ended with "Agreement of Aguas Claras" guaranteeing consultation.
February 24	Pastrana announces preliminary agreement to withdraw government troops, without specifying location or geographical confines.
February 25	Leaders in southern Bolívar state that "Aguas Claras" has been violated and that they will prevent zone there.
May 10	Blockade in southern Bolívar against zone; trade with Venezuela cut off; 15,000 participants.
May 25	Blockade ends after government agrees to consultation before considering any zone. Not clear if referendum or "*concertación.*"
June 12	*Asociación Civil para la Paz de Colombia* announces its opposition to a zone anywhere in Colombia.
July 14	Pastrana states that he is thinking of the convention in a foreign country because of the violence in southern Bolívar.
September 11	*No al Despeje* states that it will respect demilitarized zone if ELN has cease-fire in entire country, liberates all kidnapped, and puts all troops in three municipalities (Castaño had made same promise).
November 30	Strike called by *No al Despeje*.
December 14	In Havana ELN and government sign Preagreement for the "encounter zone."
December 20	Strike in southern Bolívar.

Continued on the next page

Table 7.1. *Continued*

	2001
January 15	ELN, government, and Friendly Countries agree that there will be no demilitarized zone in Bolívar without previous consultation with civil society.
January 16	Government fails to convince *Asociación Civil para la Paz* and *No al Despeje* of the convention in southern Bolívar. Pastrana states that he will push on with ELN anyway.
February 15	Thousands block roads in southern Bolívar. Pastrana blames it on paramilitaries.
February 16	Minister of Interior threatens use of "rational and democratic" force. Blockades removed several days later.

did the same to the highway between the national capital and Medellín. In addition there was a strike on the ships between Barrancabermeja and southern Bolívar, closing businesses in the area. One of their spokespersons said that they would lift the blockade only when the government promised not to establish a demilitarized zone in the area. Meanwhile an NGO charged that the AUC was paying people to be in the protest.[32]

The government replied that it would be a coexistence zone rather than a demilitarized one and guaranteed that the inhabitants of southern Bolívar would be allowed to participate in the process. After six hours of negotiation the minister of the interior and the Bolívar leaders signed the "Agreement of Aguas Claras," which included in its eleven points that group called *Asociación Civil para la Paz de Colombia* (Civil Association for Colombian Peace), known as Asociapaz, would be created and would represent the southern Bolívar farmers in peace matters. Asociapaz would first appear on February 22 at the installation of working tables in Santa Rosa del Sur, where it would have its headquarters.

Most of the points of the agreement were to clarify that there would be no demilitarized zone in the area. Rather it would be a "coexistence zone" and farmers would be participants in its definition.[33] As will be shown below, this agreement did not settle the problem of the participation of the Bolívar farmers.

On February 22 the eleven working tables that the government and the Bolívar leaders had agreed upon were opened in Santa Rosa. While public discussions there in the following days were on economic plans for the region, in the halls the subject had to do with the possibility of ELN presence in the region. One of the Asociapaz leaders, with promise of confidentiality, stated to an *El*

Tiempo reporter, "The coexistence zone is one where the people live, work, and have had control for many years; then, how are we going to ask the farmers that they leave their lands so that the ELN people can come to it for the dialogue? No, that cannot be. We are ready to collaborate with the ELN far from the south of Bolívar, as long as they are unarmed. The government should offer them security."[34]

The complicated nature of the ELN–civil society–government attempts at talks had clearly become a situation of at least four actors by then. Alfredo Rangel Suárez pointed out this change very clearly in an op-ed column in *El Tiempo* when he stated:

> The weakening of the ELN has given to the self-defense groups, at least temporarily, the possibility of getting their hands into the peace process. Showing a capacity to mobilize and organize the masses that until now had been shown only by the guerrillas, the paramilitaries have established themselves as the third actor which one has to consider if having a national convention in southern Bolívar is still being considered. . . . With things this way, the situation is complicated for the ELN because it finds itself in a horns-of-a-bull type dilemma because both alternatives are undesirable. It either insists on the coexistence zone in southern Bolívar, but then it would have to agree to the conditions and the location that the farmers and the paramilitaries accept. Or it abandons this demand, even after having said that it was its last word, and resigns itself to a process in another area, with which it would be recognizing the de facto power of the area.

This dilemma was being reflected, Rangel suggested, in an internal division within the subversive group, between a hard line that insisted on the southern Bolívar zone and a soft one that wanted the process to start, even if it was elsewhere.[35]

The following weeks were ones of various discussions—of government and ELN leaders in Caracas and of community, government, and paramilitary leaders in southern Bolívar, although in that case the communications were indirect rather than face-to-face. At one point AUC leader Carlos Castaño offered to remove paramilitary forces from the municipality of Tiquisio, with High Commissioner Ricardo replying disingenuously "The government determines alone in which part of the country the guarantees can be established for the holding of the convention."[36]

In late March the ELN stepped up its terrorist activities, bombing eleven electricity towers. This led an *El Tiempo* journalist to compile ten reasons that, according to experts, the demilitarized or coexistence zone had become the "Achilles Heel" of the negotiation:

1. The case of El Caguán of FARC and the alleged misuse of it.
2. The choice of southern Bolívar, because of the presence of AUC and FARC troops there as well as its economic importance.
3. Lack of international interest, since the ELN does not profit from the coca cultivation and marketing.
4. The weakness of the ELN.
5. The illusion of a military victory, as the ELN is weakened even more.
6. Lack of an ELN policy proposal, having had only the slogan of "Victory or Death."
7. Lack of a vertical command structure of the ELN, with decisions made by consensus.
8. Lack of clear leadership since the death of Manuel Pérez.
9. Agreements reached by the ELN with the Samper government, making it secondary to the Pastrana administration.
10. A veto by FARC, which did not want its peace process overshadowed by the ELN National Convention.[37]

In April the ELN continued calling for the National Convention, as a place "that would allow all Colombians to reflect on the gravity of the crisis in which Colombia lives and based on that reflection to understand what the structural problems that the country suffers are." The National Convention would lead to new leadership based on the idea of change and the direction that would lead to a "more just, more egalitarian society, with more democracy, with more participation and where all Colombians have the responsibility for the model of society that we intend to construct." Of course this convention would include "especially the national majorities that historically have been excluded." However, there was nothing specific about the composition of the convention, nor its location.[38]

Later in the month President Pastrana made headlines in the wire services when he announced a preliminary agreement to withdraw government troops from a northern region as a condition for opening peace talks. However, he announced neither a timetable nor the geographical confines.[39] Bogotá newspapers also heralded the accomplishment when they stated: "After eighteen months of horse-trading between the government and the ELN yesterday it was decided to create an encounter zone, in southern Bolívar and northeast Antioquia." The zone would be 4,725 square kilometers and although the armed forces would leave, civilian authorities would remain. The zone would be in existence for about nine months and it would be verified by an international commission.[40] The ELN agreed that they would not escalate the conflict during the National Convention. Further, the guerrilla group would respect the civil, judicial, and ecclesiastical authorities in the zone. International verification would be carried out by a commission made up of Spain, Norway, Cuba, and Venezuela. The zone would be returned to the government after the process was over. Kidnapped people would be freed. The ELN would carry out a substitution of illicit crops in the zone; and the National Convention would first consider a prisoner exchange.[41]

Local reaction in Bolívar was immediate. Prophetically one resident of San Pablo said, "Forget about it. Here we won't allow a demilitarized zone."[42] Government offices in Bolívar were seized by some eighty farmers who had come from Simití to protest that "with the demilitarization of San Pablo and Cantagallo the Agreement of Aguas Claras was broken, in which it was determined that the government would consult with civil society in the case of a demilitarized zone."[43] One of the spokespersons of Asociapaz stated "After this announcement people are ready to march and to protest the demilitarized zone, because it is clear that no one wants it, we all want to live in peace and calmly without the domination of any armed group."[44]

Several days later the facilitating commission arrived in San Pablo and Cantagallo (Bolívar) and Yondó (Antioquia), in an attempt to end the strike that had begun the day the zone was announced. This came after some inhabitants of the zone announced that paramilitary representatives had come to their villages, demanding that they close their businesses and enter the protest.[45] Former foreign minister Augusto Ramírez Ocampo said that he came as a member of civil society, not of the government, and added, "Like you we want a peace without guns, with social justice and for that reason the conditions must be established so that those who need to talk can do so, with the necessary safeguards. . . ." Nevertheless, there was no apparent change of the viewpoints of the citizens of the three towns.[46]

In the first weeks of May the ELN stated that they would respect the rights of the zone's inhabitants, that the national constitution would apply there, that trade would continue freely, that they would respect human rights and international humanitarian law, and that they would not recruit minors. Nevertheless the inhabitants of the three municipalities planned more protest marches, in which over 50,000 people reportedly participated. A spokesperson for the protesters put in very clearly: "The 'no' to the demilitarized zone is not negotiable, as we have been saying for some time now."[47] The effect of the strike was to close the major highway passing through the area, and in so doing it paralyzed trade with Venezuela. Other municipalities joined the directly affected three.

Finally High Commissioner Gómez traveled to the area and stated that he would negotiate with the protesters only when the highway was no longer blockaded. Carlos Arturo Clavijo, general coordinator of the protest, replied "The only thing we asked the government was that the constitution be applied . . . There was no agreement with the High Commissioner, and therefore we decided to continue with the blockade and we will talk again when the Government considers it appropriate, because that is their decision."[48]

On May 16, the blockade began again, after one day without barricades, with even more individuals participating than before. A week later the high commissioner and the minister of the interior met with Bolívar officials in Bucaramanga, at which time officials from the Magdalena Medio region announced, "If the national government insists in this matter, we—the mayors, the members of municipal councils, and the office secretaries of Magdalena Medio—will declare ourselves in civil disobedience and will resign from our posts."[49] At one point the president of the association of mayors of Magdalena Medio was even more emphatic, saying "We are capable of fighting a war in southern Bolívar," while a councilperson was even more forceful: "We are not going to let ourselves be defenseless so that we can be killed. If this [demilitarized zone] takes place, there is going to be a civil war."[50]

On May 28 the crisis was ended at least temporarily when High Commissioner Gómez, after meeting with ELN leaders, stated that the government would consult with the affected communities before formalizing any agreement with the guerrilla group for a demilitarized zone.[51] The blockade was lifted, although as time would demonstrate there was a lack of specificity in what "consult with" meant. Local leaders wanted it to be a popular vote, but the draft agreement stated only: "The government promises not to decree or authorize demilitarized zones, zones of coexistence, sites for encounters or anything similar or to remove public forces from any site within the national territory until it consults with the community directly affected and with its zones of influence by means of the mechanisms contemplated in the constitution and the laws."[52] Although details had made it into earlier agreements, Theme V was clear here and the blockade was reinstated after it was clear that the government did not interpret the agreement as a popular vote of the affected areas.

In June 2000 the ELN and the Pastrana government reached another agreement on procedure, in this case by approving a list of five countries who would be "friends and facilitators" of the process. As the agreement stated, "The group of friends and facilitator countries will have as its principal function that of lending more security and body to the agreements of the two sides, in its quality as an honor witness to the agreements that are reached during the process of negotiation."[53] The countries named were France, Spain, Norway, Switzerland, and Cuba.

Yet the stalemate in Bolívar continued. By July the national government was interpreting "popular consultations" as town meetings, while the inhabitants continued their insistence on plebiscites. Hoping to win over the residents, the Pastrana government arranged for local officials to visit the FARC demilitarized zone, so that they could talk with their counterparts and other locals. That effort backfired when the officials returned home with reports of extortion, forced recruitment of teenagers, summary executions, and other FARC abuses. A pharmacist from San Pablo said, "We can see for ourselves what happened down there, and we've been contacted by people down there who tell us that we should fight by all means to prevent what happened to them from happening to us. The FARC zone has become an independent country, and we don't want that happening here."[54]

In late July 2000 the government met with representatives of the ELN and civil society in Geneva. While the long-range goal of the assembly was "to begin to build mutual confidence after nearly 40 years of conflict" and to work towards a cease-fire, the immediate goal was to create a place for the National Convention.[55] That zone, whatever it was called, was a "hard bone to chew," as former foreign minister Rodrigo Pardo put it. As Pardo stated, "The only way one could make a demilitarized zone viable today for the ELN is an agreement about the conditions and mechanisms of verification that do not exist in Caguán."[56]

The membership of civil society was diverse at the Geneva meeting—members of racial minorities (indigenous and *afrocolombiano*), small farmers, youth, women, priests, union members, people from cooperatives, environmentalists, and businesspeople. Four major topics were to be, including negotiation between the government and the ELN, the National Convention, the chronology of the process, and the logistics for the Convention.[57] At the meeting the ELN proposed that there be two parallel sets of talks, one between the guerrilla group and the government and the other in the National Convention. The agenda of the Convention would include ten items, among which were the economy, politics, the environment, relations with multinational corporations, petroleum, human rights, and international law. Each of the processes would last nine months.[58]

The meeting concluded with the Declaration of Geneva, which called upon the friendly countries to assist in finding the necessary conditions for a negotiated settlement between the government and the guerrilla group. It also considered the National Convention to be "indispensable" and called on all sides to observe international humanitarian law. It was reported that the "vast majority" of the participants did not think that this was just another "catalogue of good intentions." High Commissioner Gómez stated "Here the thesis that dialogue is the solution has triumphed." ELN leader Antonia García added, "This has been a success because we have accepted the thesis that the political way is better than violence."[59] Participant Samuel Moreno was less optimistic: "We had many expectations from such a long trip. We hoped for better results." The two sides still had opposite views of where the National Convention should be, the government favoring Cuba while the ELN despite everything that happened, asking for southern Bolívar.[60]

Events in Colombia explained the lack of more progress in Geneva. Right before the meeting began, news began arriving from southern Bolívar that the AUC was attacking the very area where the ELN had been meeting with the government and with foreign officials and where the ELN had proposed the encounter zone. Reports of the number of deaths vacillated, and each side had nervous meetings. Then while the Geneva meeting was taking place, the ELN delegates there lost contact with its leaders in southern Bolívar. The agreement signed was preferable to nothing, which seemed very possible.[61]

Francisco Santos, one of the civil society representatives, thought that each of the three actors could do something to make the process work better. The ELN should agree to the "humanization of the war," that is, the end of kidnapping and terrorist acts. The government should make sure that its armed forces were more than observers when there were major paramilitary attacks, and should take actions to prevent them. Civil society, for its part, should recognize its limits. It could accompany, facilitate, promote, and pressure, but it could not negotiate.[62]

Conclusions: The Optimism of the Geneva Agreement

The process between the Pastrana government and the ELN had many difficulties. Although the period analyzed in this chapter ended optimistically with the Geneva agreement, an analysis of points of that agreement does not necessarily lead to hopefulness. Figure 7.1 shows the vicissitudes of the Pastrana talks with the ELN through July 2000. Many positive things happened (such as including details in some documents and the naming of the friendly countries), but negative ones were common also (especially local opposition to the national convention in southern Bolívar). Also negative were the bellicose activities of the ELN and the disruptive actions of civil society in southern Bolívar.

Three generalizations can be made about the ELN-government talks during

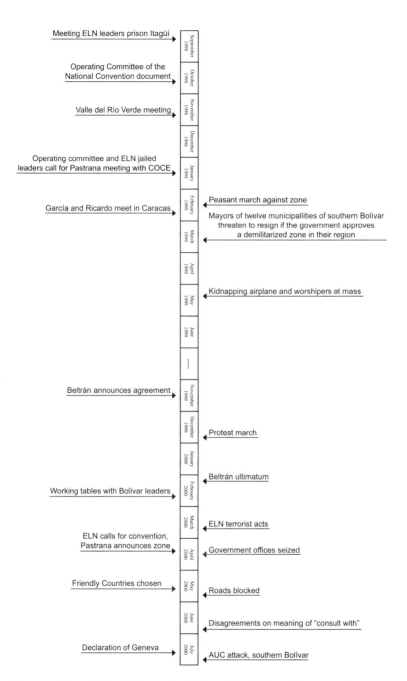

Figure 7.1. Negotiations between the ELN and the Pastrana Government, September 1998–July 2000.

this first period. First, the conversations with the government were suspended twice because of activities of one side or the other on the battlefield. Second, the National Convention was not held in large part because of difficulties in finding an area in which there was a bilateral ceasefire and in which the necessary guarantees would be given to all the participants. Finally, just as in the case of FARC, all of the agreements made with the ELN were on procedural rather than substantive matters.

To analyze the Francisco Santos statement quoted above, I think several major points need to be made. First, "humanizing the guerrilla war" is an oxymoron, the nature of which had been stated clearly by Armando Borrero, former presidential counselor for National Security, in an interview with Juan José Ramírez: "A guerrilla group that respects international humanitarian and human rights is a guerrilla group that has already made peace. If the guerrilla group accepts international humanitarian rights it would remain without a way to finance itself and for that reason it's going to be difficult to carry out this objective of the agenda."[63] As later events were to show, the ELN needed kidnapping as a way to raise money if it wanted to survive. If the ELN did not kidnap (and wasn't in the drug business), it would need income from some other source.

Second, it should be pointed out that the Pastrana government was doing one thing that the ELN wanted in southern Bolívar—it was removing army troops from the proposed encounter zone. In a sense that was surprising, since many in the military thought that the ELN could be ended militarily.

Third, that the AUC moved into the area as a result of the military's leaving is hardly surprising. And the ELN could not have the army removed and then expect the army to protect them from the AUC.

Finally, if civil society could not negotiate, why was the ELN so insistent on having a "national convention"? And why was FARC so determined to have the very similar national hearings?

By early September the situation seemed mixed, one report stating that President Pastrana considered the ELN peace process "going better than ever" and that formal negotiations were possible very soon. ELN military leader "Antonio García," in an interview in *El Tiempo* was less optimistic, saying, "The government lacks interest in giving a real push to the dialogue process with the ELN." When becoming more specific, García made it clear that the insurgent group still expected the National Convention to take place in the three municipalities that had been discussed for some time; he also made it clear that keeping kidnapping hostages until ransoms were paid was a "cost of war," and that kidnapping could stop only if there was "a change of financing."[64] As will be seen in chapter 8, the ELN was asking the government to pay it for not kidnapping people.

Yet there was some small reason for optimism. An NGO had appeared in Bolívar. Named simply *No al Despeje* (No to the Demilitarization), its leaders agreed with the national government that three municipalities in the south of Bolívar could be used for the National Convention. But they agreed to it only if the ELN would agree 1) to put all its troops in that area, 2) to a national ceasefire, and 3) to the freeing of all the kidnapped victims. The same proposal had been made by Carlos Castaño a few months previously.[65] There was no immediate reply from the guerrilla group.

There is no doubt that the attempts to set up the *zona de convivencia* (coexistence zone) failed largely because of mass demonstrations and blockades by thousands of people in southern Bolívar. No doubt paramilitary groups played a role in those mobilizations. However, there is disagreement about whether it was the *paras* or the citizens who played the major role.

One sociologist interviewed stated: "I have some good contacts with the No al Despeje group. While there is no doubt that AUC played a role in the public manifestations against the zona de convivencia, the No al Despeje group insist that they took the major role in mobilizing the people."[66]

Another interviewee stated: "There is no doubt that the *paras* assisted in the Southern Bolívar demonstrations: They made no effort to hide it."[67] Along the same lines, Mauricio Romero describes how everyone had to attend a meeting called by the AUC (with the exception of one person of each family who could remain at home). At that meeting an AUC leader, in his camouflages, stated that they were not a group outside of the law, but rather, "We are here to help and organize the communities." Later he warned that southern Bolívar would become like the FARC demobilized zone.

> Your daughters will be forced to be the women of the guerrilla fighters. Are you going to allow the ELN to fortify itself here again when we have almost finished them off? We do not ask for anything, we are only here to ask for your moral and physical collaboration to go out on the march. We are here because the people have asked for protection.[68]

There is little doubt both sides are correct to a certain extent, the two combined appropriately by Mauricio Romero, whose conclusion about this matter is: "In the case of the ELN, the so called 'coexistence zone' in the Magdalena Media area agreed to by that guerrilla organization and the government of President Pastrana was sabotaged by the AUC, working together with municipal governments, ranchers and businesspeople of the region, and organizations of the very state."[69]

Whether from the civil society, the paramilitaries, or a combination of the two, the ELN case shows an important variation from that of the FARC in Theme IIIa—there was much more opposition to President Pastrana's peace process. There were at least three basic reasons for this. First, there were many more people in the potential coexistence zone in southern Bolívar than there were in the FARC zone in the Orinoco eastern plains and Amazon rain forest. Second, the proposed area for the ELN was strategically important because of petroleum and transportation routes. (Although it was in a coca-producing area, the FARC demilitarized zone was not between economic centers.) Finally, FARC asked for a demilitarized area in a part of the country that they had long dominated. The ELN, on the contrary, asked for a site for the National Convention in a region that was controlled by the paramilitary forces, although the guerrillas had previously had power over it.

8

The Failure of the ELN Discussions

After the agreement in Geneva, the discussion of the peace possibilities moved to other venues. Over the months that followed, the government talked with ELN leaders in southern Bolívar, Caracas, and Havana. Agreements (sometimes so tentative that they were called "preagreements") were reached, but in the end it was impossible to carry them out. In southern Bolívar the issues discussed in the previous chapter continued—discussion of what consultation meant, threats of strikes, and actual strikes. In the end, the peace process with the ELN was a failure just like the one with FARC was, albeit for slightly different reasons.

In this chapter I describe and analyze the happenings between September 2000 and April 2002. The first part shows the hopes and the failures, analyzing the process using the themes presented in chapter 1, including Ib (the national military opposing the president's policy), Id (opposition of regional governments and groups to the course of action), and the constant blaming by each side of the other for the failures (IIIc). This chapter ends with major conclusions about why the Pastrana government failed in the ELN peace process.

The Search for a Demilitarized Zone after the Cali Kidnapping

The peace process with the ELN suffered serious problems after the September kidnapping of fifty-seven parishioners during a Roman Catholic Mass in Cali.

This immediately led the Facilitating Commission of Civil Society to call for meeting with ELN leaders, while the board of directors of the *Asociación Nacional de Industriales* (ANDI, National Association of Industrialists), the strongest Colombian economic interest group, called on the government to end all negotiations with the guerrilla group until the hostages were released. Further, the ANDI board stated that no representative of the group would participate in meetings, as they had in Mainz and Geneva, until that release.[1]

It is not surprising, in light of the kidnappings, that governmental and civil society contacts with the subversive group were rare in the following months. Apparently there were some meetings in October, although both sides were very secretive about them.[2] In mid-November Commissioner Gómez, accompanied by representatives of civil society and of the Friendly Countries, met with ELN leaders in southern Bolívar,[3] while at roughly the same time representatives of *No al Despeje, Asociación de Municipios para la Paz del sur de Bolívar* (Association of Municipalities for Peace in Southern Bolívar), and ranchers began meetings, with the renewed goal of preventing a demilitarized zone in the region.[4]

In December activities picked up. First, the ambassadors to Colombia of the five Friendly Countries presented a plan for a demilitarized zone in southern Bolívar. The proposal went to lengths to demonstrate that the sector differed from the FARC area. Most notably it was to include an international verifying commission which would include the five countries, as well as others.[5] Then in mid-month the government had a secret meeting with ELN leaders in Havana, the purpose of which was to "unfreeze" the talks. In the meeting the two sides discussed the possibility of a demilitarized zone in southern Bolívar,[6] which lead Asociapaz representatives to state that "the government is talking behind our backs."[7] Hundreds of farmers from seven municipalities in southern Bolívar marched against any demilitarized zone in the area the following day.[8]

As the month ended, Commissioner Gómez met with Asociapaz representatives to discuss the draft agreement reached with the ELN in Havana. President Pastrana said, "The idea is that we can set up an encounter zone very quickly, that we can begin the process of negotiation, and—as the ELN has stated—we hope that in nine months we can consolidate the peace process."[9] The president of Asociapaz quickly replied that the agreement would not be reached in "six days or two months." More lyrically the mayor of Cantagallo added, "Things are not simple for an encounter zone. There is nothing concrete yet and the actors in conflict should take off their costumes, their masks and outfits that they have always worn."[10] Both of these statements demonstrate the ongoing conflict between the central government and regional and local officials and members of the public (Theme Id).

One of the difficulties was that piecemeal information, usually based on rumors, was the currency of the day, as the government had not released its draft agreement. It became probable that the zone had changed, that there would be international verification, that there would be a civic police reporting to the mayors, and the judicial authorities would be allowed to remain. In this context Asociapaz president Celso Martínez called for the draft to be released, so as to avoid speculation and half-truths.[11] In the proposed zone, hardware store owner Pedro Gutiérrez was more pessimistic and defiant: "The civilian population has armed itself, quietly and strongly. As soon as the president says there will be a [clear zone], we will begin our war."[12]

In January the outline of the draft plan was published in Colombian newspapers. Perhaps indicating learning from the FARC case, the agreement attempted to avoid lack of specificity (Theme V). As shown at the same time on the government website, among its eighty-four rules, the major points included that the encounter zone would have as its only purpose the carrying out of the "National Convention" and the "Negotiating Table" between the government and the ELN. A permanent verification commission—made up of 150 Colombians and foreigners—would live in the area to guarantee the agreement. There would be no violations of liberties and rights guaranteed by the constitution. Religious institutions would be respected.

Judicial and police authorities and mayors would remain in the area. All threats and intimidations against the inhabitants would be prohibited, as would taxes by the ELN. The zone, made up of the administrative centers and two additional areas of the municipalities of San Pablo and Cantagallo, would last for nine months. It could not be used for the ELN to mount attacks. Although the ELN would remain armed, a civic police would be created.

Inhabitants of the area would be consulted about the preagreement, although there was no operational definition of this consultation. The government also promised a development plan for the region. The plan would be financed in large part by the Friendly Countries. The national army and police would be close to the zone, to guarantee that the National Convention and the direct negotiations could be carried out without the interference of the paramilitaries.[13]

Several days later Mauricio González, vice minister of the interior, met with No al Despeje and Asocipaz representatives, but failed to come to any agreement after several hours of meetings. His conclusion was: "As we have said umpteen times, this is a process that is going forward. We are going to have a meeting with the Central Command of the ELN and the Friendly Countries, and afterwards we are going to consult the communities once again." President Pastrana added, "We have talked with them [the community leaders] and we will talk to them again, but the process with the ELN will go forward along the guidelines mapped out in recent meetings." However, spokespersons for No al Despeje and Asocipaz were firm: there would be rebellion in the communities if the government tried to have the National Convention there. The president of Asocipaz stated, "We are angry with the high commissioner because he thinks that he is the sole owner of truth and he has never gone to the zone to listen to the communities. The arrogance with which they want to carry out the process is not going to lead to anything good."[14]

The Conflict Intensifies: February–April 2001

The following three months were a time of disagreements between the parties, mobilizations in southern Bolívar, Operation Bolívar (a military incursion, the goals of which were disputed), military withdrawal, increased paramilitary presence in Bolívar, an ELN conclusion that the talks with the government were "in a tight place," and the insurgent group's "freezing" of the talks. In this process the complex dynamics of the peace process with the ELN became even more apparent.

The period began when, on the first Sunday of February, thousands of inhabitants of southern Bolívar rejected the creation of a demilitarized zone: some 12,000 people filled the streets of San Pablo, in a peaceful protest to oppose the plan.[15] This showed clearly that, while the preagreement signed in Havana might have made it seem that the process was finally taking off, nothing could have been further from the truth. Indeed positions were hardening. This hardening was seen in at least three sets of relationships—between Pastrana and the armed forces (Theme Ib), between the government in Bogotá and the inhabitants of southern Bolívar (Theme Id), and between the drug dealers and paramilitary groups.

One of the problems which President Pastrana had apparently not anticipated was within the government; this first emerged in sharp disagreements with the commander of the army, General Jorge Enrique Mora. While this disagreement might have been only verbal in early February,[16] it took concrete form in the military incursion discussed below. As one interviewee said (stressing Theme Ib), "The case of the ELN shows how bankrupt the Pastrana policy was. He could not set up demilitarized for them because of the military opposition to it."[17]

The continuing problems with the inhabitants of southern Bolívar were shown when the inhabitants of San Pablo issued an ultimatum demanding that the President attend a forum on the peace process in that town. Pastrana rejected that ultimatum. However, as shown below, this was just the beginning of worsening relationships between the president and the affected inhabitants. Meanwhile in Bogotá members of civil society learned about the complicated nature of Bolívar, which had its share of both drug dealers and paramilitary squads.[18]

All of these factors came to a climax in mid-February. The conundrum began as before, when thousands of farmers blocked one of the country's major highways, to protest the encounter zone, despite President Pastrana's stern warnings not to do so: "We are not going to allow paramilitary groups, as we know they are behind these protests, to paralyze the entire country."[19] The next day the government ordered that the blockade be lifted and threatened "the rational use of force." Minister of Interior Humberto de la Calle stated "You have a last chance to withdraw. We are going to clear up the highways immediately by the rational and democratic use of force." He added, "A situation of opposition to the state is being shown and the state is going to reply in conformity to the juridical norms. We are going to lead a massive action against the promoters of the blockades."[20]

After a tense four-day standoff with the army, on February 18 protesters dismantled the roadblocks. However, protest leaders warned that they would retake the roads if President Pastrana refused to meet with them.[21] The government had promised not to decree a encounter zone without first having "a process of dialogue and citizen participation." The government also promised not to undertake police action against the protestors.[22]

The process was further complicated when AUC leader Carlos Castaño acknowledged that he had helped the farmers of southern Bolívar in the blockade and threatened to intervene militarily if there were no consultation before a demilitarized zone. However, according to Castaño, "It is not true that the AUC directed that social protest, but neither can we be separated from it. In some way we represent authority of the South of Bolívar, a region that we control politically and socially. I accept that we contributed through farmers and coca growers, to help these people with the protest. But this cannot be used to make the protest illegitimate because it is just. The leaders of Asocipaz are independent."[23] As I pointed out in chapter 7, the relationships between the paramilitaries and the civil society groups were debatable, although Castaño's statement shows that he thought that the AUC was in control.

In early March the ELN suspended the peace talks because of the military campaign begun in Bolívar the previous month. ELN leader Pablo Beltrán stated that the ELN doubted the true motivations of the military exercise because the bombing and drug fumigations were not directed against the paramilitaries and drug dealers, but against the establishment of the encounter zone.[24] The talks resumed in early April, with the goal once again of establishing the encounter zone. Not so coincidentally, the renewal came as the national military withdrew from the region after a month of activities.[25]

The dynamics of the Colombian political economy then demonstrated the adage from physics that "nature abhors a vacuum." In the Colombian political case the absence of the government (both the military withdrawal and the imminent encounter zone) led AUC leader Castaño to pressure civilian groups in southern Bolívar to take actions. Celso Martínez, president of Asocipaz replied that "Asocipaz does not accept pressures from any group outside the law, or from the government, or from any international organization."[26] Time was to show that Castaño learned the lesson. The next time, AUC was to take action without consulting people in southern Bolívar.

In early April representatives of the ELN failed to appear for a scheduled meeting with counterparts from civil society, the government, and the international community—including representatives of Germany, Canada, Japan, Portugal, and Sweden. The insurgent group's excuse was that there were no guarantees, a justification that the government rejected.[27] Perhaps more revealing was the statement of Beltrán's statement in a radio interview with *El Tiempo*. When asked about the state of the dialogues with the government, the insurgent leader replied with a clear statement of Theme IIIc: "The process is in a stalemate, neither advancing nor receding. The government has stated that it is going to confront the paramilitary squads but it has not done so; they decided to carry out fumigations and from the paramilitary bases they have added the areas chosen for the encounter zone to those under their military control. Hence, the ball is in the government's court."[28]

By April southern Bolívar had become a battleground. AUC troops pushed even harder than before to eliminate the ELN, effectively stalling plans for the National Convention. The national military promised to reestablish order, and as former peace negotiator Daniel García-Peña stated, "The dispute now has become one between the state and the paramilitaries over the zone."[29] In a letter sent by the ELN negotiators to the ambassadors of the Friendly Countries and the Facilitating Commission, the insurgent leaders stated that the dialogue was "in the worst predicament since the beginning of the government of Andrés Pastrana." They added, "That there are problems in this path of searching for a political solution to the conflict is not new; what is new is after the repeated violations of the dedicated word we find no commitment in the government to continue the dialogue . . ." Later the ELN leadership added, "It is impossible to convoke new meetings between the teams of the government and the ELN while the paramilitary squads are in the sites traditionally used for those encounters."[30] It is not clear what the ELN leaders meant by "traditionally used for those encounters," as there had been none.

In effect the AUC had militarily seized the 1,500-square-mile region that Pastrana had planned to use as the encounter zone for the ELN. Further, AUC commanders made it clear that they had no intention of turning the area over the ELN.[31] Hence it was no surprise when the ELN suspended indefinitely the dialogues with the government in mid-April. The danger of what was happening was more than problems with the ELN negotiations. As analyst Alfredo Rangel Suárez perceptively pointed out in *El Tiempo,*

> What is at play is something much more important than the quirks of an armed guerrilla group that is in clear political and military decline. It is the legitimacy and public credibility of a peace process which is interfered with in an unprecedented way by private armed groups that are in conflict with the state not only about the monopoly of arms but also about the counterinsurgency battle. A peace process with the ELN that had to be carried out in some other place because of the armed pressure of the paramilitaries would be the equivalent to the capitulation of the state, which would open immense possibilities that would condition the peace processes in the future.[32]

Fits and Starts of Mid-2001 to Progress at the End of the Year

A new attempt to set up the encounter zone was made in May 2001 when the Friendly Countries stated that the conditions were ready for it. Yago Pico de Coaña, Spanish ambassador and coordinator of the countries, said "We consider that the agreement and sufficient bases exist, on the part of the government, in order to overcome the existing difficulties and in agreement with the ELN the encounter zone in southern Bolívar can be decreed in the shortest time possible." In addition Commissioner Gómez stated that the government was ready to make decisions, but that the ELN needed to "thaw out" the frozen process. And the minister of defense, Luis Fernando Ramírez, added "There is much good will of the government and we have much good will also."[33] If the "we" in the Ramírez statement meant the military, it was disingenuous in the case of a minister of defense who was a civilian.

All of these optimistic statements were countered immediately by ones to the contrary from leaders of both Asociapaz and No al Despeje.[34] Several days later a forty-eight-hour protest was held in southern Bolívar. Some people threatened to arm themselves, although Asociapaz leader Celso Martínez rejected that tactic. The ELN also were pessimistic about the encounter zone. In a letter to Commissioner Gómez insurgent leaders stated that both the military's maneuvers and the actions of the paramilitary squads in southern Bolívar made peace impossible.[35]

At the end of May President Pastrana announced that he was prepared to meet personally with ELN leaders, in order to give a push to the peace process, stating it again two weeks later, in early June.[36] Later in the same month he added, "I have said and I want to say again that as President of the Republic I am prepared to meet with the leaders of the ELN to begin this process because I believe in clear possibilities of peace with that group."[37] This was an attempt to use the same method of personal contacts, which he had used various times in meeting with FARC leader Tirofijo. However, the Pastrana-ELN meeting never took place.

The response of the ELN to this idea came from third-in-line Beltrán, when he stated that the only way to resume the talks was by setting up the encounter zone. In keeping with Theme Ic, there was also a report that there was a group within the insurgency that thought that there were no possibilities of the National Convention during the Pastrana presidency. It would have to wait for the next administration.[38]

In late July, after three months of suspended dialogue, the two sides met again in Puerto Ordaz, Venezuela. The meeting began in a tense atmosphere as the insurgent representatives distributed a document which recounted their frustrations, accusing the government of breaking its promises, of aggression in the areas chosen for the National Convention, for not being united in its positions, and of connivance with the paramilitary squads. In reaction to those "it wasn't us" statements, Adjunct Peace Commissioner Jorge Eastman had already discovered the uselessness of replying to these accusations; instead he insisted that the government was ready to do everything it could to make the National Convention possible. Eastman proposed a timetable for thirteen weeks of constant work, including a meeting of Pastrana with ELN leader "Gabino," the naming of negotiators by the government and the ELN, the decree of the encounter zone, and the relocation of the military and the police.[39]

Even as the meeting was continuing in Venezuela, on August 7 President Pastrana suspended the talks with the ELN. In his version of Theme IIIc, he said that just as negotiators were on the verge of establishing the ground rules for the formal peace talks, ELN officials made new demands and rejected a series of new government proposals. He added: "Faced with the obstinate position of the National Liberation Army to keep the process frozen, I've decided to suspend the talks."[40] Commissioner Gómez hastened to add that the suspension was not a triumph of the paramilitary groups or "of Asocipaz or the other movements, which we have never considered representative. We do not know exactly whom they represent."[41]

In a lead editorial, *El Tiempo* had a clear explanation of the failure of the peace process—it was the pigheadedness of the ELN. As they stated,

In effect there was no other solution in face of the intransigence of Gabino and his boys, who did not want to accept anything different than a demilitarized zone in southern Bolívar, in the municipalities that they had chosen, on the shores of the Magdalena River and in front of Barrancabermeja.

It was in that region that the ELN was born . . .

From southern Bolívar they were expelled by the AUC and since then (1997) they have been in exile in the San Lucás mountains; what they searched for now was, while they continued destroying the national infrastructure and kidnapping fellow citizens, the state to dedicate its efforts to win the war that they lost, that is, to expel the AUC from the sacred territory, to regain it.[42]

While it was not immediately clear what the differences were between a "freezing" and a "suspension" of the talks, it soon became clear as the government decreed an end to the political status of the group and issued new arrest warrants for the leaders. While at one point it appeared that the ELN was trying to use the good offices of the Catholic Church to get the conversations going again, they soon made it clear that they would wait for the next president. This was because they considered the Pastrana government to be "high-handed and arrogant."[43]

Despite all this, by early November both sides started feeling out the other about the possibilities of resuming talks. Pastrana went first, albeit somewhat defensively, when he stated "We never closed the door."[44] A few days later the ELN announced that it was ready to reactivate the dialogue with the government.[45] A week later the two sides announced that meetings would begin soon in Cuba. Commissioner Gómez demonstrated his optimism when he stated, "We have made a lot of progress. The ELN said that there are no conditions, and we have taken that positively." He added that he hoped that the meting would produce good news for the country.[46]

At the November meeting in Cuba the major accomplishment was the adoption of the "Agreement for Colombia," whose seven points are the following:

1. To formally reinitiate the dialogue through an agenda of transition until the end of the present government.
2. To stimulate meetings between the two sides and distinct sectors of society.
3. To bring about encounters between the two sides and the presidential candidates with the goal of fortifying peace as a policy of the state and to guarantee the continuity of the agenda.

4. To carry out thematic forums outside of Colombia, to bring about initiatives and proposals about specific themes such as international humanitarian law, natural resources, and others agreed upon. The conclusions of the forums will allow ideas and proposals for the National Convention during the next administration. In the next meeting we will establish the work schedule.

5. To promote the celebration of a Summit for Peace with the participation of diverse sectors of society and the international community to evaluate the accomplishments, wise moves, and obstacles that have been faced in the process between the ELN and the national government.

6. To carry out working rounds between the spokespersons of the two sides about the following themes:
   a. Cease-fire and end of hostilities
   b. Measures for the reduction of conflict
   c. Problems of the energy sector
   d. Analysis of the conclusions reached in the forums
   The first round will take place on December 12 in Havana.

7. To establish a mechanism so that regional peace initiatives are studied by the spokespersons of the two sides, who will be in charge of directing them and articulating them in the peace policy of the National Government and the Central Command of the ELN.[47]

In this seven-point accord the two sides agreed to begin a series of working meetings on December 12, in which the first theme would be a cease-fire and end of hostilities. It is clear that the decision was made to avoid the contentious point (where the National Convention would be) and to state clearly that it would not occur until the next government. It is also interesting that, comparable to the national forums of the FARC process, forums would be held to talk about substantive issues. While it was not clear who would go to these foreign meetings, it was clear that they would not be in Colombia. Finally it is of note that there was clear agreement to put the discussion of the cease-fire first— something the government had not been able to do in the FARC negotiations.

Yet when it might have seemed that momentum had finally been started for peace talks with the ELN in Cuba, events in Colombia interfered. The first came when ELN leader Nicolás Rodríguez suggested that there were relationships between the armed forces and the paramilitary squads. This, according to Commissioner Gómez was "vile slander" against Vice President and Minister of Defense Gustavo Bell Lemus.[48] The second event was the assassination of labor leader Aury Sará, which leaders of the ELN also blamed on Bell.[49]

Nevertheless the two sides met again in Havana in mid-December, releasing a joint statement to "contribute to the celebration of Christmas and the New Year in an atmosphere of peace and tranquility."[50] The ELN and the government had agreed on a "Declaration of Havana," shown in Table 8.1. This was another timetable, intended to take the negotiations almost to the end of the Pastrana government.

While some parts of the Declaration are simple repetitions of the Agreement for Colombia, a little more specificity was added, such as specific dates of the forums (even though one might ask if two or three days were sufficient for discussion of such complex matters with more than fifty people present). With this document, the government declared the formal reinitiation of the process of dialogue and negotiation with the ELN and gave the insurgents political status once again, as well as recognizing nine of its spokespersons as representatives in the process and hence suspending arrest warrants against them.[51]

The New Year began with bad news when the ELN accused the military of stepping up actions during the unilateral cease-fire the insurgents had declared— and they probably had indeed done so. In a communiqué leader Nicolas Rodríguez said that the actions raised "grave questions for a real peace process."[52] Nevertheless the government and the ELN renewed their dialogues in Havana the next week, in what Colombian ambassador Julio Londoño disingenuously called a "positive environment."[53] That the atmosphere was far from promising was shown when in the first days of the talks the Central Command of the insurgent group allowed as how it would not continue the discussions if an international commission did not verify what was taking place in the Catatumbo region, where they alleged small farmers were being killed by paramilitary squads.[54]

Nevertheless by the end of January there was another period of optimism. More than seventy representatives of civil society traveled to Havana for the Summit for Peace. María Emma Mejía, a member of the Facilitating Commission, said, "We are talking in black and white: there is no space for an encounter zone, or a 'National Convention,' that is, there is no political space for a formal negotiation. But what it is about is trying to get some type of special agreements."[55]

The "Declaration of the Peace Summit," issued on January 31, 2002, was such an agreement. In it the two sides first recommended the creation of a joint government-ELN commission, with the addition of representatives from the Group of Friendly Countries and representatives of the Secretary General of the United Nations, the Roman Catholic Church, business groups, and political parties. The purpose of this commission would be to propose a timetable for the discussion of the removal of minors from the armed conflict; investments in the conflict zones; respect for electrical, transportation, and petroleum infrastruc-

Table 8.1: Declaration of Havana, December 15, 2001

1. To celebrate in Havana on January 30–31 a Summit for Peace with the purpose of evaluating the accomplishments, wise moves, and obstacles that have been faced in the process between the ELN and the national government. For that meeting the two sides will invite representatives of Colombian society and the international community who, having had connections with the peace process, have made significant efforts for its development.

2. To carry out, according to the following schedule, between the months of February and June 2002 five thematic forums outside of Colombia with the goal of encouraging the exchange of initiatives and proposals about the following themes:
    i. International Humanitarian Law, February 25–27, 2002
    ii. The State and Participative Democracy, March 25–27, 2002
    iii. The Agrarian Problem, Drug Trade, and Substitution of Illicit Crops, April 29–May 1, 2002
    iv. Energy, Mining, and Hydrocarbon Resources, May 27–29, 2002
    v. The Economy and Social Problems, June 24–26, 2002

   The places for the forums will be agreed upon by the two sides. A minimum of fifty people will participate in each forum, including representatives of the government and of the ELN, six experts in each theme, as well as some invited people with knowledge of the theme.

3. To have a meeting with the Commission of Notable People, in Havana on December 21, with the purpose of analyzing the report made in the peace process between the government and FARC.

4. To hold work rounds in Havana and Caracas that have the objectives of:
   • projecting and advancing in the agreements made in the Agreement for Colombia
   • making progress in the development of the agenda proposed in the agreement by discussing the following themes:
    i. Cease-fire and end of hostilities
    ii. Measures for the reduction of conflict
    iii. Problems of the energy sector
    iv. Analysis and discussion of the conclusions reached in the forums

5. To thank the Group of Friendly Countries for their work of facilitation and help and to invite them to attend a coordination meeting during the following work round.

6. For the efforts of fortifying and making agile the actions and activities of the Commission of Civil Facilitation, the two sides will determine a charge so that the work of this commission might be harmonious with the dynamics of the transition period.

ture; analysis of policies for the previous themes; study of the experiences of regional humanitarian rapprochements; suspension of fumigations and carrying out of programs of substitution for illicit crops in specific regions; localization and eradication of antipersonnel mines; agreement of the state to develop with concrete acts its obligation of combating paramilitarism; and attention to the victims of displacement and the formulation of policies of prevention and to return people to their homes. The commission was to report its recommendations to the dialogue table prior to its next scheduled meeting four weeks later, on February 25–27.[56]

The Declaration had three additional points. First, it called for the United States to become a formal observer of the process. Second, it called for the Friendly Countries and the United Nations to sponsor "programs of formation and pedagogy of peace in the diverse information media" in Colombia, since those media had so much effect on the formation of opinions. Finally: "It is imperative to consolidate a peace policy of the state that permits that, at the end of a quadrennial and the beginning of another, the peace process might not suffer interruptions." Hence civil society would be the way to rectify this problem.[57]

The optimism of this period lasted for more than a month. At the end of February President Pastrana said "We are working. This is a willingness to advance on the part of the Ejército de Liberación Nacional [the same as the one that] exists on the part of the government. I hope that the Commissioner returns tomorrow and that we can have a dialogue here in Bogotá and that we can see how and in what form we can make progress in the process of negotiation with the ELN.[58]

As March began both sides were talking positively. ELN leader Beltrán said from Havana that the two sides were talking about the immediate viability of a truce.[59] Although Commissioner Gómez said that he did not want to raise false expectations,[60] by the second week of the month Colombian newspapers were reporting that the two sides were studying a bilateral truce with international verification.[61] Indeed, on March 12 a joint communiqué put it in six points:

1. Given the situation in which the country is living, it is necessary to reaffirm that a political solution to the conflict is possible. For that reason we have begun the study of a truce agreement that might be converted into a tangible fact of peace for Colombians.
2. The truce is not a definitive peace agreement. It is the first step to acclimate the development of a peace process that might lead to a political solution with social justice.

3. The truce will include aspects that reduce the intensity of the conflict and will imply an immediate relief for Colombians.
4. The truce will have international verification and the mechanisms of implementation are being analyzed.
5. At this moment the two sides are consulting and once concluded, they will continue their rounds of work in Havana.
6. We invite all Colombians to help in this effort.[62]

This progress was due, no doubt as León Valencia pointed out, both to the pressures of civil society and the international community and to the greater attention that the government could give to the ELN process since the peace process with the FARC had been terminated a few weeks earlier.[63] Nevertheless the events of the following three months demonstrated, as had been shown in the FARC process, that "the devil was in the details."

The first detail was raised by ELN leader Pablo Beltrán when he brought up the question of how the ELN was going to be financed if they were no longer kidnapping and committing extortion. He said, "In the measure that the ELN develops a political and social program, and acts during the truce as a movement in opposition to the regime, it will need financing, such as occurs with European parties."[64]

The second detail came when ELN military chief Antonio García stated that the insurgent group could only enter a truce if the government opened public hospitals; resolved the crisis in public education, guaranteeing the labor stability of the professors and the punctual payment of their salaries; reduced the prices of public services and froze the prices of the "family basket" of basic groceries; financed the return of displaced people to their lands, with protection; suspended fumigations in drug areas, repairing lands damaged by the fumigations and developing crop substitution programs; and halted congressional plans that would harm the national social interest.[65]

The third detail came when the ELN refused to have its troops concentrated in special areas. On the contrary, they argued, "In essence the truce would be to silence the arms and leave them in the hands and places where they have always been. The armed forces do not agree to immobilization and we discard out of hand any suggestion that our guerrilla forces demobilize."[66]

A fourth detail had to do with the 200 or so individuals whom the ELN were holding as kidnapping hostages. The insurgent group suggested that the ransoms be paid by the government, a request that was immediately rejected by President Pastrana. Commissioner Gómez put it categorically: "It is juridically, ethically, and morally impossible."[67]

Table 8.2 shows the differences between the government and the insurgents

Table 8.2: Differences in ELN and Government Truce Proposals, April 2002

ELN	Government
Necessary that ELN has money for "political and social activities" in its zone of influence	Does not accept the "political and social activities" fund, but states it is under discussion
Necessary that a fund be created so that the ELN would not be broke if the truce is not extended	Rejects the idea of a fund for the ELN should the truce not be extended
Necessary that the ransoms of the kidnapped hostages be paid by the government	Rejects paying ransoms for kidnapped hostages
Necessary that the ELN troops stay where they are	Believes that ELN troops must be concentrated in specific sites

Source: "Gobierno no pagará rescate por secuestrados del Eln," *El Tiempo,* April 3, 2002.

in early April, after the ELN had backed down from this demand. The events of the subsequent three months demonstrated that although there were points of agreement—the guerrillas would be subsidized during the truce and international verification was necessary/appropriate—there were two insurmountable details: whether or not the government should set up a fund to pay the ELN if the truce were not extended and where the ELN troops would be located. As had been seen in the negotiations of the early 1990s,[68] the latter was one of the key bones of contention. The two sides met to discuss it again in mid-April, Commissioner Gómez reporting afterwards that there was no agreement on the issue.[69] Later ELN leader Nicolás Rodríguez said that the insurgent group was quite prepared to end "every kind of hostility" if the government "promises to respect the territories historically occupied" by the rebels.[70]

On May 30, 2002 President Andrés Pastrana suspended the process, stating:

Today I have to inform the nation that, despite all the efforts that my government has made, once again the ELN has failed the country, has failed Colombians, has failed peace, and has failed the international community. . . .

We did everything possible and we put all of our part. We even offered the possibility that the leaders of this group who were in jail could temporarily leave it and travel to various places inside and outside of the country, to encourage agreements. But that was not enough.

> We Colombians are tired of negotiations without concrete results. The scheme of dialoguing amidst conflict is exhausted.[71]

Commissioner Gómez indicated what the final straw was really two points. First, the ELN had asked for financing during the truce that was impossible. Insurgent leaders suggested that the ELN had 10,000 troops, while the government thought the number was "substantially less." The bottom line of the ELN for six months was government support of US$40 million, "an impossible figure for the Colombian government."[72]

The second straw was the constant problem of location of the rebels during the truce. Gómez said, "The ELN did not accept the different formulas that the government proposed so that their troops would be located in some zones so that the international verification that had been agreed upon could function. The ELN considered that they could not lose what they called military mobility. That made the truce absolutely impossible. In order to advance in a truce, one should leave military mobility behind to begin political mobility. If that is not done, verification is impossible."[73] The commissioner later suggested that FARC had pressured the ELN not to accept the truce and that the smaller guerrilla group was likely to be absorbed by the larger.[74]

Conclusions

This chapter has shown the escalating difficulties of the Pastrana peace process with the ELN. They are shown in Figure 8.1. Although there were some efforts to get more details in the agreements (Theme V), problems remaining included both sides blaming the other for the difficulties (Theme IIIc), the Colombian military's opposition to the process (Theme Ib), and the opposition of regional governments and organizations (Theme Id).

In addition there were a number of reasons for the failure of the peace process between the Pastrana government and the ELN. Most basically the priority of the Pastrana government was constantly the FARC negotiations and those with the ELN always played a secondary role. This was true for at least seven reasons.

First, the ELN was much smaller and less of a threat to the country than FARC. It had gone through a number of setbacks in the preceding years—defeats by paramilitary squads and the national army, the capture of about one thousand members in the previous two years, as well as about 100 desertions, and the death of their leader, Manuel Pérez, which made it necessary for the movement to reorganize and change its policies.[75] There were disagreements

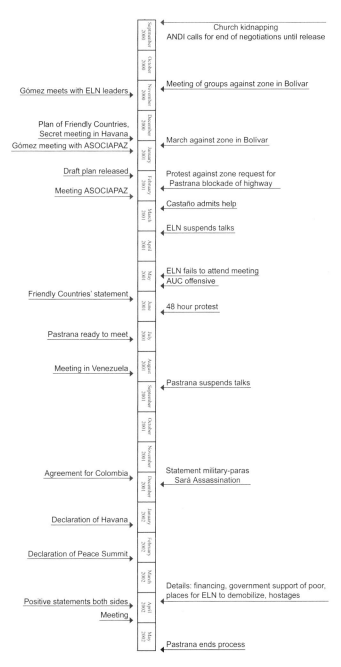

Figure 8.1. ELN negotiations, September 2000–May 2002.

over who the new leader should be. Individual ELN fronts began doing whatever they wanted.[76]

Secondly, FARC was involved (although exactly how was a matter of controversy) in the illicit drug trade while the ELN allegedly was not. Hence FARC was a much greater concern for the government of the United States than the ELN was.

Third, as shown in chapter 2, the process with the ELN had begun during the Samper years. Although officials of the Pastrana government have denied that this was important, we know from other sources that Andrés Pastrana wanted to do something to assure his place in history, not to help with that position of the man who had defeated him in the 1994 presidential election.[77]

Fourth, this peace process was not as key to the Pastrana government as the FARC one because of the desire of the ELN to negotiate with civil society, not the government. The confusion over what "civil society" meant has already been shown in chapter 2 and has become even more apparent in the last two chapters.

Fifth, the ELN was taken less seriously because they did not have a military leader of the quality of El Mono Jojoy. "Nevertheless, it was a mistake that the Pastrana government did not begin with the talks earlier."[78]

Sixth, to a certain extent the ELN was less important because the Pastrana government assumed that, if it were successful with the FARC, the ELN would follow almost automatically. Of course this hypothesis cannot be tested, simply because the Pastrana government was not successful with the FARC.

Seventh, the ELN was being defeated militarily by the AUC. Whether or not the paramilitary group was working together with the armed forces, there seemed to be no reason to offer much to an insurgent group that was being defeated—especially one that still acted like it had a chance to win.

Colombian political scientist Alfredo Rangel anticipated the failure, although he wrote long before it was a fait accompli. He put the blame on both sides, with the following words:

> In the ELN case the lack of clarity of goals was evident publicly even before beginning contacts with the government to define the conditions to carry out the National Convention and, what is even more worrying, the lack of unity about their goals. . . . Also it has been obvious that the divisions that always have existed within the ELN have been added to with another: between those who want to push the accelerator to the peace process and others want to put on the brakes. This was noted in the case of the demilitarized zone. While for some it was optional, for others it was indispensable.

Yet, Rangel continued, the government likewise had to share the blame:

> On the side of the government it is commendable that they might have adopted a firm stance, but flexible at the same time, about the conditions for the convention: not considering the demilitarized zone, but offering various alternatives to guarantee the security and logistics of the event. Nevertheless, discarding categorically any possibility of demilitarizing areas in the future and stating in general terms that "there will be no more demilitarized zones" is an attitude that leaves an adversary who deserves a more cautious attitude against the wall.

In conclusion, then,

> Without any doubt the premature paralysis of this process is due to the combination of two factors: The necessity of the government to show itself to be tough and the necessity of the ELN to not appear soft. The government because the errors in the handling of the process with the FARC have led to questioning from public opinion, doubts in the United States, and precautions from the armed forces. And the ELN because in comparison with the FARC it continues suffering the younger brother complex and it does not want to begin its process with fewer accomplishments than its older brother.[79]

Perhaps Eduardo Pizarro Leongómez best captured the problem of the ELN in the peace negotiations with the Pastrana government. After summarizing all of the above problems, he concluded:

> Facing this somber panorama the ELN decided to play in the political arena, as an alternative to its unavoidable military weakening. . . . [T]heir proposal for a National Convention not only was born in a derisory political moment, but, under an inconvenient blueprint under which to accomplish a successful peace process. In a few words, it was a dreadful proposal.[80]

PART THREE
Conclusions

In Part I of this book I presented the historical background to the Pastrana peace process and proposed characteristics of the Colombian political economy that should be considered in the description and analysis of the process. In Part II I presented that description and analysis, later presenting specific conclusions about why the Pastrana peace process failed with the FARC (chapter 6) and the ELN (chapter 8). The purpose of this last section is to present conclusions at a higher level of generality: what was it about Colombia, the Colombian government (or the Andrés Pastrana administration), or the guerrillas that made it impossible to negotiate a peace agreement with either group? Why was the Pastrana peace process a "chronicle of a failure foretold"?

At one level this task is very simple: If we make the rational actor assumptions—that a limited number of unified actors were making decisions based on cost-benefit analysis—then neither Pastrana and the FARC leadership nor the president and the ELN leadership arrived at a "hurting stalemate." I. William Zartman defines that stalemate as ". . . where each side is willing to change policies only if it believes that it cannot achieve its desired ends by violence at a tolerable cost and that its relative position will decline in the future. The hypothesis would be that a stable agreement is possible only if *both* sides believe this at the same time."* This can be a tautological argument, having little value unless we attempt to explain why no hurting stalemate was reached.

Further, even if one uses this rational actor model, there is a problem of measurement. The Colombian conflict is not a conventional war in which one can look at fairly objective factors like number of troops or weapon systems. Eduardo Pizarro shows this problem when he emphasizes three characteristics of the "negative tie," as he called it in 2004. First, the armed forces have had a clear strategic superiority throughout the entire struggle. But second, the armed forces have never been able to win the war, despite that superiority. Finally, the

---

* I. William Zartman, "How Civil Wars End: Questions and Methods," in *Stopping the Killing: How Civil Wars End,* ed. Roy Licklider (New York: New York University Press, 1993), 16, emphasis in the original.

"negative tie" had been broken, for example between 1994 and 1998 when FARC changed to a war of movements.**

But why has there been no peace accord in Colombia? This is the subject of chapter 9. To answer that question, after comparing the socioeconomic and political differences of the country that failed (Colombia) with the two countries that succeeded (El Salvador and Guatemala) I turn to an analysis of the Colombian political economy.

** Pizarro, 331.

9

Why the Pastrana Peace Process Failed

Peace negotiations succeed when each side realizes two things: that they cannot win the conflict militarily and that it is too costly to continue it. Whether called a "mutually hurting stalemate" or a "negative tie," the situation as been described in the following way in the Conflict Management Toolkit of the School for Advanced International Studies' Conflict Management Program:

> Either by their own conviction or through the influence of others, leaders can perceive themselves to have reached a hurting stalemate, where violence takes too great a levy without bringing sufficient gain. If both parties consider the continuation or escalation of violence to be more costly than peaceful alternatives, a mutually hurting stalemate has been reached. This mutually hurting stalemate creates a window of opportunity—a ripe moment—for negotiations.

So the Pastrana peace process failed because there was no mutually hurting stalemate. But that is a mere tautology unless I can explain why the negative tie did not occur. There are two possible methods to get beyond this tautological statement. One is through comparative analysis; the other is through investigation of the characteristics of the Colombian conflict at the micro level.

Comparing Colombia to El Salvador and Guatemala

The first way to attempt to find an answer to why the Pastrana peace process failed in Colombia is to compare it with the successful peace processes in El Salvador and Guatemala.[1] There were similarities of the civil wars in those two Central American countries to the one in Colombia. For that matter, Marxist insurrections emerged against many Latin American governments in the 1960s and 1970s, with—besides Colombia—Peru and Nicaragua most seriously affected. In some countries the rebellions never amounted to much (Ecuador, for example), and in others the governments defeated them militarily. Perhaps the most notable case of that was the defeat of the *Sendero Luminoso* (Shining Path) guerrillas in Peru.

Where the guerrillas succeeded, as the Sandinistas did in Nicaragua, they were then faced with an insurgency against *them,* the new government. And in the case of Nicaragua, the counterrevolutionaries (*contras*) were encouraged and financed by the Reagan administration in the United States.

One thing similar in Colombia, El Salvador, and Guatemala is that Marxist insurrections began in the name of ending socioeconomic inequalities in income, land tenure, and social capital. In searching for the reasons that El Salvador and Guatemala ended in negotiated settlements and Colombia did not, my "independent variables" are factors about the country—size, ethnic makeup, and wealth, as well as the nature of the political regime before the insurrection and the nature of the financial base of the guerrilla groups.

Table 9.1 compares certain demographic characteristics of the two Central American countries with Colombia. While the comparisons are from 2004, the same magnitudes would have been seen in comparisons at the beginning of the conflicts. The table shows notable differences. Colombia is so much larger than the other two countries, ten times the size of Guatemala in area and more than fifty times the size of El Salvador. In population Colombia is three times the size of Guatemala and more than six times that of El Salvador. By 2004 one source reported that the Colombian military had as many helicopters as El Salvador had at the end of its civil war, indicating clearly that the Colombian military was far from being as prepared as the Salvadorian military for the counterinsurgency conflict it faced.[2]

There are also important qualitative differences among the three countries. One was the nature of the regime against which the Marxist insurgencies took up arms. In the case of Guatemala, governments had (with the exception of a short period in the 1950s) been of military dictators. In El Salvador there were elections, but through the 1970s they were fraudulent with the winner consistently being the candidate of a military-sponsored political party. Furthermore,

Table 9.1: Comparison of Colombia with El Salvador and Guatemala

Country	Area (sq km)	Population	GDP per Capita	Income Distribution (gini index)	Ethnic Diversity
GUATEMALA	108,890	14,280,596	$4,100	55.8	Mestizo 55%, Amerindian 43%, whites and others 2%
El SALVADOR	21,040	6,587,541	$4,800	52.2	Mestizo 90%, Amerindian 1%, white 9%
COLOMBIA	1,138,910	42,310,775	$6,300	57.1	Mestizo 58%, white 20%, mulatto 14%, black 4%, mixed black-Amerindian 3%, Amerindian 1%

Source: Central Intelligence Agency, *The World Factbook 2004,* http://www.cia.gov/cia/publications/factbook/.

there was repression in the countryside, not only from the armed forces but also from a government organization of informants. While some might argue that the Colombian paramilitary groups were quite similar, in El Salvador the Republican National Organization (*Organización Republicana Nacional,* ORDEN) was founded by and reported directly to the national government unlike the AUC, whose relationship to the Colombian military was very much looser and more indirect. This opinion was shared by a Colombian political scientist who has studied the Central American cases, as well as that of his own country. In exchange of emails he stated "I do not see a similarity between ORDEN and the paramilitary troops here."[3] As pointed out in chapter 2, AUC leaders claimed their organization was the first time in the history of the Americas that a nationwide antiguerrilla organization was built, in which neither the government, nor the upper class, nor the multinationals participated.[4]

The second qualitative difference was that the rebellion in Colombia was against a more "democratic" government. However, Colombian democracy before 1954 was plagued with corruption and violence. Between 1958 and 1974 it was the power-sharing accord between the Liberal and Conservative parties that constitutionally gave each party half of each elective and appointive body and alternated the presidency between the two every four years. During those years, no other political party was legal, leading some to argue that many emergent social groups were hence disenfranchised. Between 1974 and 1991 the president was constitutionally required to give "adequate and equitable" representation in appointive positions to the party of the presidential candidate who finished second. The first and second parties were always the Liberals and Conservatives, although candidates of the latter sometimes ran candidates under different labels. No matter how imperfect that democracy was, Colombia was different from Guatemala and El Salvador in that it did not have a government dominated by the military—at least, not directly.

A third qualitative difference was that the Central American insurgencies had critical foreign support. In El Salvador and Guatemala the rebels were supported by the Soviet Union and Cuba. When the Soviet Union disappeared so did direct support for the rebels and Cuba was less able to give assistance. The U.S. government supported the governments in both countries. However, with the change of the presidency from Ronald Reagan to George Bush and the end of the Cold War, so did the amount of support for the government of El Salvador. The U.S. Congress cut aid to the Salvadoran army by 50 percent in 1990.[5] And in the case of Guatemala, foreign lenders let it be known that economic aid for the country would end if a peace agreement were not reached.[6]

So clearly, one side of the Colombian conflict did not reach the point of a "hurting stalemate" because of the end of military governments as had happened in El Salvador nor because of the threat of its loss of foreign financial support as in Guatemala. And while in the 1960s and 1970s Cuba and the Soviet Union did play important roles in the early support of the FARC and ELN, by the 1980s other ways to support the guerrilla insurgencies had been found. In the case of the ELN those sources were extortion and kidnapping ransoms, while the FARC had those resources plus large sums of money coming from the drug industry. In mid-2004 the Colombian government estimated that FARC was receiving COL$1 billion (or almost US$300 million) every three months from cocaine alone[7]—or US$100 million a month, more than enough for the guerrilla war.

Unlike the Central American governments the Colombian regime was not cut off from U.S. aid or threatened by foreign conveyors of economic assistance. Indeed, as described in chapter 5, there was more U.S. military aid than ever through Plan Colombia. In addition investments of foreign multinational corporations, especially in petroleum and coal, continued in Colombia despite the violence.

Yet the results in the two Central American countries were different variants of the "hurting stalemate." As Colombian sociologist Eduardo Pizarro Leongómez argues, the conditions that led to the peace agreements were quite different. In Guatemala the insurgents had been defeated and there were fewer than 900 troops left, who were no danger to the stability of the country. "Nevertheless, influential sectors of the Guatemalan elite—with the help of the United Nations—pushed a peace process that finished successfully in December 1996." In the Guatemalan case, although the government had military superiority, it was incapable of finishing off the guerrillas.[8]

The case of El Salvador was quite different. The guerrilla forces were intact and strong. But neither side was capable of defeating the other and, in both cases, foreign financial assistance was disappearing.

In conclusion, Pizarro states,

> In a few words, in both cases the continuation of the conflict, independent of its level and intensity, had become painful for the guerrillas—who had already lost their strategic potential of obtaining political power by military means—but equally painful for the political elites. They, under the climate of internal violence, could not carry out successfully their entry into the international system that affected their possibilities of private investment, both foreign and domestic, and therefore economic growth.[9]

The most obvious conclusion from this study is that the Pastrana peace process with the FARC did not succeed because neither side had reached the conclusion that it could not win and that continuing would cost too much. As I pointed out in chapter 2, FARC began a what it called a "war of movements" during the Samper government—changing from hit-and-run tactics to attacking military bases and small cities. Never had the guerrilla group seemed stronger; never had the armed forces appeared weaker. Hence a retired military officer in an interview stated the general conclusion very clearly, albeit in more general terms: "The problems with governments before Uribe is that they negotiated from a weak position. That is not a good thing to do." In addition "FARC had no intention of peace. As in the case of Belisario Betancur, they wanted an opportunity to get stronger. There are FARC documents that show that this [coming to the negotiating table] was a war tactic, not one for peace. FARC was strong and was coming off many victories during the Samper years."[10]

On the other side, the Colombian government believed that there was reason to continue the war against FARC. Plan Colombia had been set up with the assistance of the United States government and the Colombian military was going through one of its most profound changes in history, with more troops, weapons, and training than ever before. Eduardo Pizarro arrives at the same conclusion when he explains the first lesson of the Pastrana failure in the following words: "It is indispensable to guarantee a clear and rigorous military superiority of the Colombian state in the medium range, as a condition for a successful negotiation with the armed groups."[11]

The costs to the Colombian government from the war with FARC were considerable, and while the number of deaths from the guerrilla warfare was large (one estimate is 50,000 since 1980), it was in no sense comparable to the 70,000 in El Salvador and the 150,000 in Guatemala, especially as a percentage of the national populations. The economic costs were also considerable in Colombia, but not to the degree of El Salvador or Guatemala. In the major cities, besides having to pay taxes to help wage the war, citizens have been rarely affected. Colombian political scientist Angelika Rettberg, referring to the 2003 FARC bombing of the exclusive El Nogal club in the north of Bogotá, points out, "The attack against El Nogal represents an escalation of the Colombian conflict. Downplayed for decades as a rural phenomenon, the conflict has begun to seriously affect overall business prospects in the country, even in the cities." Based on various authors she concludes that the overall cost of conflict to the Colombian economy has been between 2 and 4 GDP points per annum. She adds that, while the specific cost to the business community is difficult to establish and varies by sector, several indicators suggest this cost has been climbing. This is revealed "by rates of capital flight, rates of infrastructure destruction, kidnappings of business executives, and tax payments to support the war effort, among others."[12]

In addition, one can look at the cost to the individual taxpayers of Colombia. In mid-August 2004 Colombian newspapers reported that a study by the U.S. Congress concluded that tax collection in Colombia is one of the lowest in the world, only 10 percent of gross domestic product in 1998, as compared to twice that much in the United States. While the president of the National Association of Industrialists pointed out that by 2003 taxes were up to 14.4 percent of GDP, the government responded that many other Latin American countries were higher.[13]

Yet there is no way to avoid concluding that the conflict has negatively affected the Colombian economy. The National Planning Department reported in early 2005 that it had cost the country COL$16.5 trillion in the previous five years. Further there were human as well as economic costs. Between 1999 and 2003, 1,179 members of the police force and 1,265 members of the armed forces had died.[14]

In the case of the ELN, the analysis is a bit more ambiguous than of the FARC. Clearly the ELN was on the decline militarily. Yet it seemed to have considerable resources through kidnapping and extortion of multinational corporations, particularly in the energy field. Perhaps it was for that reason that it clung so stubbornly to the idea of a "National Convention." On the other side the Pastrana government probably did not press on peace negotiations more because the ELN was obviously being defeated, either by the official armed forces, the paramilitary squads, or the intentional or unpremeditated cooperation of the two. One interviewee stated that he knew of one attack, in which the armed forces pushed the ELN guerrillas into an area, knowing that in that region the paramilitary forces would have them surrounded.[15] Another stated it plainly: because they thought they could win the war, the Colombian military had not allowed the Pastrana government to negotiate peace with the ELN.[16]

So in both cases we reach the same conclusion: that there was no "negative stalemate" as there had been in the two Central American countries. In the case of the FARC negotiations both sides still thought that they could win the war. In the ELN case at least the Colombian government still believed that it would be victorious.

All of these conclusions are based on a small number of participants in the negotiations—the Colombian government, FARC, ELN, and, on occasion, the U.S. government. The descriptions in this book have shown that the Colombian world is not nearly so simple.

The Colombian War System

The Colombian war is not one of several but rather of numerous participants. As I have shown above in what I have called "Theme I," at times there was a clear division between President Pastrana and the military. At others the same division was just as real if not as noticeable. I have also suggested that at times various FARC or ELN fronts were carrying out actions without prior specific approval of their respective leaders. Along the same lines, one interviewee suggested that the self-defense groups were united in the AUC only in name, with considerable regional variations.[17]

In addition, Colombia had experienced so many years of civil war that the de facto system was quite different from that formally stated in the Colombian constitution. The government in Bogotá is far removed from national reality at times. As one interviewee put it, punning on the fact that the elevation of the capital city is 2,600 meters, "Bogotá is 2,600 meters above national reality. Inhabitants of the city do not realize what is going on in the rest of the country. For example, there are paramilitary groups in Medellín, Barranquilla, Cartagena, and other cities. But not in Bogotá—at least not yet."[18]

The other set of conclusions, then, is based on the geographical complexity of Colombia and the political economy that resulted from more than forty years of counterinsurgency warfare. President Pastrana was within his constitutional rights when he stated official peace policy; however, that did not necessarily mean that the military or regional governmental leaders or economic elites would follow his course of action. This came from the geographical diversity of the country, leading to different groups maintaining de facto power in diverse parts of the country, the "political archipelagos" introduced in chapter 1.

Using different terms, a number of scholars have pointed to these divisions, albeit with emphasis on different features of the conundrum. For example Marc Chernick, writing at the beginning of the Pastrana years, captured this situation well when he stated the following:

> Objectively, the conflict does not seem more intractable than many other armed rebellions around the globe. The conflicts did not arise as a result of ethnic or racial exclusion. To judge from past negotiations and public demands, the ideological differences are not great, nor are the guerrilla demands excessive, comparatively speaking. Yet as time and history pass, the ability to negotiate successfully seems to recede. The guerrillas are more entrenched at a local level, and have greater military projection throughout the national territory than at any previous period in the conflict. The state, having expanded in its counterinsurgency apparatus and having abetted or acquiesced in the arming of paramilitary forces to confront the guerrillas further, has contributed to the loss of state cohesion and to the privatization and fragmentation of its monopoly on arms. Political violence now revolves around territorial control and competition over small pieces of political geography—a finca [farm], a neighborhood, a municipality, or a region—among those diverse armed actors. Civilian populations are the target of this competition. The old dynamics of leftist insurgency directed against the state has increasingly given way to a class of multiple armed actors vying for strategic control of local territory.[19]

This complexity of the Colombian system and how it makes conflict resolution difficult includes at least four characteristics, as has recently been shown in the works of Philip Mauceri, Mauricio Romero, Ricardo Vargas, and Nazih Richani. Even though they stress different aspects of the Colombian situation, all four argue that regional differences led to political, economic, and social structures in Colombia which have included regional and individual patterns of behavior that did not favor the Pastrana peace process—or any other peace process for that matter.

The Disunified Elite

Philip Mauceri argues that the peculiarities in Colombia are explained by the nature of its elites and their relations with both the state and its weak links with the state in general and the armed forces in particular. He argues that this comes from four key elements of the structure of Colombian elites.

First, Colombian elites come from a heterogeneous economic base, which is a reflection of economic diversity. The economic groups based on mining, coffee, ranching, and petroleum are separate. Second, those economic differences are reinforced by regionalism and lead to different perceptions of society, politics, and economics. Third, this diversity has made it difficult for the economic elites to agree on a common political project and has prevented the development of a single hegemonic class. Since the National Front ended in 1974, despite the new constitution of 1991, there has been an additional fragmentation of the political elite.

Finally, there is the strong antimilitary sentiment prevalent in Colombia since even before its independence. This is reflected in the social distinction between civilian and military elites, the lack of a nation-building ideology of the armed forces, and the lack of challenges to the civilian elite.[20]

Mauceri concludes that the differences of counterinsurgency policy in Colombia and Peru came from divergences in elite structure. As he states it, "In essence the historical differences of these two different elites shaped their relations with the state and other political actors, which in turn created and/or limited their abilities to construct alliances and adopt the visions needed to deal with insurgent challenges."[21] I would add that, for the same reasons, one might argue that the elite were unable to adopt a vision to deal with peacemaking.

Businessmen of Coercion

Mauricio Romero begins his excellent study of paramilitary or self-defense groups in Colombia with a political explanation of those vigilante groups: he uses the concept of "businessmen of coercion, which refers to individuals specialized in the administration, deployment, and use of organized violence, which is offered as merchandise in exchange for money or another kind of value."[22] The purpose of Romero's study is to underline an aspect that previously had not been studied specifically before—that the number of "businessmen of coercion" grew especially during peace negotiations and democratic openings, concurrent with weakness and decentralization of the government.

In the case of peace negotiations, this happened for three reasons: First, regional elites disagreed with the peace processes and challenged them publicly, while being silent about violence against the popular sector. Second, drug traffickers who had become landowners promoted private groups to attack suspicious civilians. Finally, the armed forces rejected the negotiations with guerrillas, publicly opposing them and privately using counterinsurgency tactics against civilians as "auxiliaries of the guerrillas."[23]

In his study Romero empirically finds four periods of rapid growth of the paramilitary squads. The first was in 1982, when President Belisario Betancur began the first peace process. The second was in 1988 with the first popular election of mayors. The third was in the early 1990s with the combination of a constituent assembly, a peace process, and the later return to even more guerrilla violence. The last was in 1998, with the election of Andrés Pastrana and the peace processes described in this book.

Romero's conclusion about the Pastrana peace process is as clear as his data are convincing: "That divorce between the politics of negotiation of the presidency with the guerrilla groups, in face of the concurrent opposition of the military organization and the regional leaders, produced a situation close to what Paul Oquist has called a 'partial collapse of the state,' in which the drug dealers, working with the local elites who were opposed to central authority, took advantage of those new institutional and political conditions to construct a paramilitary apparatus."[24]

Esprit Mafioso

Ricardo Vargas bases his analysis of the Colombian dilemma on the "esprit Mafioso" that the illicit drug industry led to in the country. Despite the use of the term, "Unlike the Italian case, mafia power expanded as a result of the illegal drug economy in a regional environment without the need of a center. That is to say, it did not require a mediating role with the state; on the contrary, it strengthened its territorial control based on an illegal and globalized market." This esprit was possible because the premodern structure of Colombia's state included its "weak capacity to control territory and exercise a monopoly of force in both the city and the countryside."[25]

However, Vargas continues, paramilitary groups are not merely reactions of the economic elites to the lack of governmental protection from guerrilla groups. Rather they represent "an independent political and military project of social control that extends the economic structures linked to cattle ranching *latifundios* and an agroindustrial sector that receives capital directly from drug trafficking."[26]

In comparing the department of Magdalena on the Caribbean coast and that of Putumayo in the Amazon region, Vargas finds notable differences. He finds many peculiarities in Magdalena, beginning with important sectors of the traditional political class being directly involved in the management of drug-trafficking activities. Secondly (echoing Romero), Vargas points out that "the move on the part of the paramilitary forces in the region toward acquiring political power through electoral pressures involves them directly in the management of a series of local and regional resources." This allows the AUC "to use the cover of legitimate institutions to strengthen its private control of all aspects of citizens' lives." This makes it more likely that disputes will be resolved privately. "Finally, all of the above trends to create a situation in Colombia controlled by actors whose strategic goal is an authoritarian transformation of the Colombian state."[27]

Therefore, Vargas argues, "Colombia's armed conflict is not one involving the struggle between a modern state attempting to impose its legitimacy through the use of force and an insurgent group. The support, both implicit and explicit, by sectors of the state for private groups engaging in violence and atrocities evidences a pattern of social control reminiscent of the premodern era."[28] In that armed conflict, drug trafficking is seen in two contradictory ways—either as "a mechanism of support for the guerrillas, which thus require a strong response (the position of those who support Plan Colombia), or as a source of financing for a new structure of power, based on the intermediation of capital from drug trafficking."[29]

Vargas's conclusion is clear: peace cannot come in Colombia unless the matter of illicit drugs is settled. Or as he puts it, "The peace process effectively obscured the complexity of the drug economy, treating it as a largely marginal issue, even as its role in the dynamic of war has been increasing."[30]

The War System

In a more general study and with different terminology, Nazih Richani argues that a "war system" exists in Colombia and that such a system exists when three conditions are present, all of which obtain in Colombia: 1) the failure of institutions to mediate conflicts among antagonistic social and political groups; 2) the antagonists' success in adapting themselves to conflict through accumulating political and economic assets that make the condition of war the best possible option given the balance of power and the higher costs of peace; and 3) a balance of forces among the conflicting groups that results in a comfortable impasse. Richani uses theories of economic utility, cost-benefit analysis, rational choice, and political economy to argue that "The convergence of these three variables leads to a war system that tends to perpetuate itself; where any of these conditions is lacking, conflicts are likely to terminate faster."[31]

Richani also substantiates an argument not commonly made—that the military accepted a "comfortable impasse" that allowed it to accumulate significant resources that could not have been obtained either under peace or a high-intensity conflict. That statement, however, is based on two assumptions: that more resources were potentially available and that, if the military had been given those resources, it would have been able to win the war against the guerrillas. He also argues that both FARC and ELN decided that local and regional control was more important than control at the national level, especially given the drug money to be made in certain locations. Once again, of course, this presumes that national control was a plausible option.[32]

Richani also applies his thesis to the "dominant class." He states, no doubt correctly,

> [S]ectors of the dominant class are contemplating the deconstruction of the default hegemony, the war system, and reconstructing in its place a more "encompassing hegemony" by persuading the peasant-based guerrillas by granting them some concession as a new basis of their authority and stabilizing property rights. The price of maintaining the war system has become too high and does not measure up to the opportunities that peace could offer to important sectors of the dominant class.[33]

Conclusion: Did Pastrana Fail and How Can Peace Be Reached in Colombia?

In the past forty-one years I have gone to Colombia eleven times. Whether it was a very short trip of only a week (as two were) or a long one of a year or two (as three were), one thing has been constant: I have always left Colombia with more questions than answers. Hence I end this book with two questions—was the Pastrana peace process really a failure, and how might peace really come to this troubled country?

Was the Pastrana Peace Process Really a Failure?

The figures on violence during the Pastrana years, as compared to the last two years of the Samper government, seem clear enough. As Table 9.2 shows, every indicator shows more violence during the presidency of Andrés Pastrana. The most notable increase was in the number of displaced people, indicating increasing numbers that were caught in the cross-fire between paramilitary squads and guerrilla groups.

Nevertheless, some Colombians argue that although the Pastrana government failed in the short run to bring peace to Colombia, through Plan Colombia it began the changes that would finally lead to peace in Colombia. One interviewee said to me,

> In a certain sense, the Pastrana government did not "lose" in the peace process with FARC. There were at least three "successes" from the process. First, the process gave time to the government to build the strength of the armed forces, who had suffered serious defeats during the Samper government. Second, FARC lost international prestige. The process showed that they were not "Robin Hoods" as they had tried to portray themselves. Finally, FARC lost prestige within Colombia. The Pastrana government gave them everything but they still didn't negotiate seriously.[34]

A Colombian political scientist made the same argument, in slightly different language: "There was a change of equation after Pastrana. FARC has less legitimacy than before for two reasons. Pastrana gave them everything but they still would not make peace. Secondly FARC changed its military strategy, causing much more violence and more deaths than before."[35]

Another interviewee suggested that "war of movements" of FARC had been a mistake. To do this they had to mobilize members of their urban "Bolivarian militias," leaving a vacuum that was filled by the paramilitary troops.[36] This source made the case clearly in the following way: "The irony of the Pastrana government is, while he failed miserably in the peace process, he succeeded in the long run because of Plan Colombia. Before this Colombian governments would either negotiate or fight. Pastrana, in effect, was doing both. The genius behind this was Rodrigo Lloreda, minister of defense."[37]

This, then, was the situation in which Alvaro Uribe Vélez became president in August 2002. Uribe was elected with a different paradigm (no negotiations without previous ceasefires) and, aided by the U.S. government through Plan Colombia, attempted to strengthen the Colombian military as never before.

Table 9.2 Indices of Violence during Samper and Pastrana Years, 1996–2002

Year	Homicides	Kidnappings	Displacements	Terrorist Attacks	Number of Massacres	Victims of Massacres	Attacks on Towns
1996	26,642	1,608	625	625	110	572	67
1997	25,379	1,986	2,190	858	118	571	94
1998	23,096	2,609	8,906	748	113	677	110
1999	24,358	2,991	7,099	804	168	929	114
2000	26,528	3,706	56,119	1,037	236	1,403	182
2001	27,840	3,041	67,727	795	185	1,039	128
2002	28,837	2,986	75,730	1,171	115	680	98
AVERAGE AMPER	25,039	2,068	3,907	744	114	607	90
AVERAGE ASTRANA	26,891	3,106	41,335	944	176	1,013	130

Source: Dirección de Justicia y Seguridad, Departamento Nacional de Planeación, *Cifras de violencia 1996–2002*, Volumen 0, n° 1, http://www.np.v.co/rchivos/documentos/DJS_Documentos_Publicaciones/DJS_Cifras1.pdf.

Levels of violence went down and a constitutional amendment allowed him to be reelected in May 2006. It is too soon to conclude if he will be able to end the "political archipelagos" that made national peace impossible before.

How Will Peace Ever Come to Colombia?

It is not an easy task to decide why the Colombian war has not ended in peace accords. I am struck by the Mauceri, Romero, Vargas, and Richani arguments above that there is so much regional variation, and so many structural reasons to continue the violence, that no peace is likely to come without specific policies for particular areas of the diverse country. Indeed, academicians have not done all the studies that are needed. Note that Romero and Vargas consider only four of the numerous areas of the country.

At least four things need to be done before there is any hope of peace in Colombia. First, many more studies are going to be needed—of the paramilitary groups in the eastern plains, of the FARC in Antioquia, and of the ELN in Norte de Santander, to mention only a few—to have a complete picture of the intricacies of problem. This is necessary not only for academic completeness, but also so that the Colombian government can have a complete picture of the situation of the country.

Second, a government is going to have to be brave enough to base a peace process on those studies. Third, a considerable amount of money is going to be needed to implement the peace processes, surely more than Colombia has.

Finally, no peace process will be complete in Colombia unless it includes the paramilitary groups. Over the years the assumption in Colombia had been that, regardless of bellicose actions, it was more legitimate to negotiate with the Marxist guerrillas than it was with the paramilitary squads. The assumption was that the guerrillas had become insurgents for political reasons while the paramilitaries had started violent acts for economic reasons. This particularly seemed to be the case in the late 1980s and early 1990s when the Medellín drug group played an active role in paramilitary activities.

As a result, at least one of the reasons that the paramilitaries had not been included in the peace talks up through the Pastrana years was that Colombian law required that a group have "political status" for the government to negotiate with them. However, in December 2002 Law 548 of 1999 was modified: no longer is it necessary for groups to have political status for the government to negotiate with it.[38] Accordingly the first president who had the legal right to negotiate with the paramilitary groups was Álvaro Uribe Vélez.

That he would be different in negotiations was shown clearly by Álvaro Uribe when, in his inaugural speech, he announced that he would search for "useful dialogue" with groups outside of the law on the condition that there be a cease-fire. He added that he had asked United Nations Secretary-General Kofi Annan for "good offices of the institution to search for the dialogue" and added "within this framework we will explore humanitarian solutions that liberate kidnapped victims, which might take place after agreements that show peace as something that is possible."[39]

By a month later the paradigm had much greater specificity. There would be a program of stimuli for the demobilization and disarming of guerrilla and paramilitary troops through a "decree of internal commotion" ready to be signed by the president and his ministers. It was obvious from the beginning that certain individuals could not receive the benefits, such as those who had carried out kidnapping, genocide, acts of ferocity, and homicides outside of combat. This meant that the incentives were not for the higher-level officials of the guerrilla and paramilitary groups who had judicial processes already started against them, but instead lower levels of the groups.[40]

As I finish this book, four years into the Uribe government, it is not at all clear that the negotiations with the paramilitary groups will work, although over 30,000 troops have demobilized. One of the problems is the "discovery" that many of the para leaders are very immersed in the drug trade. Another difficulty has been the unwillingness of the former paramilitary troops to return their profits from their violent activities. Yet another is how that large a number of people would be employed.

Some progress seems to have been made with the ELN. For a while the government of Mexico operated as an intermediary between the government and the ELN, but it did not lead to negotiations. In December 2005 and January 2006 the government and the ELN began meetings in Havana, Cuba, but its results are unknown as I write this.

FARC and the Uribe government have talked about a "humanitarian exchange" of imprisoned guerrillas for kidnapping victims. Yet at one point the government wanted to negotiate by email, while the guerrilla group wanted to talk in a demilitarized zone (something the Uribe government states was not possible unless the guerrilla group declared a cease-fire). Although in late 2005 the Uribe government proposed a small demilitarized zone for a short period of time, it was not the area that FARC wanted demilitarized, so as of this writing no talks have begun since. It is not at all clear, even with a tougher stance, that Uribe will be successful.

So, will peace come to Colombia? Perhaps, but one needs to be very optimistic to think that it will come any time soon. It would be more realistic to think that peace will come only when at least three additional conditions are met.

First, ideological disagreements must be channeled through a fair, democratic process.

Second, Colombians must be able to earn at least as good an income through legitimate professions as they now do through violence and drugs.

Third, the Colombian government must do a much better job enforcing its laws than it is doing now or has done in the past. As Francis Fukuyama said in a recent book, "The essence of stateness is, in other words, *enforcement:* the ultimate ability to send someone with a uniform and a gun to force people to comply with the state's laws."[41] To put the same argument in the terms used in this book, the national government must end the political archipelagoes.

Notes

Preface

1. Based on Gabriel García Márquez, *Crónica de una muerte anunciada* (Bogotá: Editorial La Oveja Negra, 1981).

2. George Santayana, *Life of Reason: Reason in Common Sense* (New York: Scribner's, 1905), 284.

3. Throughout this book I use "paramilitary squads" as a label for private justice groups. The groups themselves would prefer "self-defense groups." My choice of the term used is not evaluative. Mauricio Romero, in his excellent book *Paramilitares y autodefensas, 1982–2003,* defines paramilitary groups as "armed groups organized to carry out operations of social cleansing and military consolidation, prior to the territorial domination of an area" and self-defense groups as "groups organized to defend themselves from an aggressor and to maintain control of a territory, without pretension of expansion," 38.

Chapter 1

1. John Leddy Phelan, *The Kingdom of Quito in the Seventeenth Century: Bureaucratic Politics in the Spanish Empire* (Madison: The University of Wisconsin Press, 1967), 3.

2. Ibid., 22.

3. David Bushnell, *The Making of Modern Colombia: A Nation in Spite of Itself* (Berkeley: University of California Press, 1993), 36–37.

4. The historical circumstances leading to these "decisions" are described in Harvey F. Kline, *Colombia: Democracy Under Assault* (Boulder, CO: Westview Press, 1995), 30–34.

5. Alfonso López Michelsen, "Del orígen de La Violencia en Colombia, *El Tiempo* (Bogotá), 14 July 1991. *El Tiempo* is a daily newspaper published in Bogotá. Its URL is http://eltiempo.terra.com.co/.

6. Fabio Zambrano Pantoja, "Contradicciones del sistema político colombiano," *Análisis Conflicto Social y Violencia en Colombia* (Bogotá: Cinep, 1988), 23, emphasis in the original.

7. Eduardo Santa, *Sociología Política de Colombia* (Bogotá: Tercer Mundo Editores, 1964), 44–48.

8. Harvey F. Kline, *State Building and Conflict Resolution in Colombia, 1986–1994* (Tuscaloosa: University of Alabama Press, 1999), 196.

9. Harvey F. Kline, "The National Front: Historical Perspective and Overview," in R. Albert Berry, Ronald G. Hellman, and Mauricio Solaún (eds.), *Politics of Compromise: Coalition Government in Colombia* (New Brunswick, NJ: Transaction Books, 1980), 68–69.

10. The term "consociational" was first used by Arend Lijphart, in his article "Consociational Democracy," *World Politics* XXI (1969), 207–25, and was skillfully applied to the Colombian case by Jonathan Hartlyn, *The Politics of Coalition Rule in Colombia* (Cambridge, UK: Cambridge University Press, 1988).

11. Francisco Leal Buitrago, "Defensa y Seguridad Nacional en Colombia, 1958–1993," in Franciso Leal Buitrago and Juan Gabriel Tokatian (eds.), *Orden Mundial y Seguridad: Nuevos Desafíos para Colombia y América Latina* (Bogotá: Tercer Mundo Editores, 1994), 132.

12. Barbara Geddes, *Politician's Dilemma: Building State Capacity in Latin America* (Berkeley: University of California Press, 1994), 18.

13. In 2004 FARC celebrated their fortieth anniversary on their website (http://www.farc-ep.ch/). There, they claim that they were founded in 1964, not 1966.

14. Eduardo Pizarro, "Revolutionary Guerrilla Groups in Colombia," in Charles Berquist, Ricardo Peñaranda, and Gonzalo Sánchez (eds.), *Violence in Colombia: The Contemporary Crisis in Historical Perspective* (Wilmington, DE: Scholarly Resources Inc., 1992), 177.

15. Medios para la Paz, "*Ejército Popular de Liberación,* EPL," http://www.mediosparalapaz.org/index.php?idcategoria=479, last accessed August 10, 2005.

16. Pizarro, "Revolutionary Guerrilla Groups," 182–83.

17. Philip Mauceri, "States, Elites, and the Responses to Insurgency," in Jo-Marie Burt and Philip Mauceri (eds.), *Elites in the Andes: Identity, Conflict, Reform* (Pittsburgh: University of Pittsburgh Press, 2004), 154–55.

18. "Pura Sangre: Después de los sucesos de Mejor Esquina, siguen las masacres en varias regiones del país," *Semana*, May 17, 1988. *Semana* is a weekly magazine published in Bogotá. Its URL is http://semana.terra.com.co/.

19. For a full account of these efforts during the Gaviria presidency, as well as the even less successful ones during the Barco years, see Kline, *State Building*.

20. "Los únicos locos que quedan son los de la Coodinadora: Entrevista Ariel Otero," *Semana,* January 6, 1992.

21. *Ibid.*

22. Armando Neira, "Aparece el MAS," ColombiaLink, http://www.colombialink. com/01_INDEX/index_historia/07_otros_hechos_historicos /0330_aparece_el_mas.html.

23. Facsimile of threat published in *El Espectador,* July 31, 1988. *El Espectador* is a bi-weekly newspaper published in Bogotá. Its URL is http://www.elespectador.com/html/ i_portals/index.php.

24. Jesús Antonio Bejarano, *Una agenda para la paz: Aproximaciones desde la teoría de la resolución de conflictos* (Bogota: Tercer Mundo Editores, 1995) 87–88.

25. Ana María Bejarano, "Estratégias de paz y apertura democrática: Un balance de las administraciones Betancur y Barco," in Francisco Leal Buitrago and León Zamosc (eds.), *Al filo del caos: Crisis política en la Colombia de los años 80* (Bogotá: Tercer Mundo Editores, 1990), 66.

26. Presidencia de la República, *El camino de la paz* (Bogotá: Consejería para la reconciliación, normalización y rehabilitación, 1989), 22.

27. Ana María Bejarano, 93–96.

28. Ana María Bejarano, 103.

29. Ana María Bejarano, 112.

30. Ana María Bejarano, 115.

31. Jesús Antonio Bejarano, 93–94.

32. Harvey F. Kline, *State Building,* 111–17.

33. Rafael Pardo Rueda, "The Prospects for Peace in Colombia: Lessons from Recent Experience," Inter-American Dialogue Working Paper, July 2002, http://www. thedialogue.org/publications/country_studies/colombia_pardo.pdf, 4.

34. Ibid.

35. Ibid., 5.

36. Interview 5, Colombian sociologist, by email, January 5, 2006.

37. Kline, *State Building,* 116.

38. Ibid.

39. "En Colombia hay poco espacio para la crítica: ex fiscal Gómez Méndez," RCN Radio, January 6, 2006. Radio Cadena Nacional publishes a daily webpage with *http:// www.rcn.com.co/noticia.php3?nt=12056* as its URL.

40. Geddes, 22.

41. Amnesty International, "The Guatemalan Peace Process Agreements: Elements most relevant to AI's concerns," http://web.amnesty.org/library/Index/ ENGAMR340241997?open&of=ENG-2M2.

Chapter 2

1. "Santiago Medina, tesorero de la campaña presidencial del presidente Ernesto Samper, fue detenido el 26 de julio por la Fiscalía Nacional," *Semana,* August 1, 1995.

2. Interview 21, private foundation official, Bogotá, July 19, 2004.

3. Interview 1, former official in Samper peace process, June 7, 2003.

4. "EL 8.000 dia a dia: Desde que se conocieron los narcocasetes no ha habido una sola semana sin noticias sobre el tema," *Semana,* August 1, 1996.

5. "'J'accuse'," *Semana,* February 20, 1996.

6. "Entrevista con Ernesto Samper," *Semana,* February 6, 1996.

7. María Jimena Duzán, "Colombia's Bloody War of Words," *Journal of Democracy,* 2, no. 1, 1991, 105.

8. Interview 5, Colombian sociologist, Bogotá, June 20, 2004.

9. "Gobierno fija bases para diálogos de paz," *El Tiempo,* November 17, 1994.

10. "'Hay condiciones para discutir agenda': Holmes Trujillo entrega primer informe," *El Tiempo,* November 18, 1994.

11. "Gobierno y FARC definirian agenda de paz," *El Tiempo,* February 12, 1995.

12. "FARC rompieron la confidencialidad: Comisionado cuestiona esta actitud," *El Tiempo,* February 22, 1995.

13. "La Uribe será sitio de primer encuentro: Gobierno y FARC discuten desmilitarización," *El Tiempo,* April 7, 1995.

14. "Hoy se destapa la baraja de la paz: Desmilitarización de La Uribe y consulta popular, temas claves," *El Tiempo,* May 18, 1995.

15. "La Uribe, Sede del diálogo: Gobierno despeja el camino para negociar con la guerrilla," *El Tiempo,* May 19, 1995.

16. "Ultimatum del Gobierno a FARC: Gobierno fija plazos para conversar," *El Tiempo,* June 23, 1995.

17. "Ejército advierte riesgos de desmilitarizar Uribe: Memorando interno del Ejército al Gobierno," *El Tiempo,* July 3, 1995.

18. "'Acatamos al presidente': F.M.: 'Aquí mando yo,' advirtio ayer Samper al referirse a la estrategia de paz," *El Tiempo,* July 4, 1995.

19. "No se ha desconocido la autoridad del Presidente: Explican comandantes de Ejército y FF.MM.," *El Tiempo,* July 4, 1995.

20. "El Gobierno precisa condiciones de paz: 'No existió crisis con militares': Botero," *El Tiempo,* July 5, 1995.

21. Conversation with a Colombian army major, Columbus, Georgia, April 1997.

22. Interview 8, official in the Office of the Vice Presidency, Bogotá, June 19, 2003.

23. Interview 4, Colombian historian, July 8, 2004.

24. "Con la salida de Holmes, el proceso de paz cada vez más a la deriva: El Alto Comisionado fue elegido en la DLN," *El Tiempo,* July 24, 1995.

25. "Uribe no será desmilitarizada: Comisión no puede negociar," *El Tiempo,* August 12, 1995.

26. "La política de paz no está archivada," *El Espectador,* January 16, 1996.

27. "Hay aval para dialogar, pero no para negociar: Las FARC plantean nueva propuesta de desmilitarización," *El Tiempo,* August 16, 1996.

28. "Las propuestas sobre la mesa," *El Tiempo,* November 5, 1997.

29. Interview 5, Colombian sociologist, by email, January 4, 2006.

30. "Solicita que sea uno de los cinco municipios exigidos por las FARC: Consejo de Paz le pide despeje a Samper," *El Tiempo*, June 12, 1998.

31. "Sería después de elecciones y en consulta con el presidente electo: Samper se da 'la pela' con despeje," *El Tiempo*, June 13, 1998.

32. "El Despeje: Los cinco municipios estratégicos," *El Tiempo*, July 10, 1998.

33. "'Diálogo, difícial pero posible,' Habla Manuel Pérez, jefe del Eln," *El Tiempo*, September 2, 1996.

34. The message referred to the Coordinadora Guerrillera Simón Bolívar (CGSB), the organization that had allowed the ELN and FARC to negotiate together during the Barco and Gaviria governments.

35. "El Gobierno define hoy sitio de contactos," *El Tiempo*, February 21, 1995.

36. "Eln ve leganos los diálogos: Insiste que 'Galán' es prisionero de guerra," *El Tiempo*, May 25, 1995.

37. "En peligro los diálogos si no hay hechos de paz: Gobierno," *El Tiempo*, July 17, 1995.

38. "Comienzan diálogos con guerrilla," *El Tiempo*, May 29, 1995.

39. "Iglesia en Colombia mediará en cita de paz en Alemania," http://www.aciprensa. com/notic1998/julio/notic386.htm. [Scroll down to article.]

40. Dirección Nacional, Unión Camilista Ejercito de Liberación, "Una Propuesta Urgente para Colombia," Montañas de Colombia, February 2, 1996, http://www.eln-voces. com/historia/pp_co_ch.htm, last visited February 17, 1996.

41. Ibid.

42. "Propuesta de Convención Nacional del ELN a las primeras jornadas por la paz y los derechos humanos en Colombia, Madrid-España," December 12, 1997, http://www. eln-voces.com/comupa/pp—co—jp.htm, last visited December 11, 1999.

43. Ibid.

44. Ibid.

45. Comisión de Reconciliación Nacional, "Paz y reconciliación," http://www.ccncol. org/p/paz.html#comision.

46. "Declaración de Viana," February 9, 1998, http://www.ideaspaz.org/proyecto03/ boletines/download/boletin03/viana.doc.

47. García-Peña was frequently referred to as the "alto comisionado" in the press. However, Samper did not give that title to anyone after the Holmes resignation.

48. "Government and ELN reaffirm Pre-agreement for Peace Document," Santafé de Bogotá, ANCOL, March 27, 1998. ANCOL (the Colombian News Agency) is what the Pastrana government called the presidential website. The URL was http://www. presidencia.gov.co. Inconvenient for this book, that URL now goes to the website of the current president, and contains no archive of the previous presidency.

49. Comando Central del ELN, Montañas de Colombia, Marzo 26 de 1.998, http:// www.eln-voces.com/comupa/pp_co_rv.htm, last visited March 30, 1998.

50. Ley 434 de 1998 (febrero 3), "Por la cual se crea el Consejo Nacional de Paz, se otorgan funciones y se dictan otras disposiciones," http://www.secretariasenado.gov.co/ leyes/L0424_98.htm.

51. Interview 15, member of the Peace Commission, Bogotá, July 3, 2003.

52. Comando Central, "Proceso de Paz, Convención Nacional: Una propuesta para la reconstrucción de la sociedad," Montañas de Colombia, April 2000. Document obtained from the Fundación Ideas para la Paz, Bogotá, June 2003.

53. Ibid.

54. Ibid.

55. "Acuerdo de Puerta del Cielo con el ELN," July 15, 1998, http://www.ciponline.org/colombia/cielo.htm.

56. Ibid.

57. Respectively, Interview 6, Colombian sociologist, Bogotá, June 14, 2003; Interview 5, Colombian sociologist, Bogotá, June 13, 2003.

58. MIPT Terrorism Knowledge Base, http://www.tkb.org/KeyLeader.jsp?memID=5347.

59. "51 días de secreto sobre muerte del cura Manuel Pérez," *El Tiempo,* April 7, 1998.

60. "Fifty Years of Violence," (originally published in *Colombia Report,* Information Network of the Americas), http://www.colombiajournal.org/fiftyyearsofviolence.htm.

61. "Convivir, embuchado de largo alcance," http://www.derechos.org/nizkor/colombia/doc/convivir.html

62. Ibid.

63. "Colombia: Paramilitares legalizados," *Rebelión,* http://www.rebelion.org/plancolombia/sodepaz090902.htm.

64. Romero, 151.

65. Orlando León Restrepo, "En una resolución, la Superintendencia de Vigilancia trazó, además, pautas sobre porte de armas en las cooperativas," *El Tiempo,* November 3, 1997.

66. "Por 5 votos contra 4, la Corte definió la suerte de las cooperativas," *El Tiempo,* November 8, 1997.

67. "Cerca de 300 pedirán cancelación de su licencia: Desmontan 289 Convivir," *El Tiempo,* July 26, 1998.

68. Scott Wilson, "Colombia's Other Army," *Washington Post,* March 12, 2001. The URL of the *Washington Post* is http://www.washingtonpost.com/.

69. Mauricio Aranguren Molina, *Mi Confesión: Carlos Castaño revela sus secretos* (Bogotá: Oveja Negra, 2002), 126–27. Castaño "confessed" to journalist Aranguren, who wrote this book. That Castaño and the AUC considered this book to be authentic was shown by the fact that it was made available on the AUC website for a while.

70. Scott Wilson, "Colombia's Other Army," *Washington Post,* March 12, 2001.

71. Aranguren, 243.

72. Ibid., 244.

73. Ibid., 246.

74. Ibid., 246–47.

75. Ibid., 247.

76. Ernesto Che Guevara, "Guerrilla war, a method," *Obra Revolucionaria* (Era: Mexico, 1973), quoted on http://www.marxists.org/archive/guevara/1963/misc/guerrilla-war-method.htm.

77. Eduardo Pizarro Leongómez, *Una democracia asediada: Balance y perspectivas del conflicto armado en Colombia* (Bogotá: Grupo Editorial Norma, 2004), 96, 98.

78. Fuerzas militares para la guerra: La agenda pendiente de la reforma militar (Bogotá: Fundación Seguridad y Democracia, 2003), 21–25.

79. Interview 19, Colombian sociologist, Bogotá, July 7, 2004.

80. Interview 4, Colombian historian, Bogotá, June 10, 2003.

81. "En Colombia no hay Estado de Derecho: D. Miterrand," *El Tiempo,* August 4, 1998.

82. Juan Manuel Santos, "El primer paso: La ONU y la paz," *El Tiempo,* June 19, 1998.

Chapter 3

1. Under the Colombian Constitution of 1991 the president is elected by an absolute majority. If no candidate obtains that in the first round, there is a second round between the top two.

2. Édgar Téllez, Oscar Montes, y Jorge Lesmes, *Diario íntimo de un fracaso: Historia no contada del proceso de paz con las FARC* (Bogotá: Editorial Planeta Colombiana, 2002), 15–25.

3. Ibid., 28.

4. Ibid., 29.

5. Ibid., 35.

6. "Carta abierta al Doctor Andrés Pastrana Arango, Presidente de la República," December 3, 1998. Document obtained from the Fundación Ideas para la Paz, Bogotá, June 2003.

7. Romero, 95.

8. Interview 13, Colombian political scientist, Bogotá, July 13, 2004.

9. This resignation was necessary according to the constitution.

10. "Andrés Pastrana Arango," CIDOB, http://www.cidob.org/bios/castellano/lideres/p-015.htm#1.

11. "Pedro Antonio Marín (Tirofojo)(FARC)" http://www.colombialink.com/01_INDEX/index_personajes/guerrilla/marin_pedro_antonio.html.

12. Álvaro Valencia Tovar, "El 7 de enero, fecha decisiva," *El Tiempo,* January 8, 1999.

13. Téllez, Montes, and Lesmes, 41.

14. "Cuatro años a la 'caza' de la paz," Posesión Presidencial, Colombia.com, http://www.colombia.com/especiales/2002/posesion_presidencial/paz.asp.

15. Laura Brooks, "Colombian President Inaugurated," *Washington Post,* August 8, 1998.

16. León Valencia, *Adiós a la política, bienvenida la guerra: Secretos de un malogrado proceso de paz* (Bogotá: Intermedio, 2002), 40.

17. "Cumbre de paz hoy en Palacio: 'Agenda con las Farc no tendrá temas vedados': Pastrana," *El Tiempo,* January 6, 1999.

18. Interview 19, Colombian sociologist, by telephone from Tuscaloosa to Bogotá, September 6, 2003.

19. Romero, 95.

20. "Análisis: El perfecto equilibrio," *El Tiempo*, January 5, 1999.

21. Interview 7, Colombian political scientist, Bogotá, June 19, 2003.

22. Interview 6, Colombian sociologist, Bogotá, June 14, 2003.

23. Larry Rohter, "Colombia and Rebel Group Begin Peace Talks," Associated Press, September 24, 1998. The AP's URL is http://www.ap.org/.

24. "Ayer fue instalada mesa de trabajo y participación para la paz de la Cámara de Representantes: Santos dice que reforma política no es cuota inicial de paz," *El Tiempo*, September 3, 1998.

25. "Los altibajos del proceso: El naciente proceso de paz con las Farc, hoy en el 'congelador', se ha movido entre la cima y el abismo," *El Tiempo*, January 20, 1999.

26. "Se precisan zonas de distensión: Compromiso de las Farc a llegar a acuerdo de paz," *El Tiempo*, September 12, 1998.

27. "La réplica presidencial," *El Tiempo*, September 16, 1998.

28. "Se inicia crucial diálogo de 90 días con las Farc. Despeje desde el 7 de noviembre," *El Tiempo*, October 15, 1998.

29. Interview 5, Colombian sociologist, by email, January 4, 2005.

30. "Una unidad es trofeo de guerra … y de paz: El pulso por el Batallón Cazadores," *El Tiempo*, November 29, 1998.

31. "Carta abierta al Doctor Andrés Pastrana Arango, Presidente de la República," December 3, 1998. Document obtained from the Fundación Ideas para la Paz, Bogotá, June 2003.

32. "El Presidente dará las instrucciones pertinentes para el retiro de los soldados del Batallón Cazadores: Pastrana instalará mesa el 7 de enero," *El Tiempo*, December 15, 1998.

33. Luis Guillermo Giraldo Hurtado, *Del proceso y de la paz*. Manizales, Colombia: Edir@ficas, 2001, 26.

34. Sergio Gómez Maseri, "Listo paquete de ayuda de E.U.," *El Tiempo*, January 8, 1999.

35. Interview 13, Colombian political scientist, Bogotá, July 13, 2004.

36. "Plataforma para un Gobierno de Reconstrucción y Reconciliación Nacional (FARC-EP), Octava Conferencia Nacional Guerrillera," April 3, 1993, http://www.contracultural.com.ar/notas/docu2.htm.

37. Interview 12, former cabinet minister, Gaviria administration, Bogotá, June 28, 2003.

38. "48 embajadores asistirán al encuentro: 'Si Tirofijo no va, el Presidente tampoco'," *El Tiempo*, December 24, 1988.

39. "El presidente Pastrana dijo que cumplirá promesa de instalar el diálogo: 'Viajaré con o sin Tirofijo'," *El Tiempo*, December 27, 1998.

40. Interview 11, political scientist, private foundation, Bogotá, June 26, 2003.

41. Alvaro Valencia Tovar, "El 7 de enero, fecha decisive," *El Tiempo*, January 8, 1999.

42. Interview 18, retired military officer, Bogotá, July 4, 2003.

43. "El Presidente Andrés Pastrana cree que las Farc buscan un espacio político: 'Por la paz lo arriesgo todo'," *El Tiempo*, January 7, 1999.

44. Diana Jean Schemo, "Colombian Rebel Chief Says Threats Made Him Miss Talks," *New York Times,* January 9, 1999. The URL for the *New York Times* is http://www.nytimes.com/.

45. "Las Farc insisten en que había un complot para matar a 'Tirofijo': 'Sí iban a matar al camarada'," *El Tiempo,* January 9, 1999.

46. Speech by President Andrés Pastrana at opening of talks with FARC, January 7, 1999, http://www.ciponline.org/colombia/past1eng.htm.

47. Diana Jean Schemo, "Colombian Rebel Chief Says Threats Made Him Miss Talks," *New York Times,* January 9, 1999.

48. "Intervención de los delegados de las FARC-UP en la instalacion de los Mesas de Diálogos," *Correo del Magdalena,* II Época número 99, week of the 18th to 24th of January, 1999, http://www.voces.org/info/resu99.htm. Last visited January 19, 1999.

49. "Saludo del Comandante Manuel Marulanda Vélez en el inicio de los diálogos con las FARC. Solución política al conflicto," *Correo del Magdalena,* II Época número 99, week of the 18th to 24th of January, 1999, http://www.voces.org/info/resu99.htm. Last visited January 19, 1999.

50. Téllez, Montes, and Lesmes, 106.

51. "¿Cómo sería su Constituyente? Farc pide pueblo para el diálogo," *El Tiempo,* January 10, 1999.

52. "En La Machaca se cocina la fórmula del diálogo: Cese del fuego, en el 'menú'," *El Tiempo,* January 9, 1999.

53. "Tregua solo al final de los diálogos," *El Tiempo,* December 31, 1998.

54. "En diez puntos está condensada su agenda para la paz, que ayer comenzó a ser discutida: Esto propone Pastrana a las Farc," *El Tiempo,* January 12, 1999.

55. Juan José Ramírez, "Hoy, segunda ronda en La Machaca," *El Tiempo,* January 11, 1999.

56. "Especialistas hablan sobre el cómo de la ejecución del decálogo propuesto por Pastrana a las Farc: Los desafíos de la agenda para la paz," *El Tiempo,* January 13, 1999.

57. Ibid.

58. Juan José Ramírez, "Análisis de las propuestas que están sobre la mesa: Hay más coincidencias que diferencias," *El Tiempo,* January 12, 1999.

59. "Más argumentos para el escepticismo, expresan políticos y analistas: 'Proceso de paz, en el limbo'," *El Tiempo,* January 20, 1999.

60. Juan José Ramírez, "Hoy, segunda ronda en La Machaca," *El Tiempo,* January 11, 1999.

61. Ibid.

62. Ibid.

63. "Carta abierta al presidente Pastrana," *El Tiempo,* January 20, 1999.

64. Ibid.

65. Kline, *State Building,* chapter 5.

66. Fernando Cepeda Ulloa, "En el laberinto," *El Tiempo,* January 26, 1999.

67. "Especialistas hablan sobre el cómo de la ejecución del decálogo propuesto por Pastrana a las Farc: Los desafíos de la agenda para la paz," *El Tiempo,* January 13, 1999.

68. Juan José Ramírez, "Análisis de las propuestas que están sobre la mesa: Hay más coincidencias que diferencias," *El Tiempo*, January 12, 1999.

69. "Les dice que la lucha contra los 'paras' no es condición para dialogar: Gobierno responde pliego de Farc," *El Tiempo*, January 21, 1999.

70. "En 19 páginas presentan su propio 'dossier' del paramilitarismo: Farc quieren caída de diez generales," *El Tiempo*, January 26, 1999.

71. Alirio Fernando Bustos, "Se inician esfuerzos por descongelar las conversaciones," *El Tiempo*, January 24, 1999.

Chapter 4

1. Téllez, Montes, and Lesmes, 119.

2. Larry Rohter, "Colombia's Offer to Rebels Appears Futile," *New York Times*, May 3, 1999.

3. León Valencia, 45.

4. Interview 12, former cabinet minister, Gaviria administration, Bogotá, June 28, 2003.

5. Interview 3, Pastrana government representative in National Thematic Committee, Bogotá, June 9, 2003.

6. Interview 19, Colombian sociologist, by telephone from Tuscaloosa to Bogotá, September 6, 2003.

7. Juan José Ramírez, "Hoy se reactiva discusión sobre el canje," *El Tiempo*, April 26, 1999.

8. "Comunicado No. 4, La Machaca, San Vicente de Caguán," April 21, 1999. Document obtained from the Fundación Ideas para la Paz, Bogotá, June 2003.

9. "Comunicado No. 5, La Machaca, San Vicente de Caguán," April 25, 1999. Document obtained from the Fundación Ideas para la Paz, Bogotá, June 2003.

10. "Comunicado No. 6, La Machaca, San Vicente de Caguán," April 30, 1999. Document obtained from the Fundación Ideas para la Paz, Bogotá, June 2003.

11. "Comunicado del Presidente Andrés Pastrana y Manuel Marulanda de las FARC, 2 de mayo de 1999," http://www.ciponline.org/colombia/990502.htm. This document is commonly known as the "Acuerdo de Caquetania" and is referred to as such in this book.

12. "Text of 'Accord for a Timetable for the Future of the Peace Process,' January 20, 2002," http://www.ciponline.org/colombia/012004.htm

13. Interview 5, Colombian sociologist, Bogotá, June 13, 2003.

14. Interview 19, Colombian sociologist, Bogotá, July 7, 2004.

15. Interview 5, Colombian sociologist, Bogotá, July 20, 2004.

16. León Valencia, 47.

17. Giraldo Hurtado, 27; Interview 19, Colombian sociologist, by telephone from Tuscaloosa to Bogotá, September 6, 2003.

18. Alfredo Rangel, "Un ejercicio más aritmético que politico: De agendas y coroneles," *El Tiempo*, May 2, 1999.

19. Interview 19, Colombian sociologist, interview by telephone from Tuscaloosa to Bogotá, September 6, 2003.

20. "Los diez puntos que llevan las Farc a la mesa de diálogo. ¿Qué es negociable y qué no?" *El Tiempo,* December 16, 1998.

21. "Una agenda completa, pero . . ." *El Tiempo,* January 12 1999.

22. "Framework Agreement for the Resumption of the Negotiating Process between the Government of Guatemala and the UNIDAD Revolucionaria Nacional Guatemalteca," United States Institute of Peace, Peace Agreements Digital Collection: Guatemala, http://www.usip.org/library/pa/guatemala/guat_940110.html.

23. For all the agreements, see United States Institute of Peace, Peace Agreements Digital Collection, http://www.usip.org/library/pa/guatemala/pa_guatemala.html.

24. León Valencia, 48.

25. Romero, 226.

26. "Colombia's Defense Minister Quits Over Concession to Rebels," Reuters, May 27, 1999. The Reuters URL is http://today.reuters.com/news/home.aspx.

27. Interview 19, Colombian sociologist, by telephone from Tuscaloosa to Bogotá, September 6, 2003; Interview 5, Colombian sociologist, Bogotá, July 20, 2004.

28. Interview 5, Colombian sociologist, Bogotá, June 20, 2004.

29. Téllez, Montes, and Lesmes, 159.

30. Ibid., 177.

31. Alejo Vargas Velásquez, "La negociación con las FARC: Tres escenarios posibles," *El Tiempo,* June 6, 1999.

32. "Hoy, nueva reunión en La Machaca," *El Tiempo,* July 16, 1999.

33. Ibid.

34. "Comisión no debe congelar los diálogos," *El Tiempo,* July 26, 1999.

35. "Dos lecturas encontradas de un mismo documento. Contradicciones de un acuerdo," *El Tiempo,* August 4, 1999.

36. "Acuerdo humanitarian, La fórmula. Las puertas siguen abiertas," *El Tiempo,* August 8, 1999.

37. "Primer no de Farc a nueva propuesta," *El Tiempo,* August 20, 1999.

38. "Carta abierta a la opinión pública," http://burn.ucsd.edu/~farc-ep/Comunicados/sep2099.html, last visited, March 22, 2000. (For a while in late 1999 the FARC website was only available through the homepage of a professor at the University of California-San Diego.)

39. "Víctor G. dice que tema no se pactó, pero el Presidente venía sosteniendo lo contrario," *El Tiempo,* September 21, 1999.

40. "'Acompañamiento, después'," *El Tiempo,* September 26, 1999.

41. "La próxima semana se instalará la negociación: Acuerdo sobre comisión de quejas," *El Tiempo,* September 29, 1999.

42. "Cinco meses duraron los acercamientos entre Víctor G. Ricardo y 'Manuel Marulanda Vélez' para acordar la fecha de la instalación de la mesa de negociación," *El Tiempo,* October 18, 1999.

43. Juan José Ramírez, "Equipos del Gobierno y de las FARC iniciarán hoy sesiones sobre agenda," *El Tiempo,* October 25 1999.

44. "Gobierno y Farc se ponen a prueba," *El Espectador,* October, 25, 1999.

45. Juan José Ramírez, "Equipos del Gobierno y de las FARC iniciarán hoy sesiones sobre agenda," *El Tiempo,* October 25, 1999.

46. Téllez, Montes, and Lesmes, 199.

47. "Gobierno y Farc avanzan en acuerdo sobre metodología," *El Tiempo,* November 5, 1999.

48. Interview 3, Pastrana government representative on National Thematic Committee, Bogotá, June 9, 2003.

49. Juan José Ramírez, "Anuncios procedimentales, en el primer día de negociación: Gobierno-FARC definen metodología," *El Tiempo,* October 26, 1999.

50. Interview 3, Pastrana government representative on National Thematic Committee, Bogota, June 9, 2003.

51. Interview 4, Colombian historian, Bogotá, June 10, 2003.

52. "Comunicado No. 3 de la Mesa de Diálogo y Negociación, San Vicente de Caguán," November 5, 1999. Document obtained from the Fundación Ideas para la Paz, Bogotá, June 2003.

53. Juanita León, "Audiencias públicas, foro para aportar a mesa con FARC: ¿Participación será poder?" *El Tiempo,* December 5, 1999.

54. "Intervención del Comandante Iván Ríos, Coordinador del Comité Temático en Representación de las FARC-Ep, San Vicente de Caguán," December 4, 1999. Document obtained from the Fundación Ideas para la Paz, Bogotá, June 2003.

55. "Intervención del Comandante Raúl Reyes, Vocero de las Fuerzs Armadas Revolucionarias de Colombia-Ejército del Pueblo, San Vicente de Caguán," December 4, 1999. Document obtained from the Fundación Ideas para la Paz, Bogotá, June 2003.

56. Interview 3, Pastrana government representative Audiencias públicas, Bogotá, June 9, 2003.

57. León Valencia, 50.

58. "Comunicado No. 6 de la Mesa Nacional de Diálogo y Negociación, La Machaca, San Vicente de Caguán," December 18, 1999. Document obtained from the Fundación Ideas para la Paz, Bogotá, June 2003.

59. "Comunicado de Tregua de las FARC, Montañas de Colombia," December 20, 1999. Document obtained from the Fundación Ideas para la Paz, Bogotá, June 2003.

60. Interview 13, Colombian political scientist, Bogotá, July 13, 2004.

61. "United States Support for Colombia: Fact Sheet released by the Bureau of Western Hemisphere Affairs," March 28, 2000. http://www.state.gov/www/regions/wha/colombia/fs_000328_plancolombia.html. In the Bush-Uribe years the stipulation that U.S. aid be used only in narcotics interdiction was removed.

62. "'Manuel Marulanda' apareció sorpresivamente en reanudación de diálogos: 'Ya se puede hablar de paz'," *El Tiempo,* January 15, 2000.

63. "Comunicado No. 8, Los Pozos, San Vicente de Caguán, 28 de enero del 2000.

Comunicado de los voceros del Gobierno Nacional y de las FARC-EP en la mesa de diálogo y negociación, Methdología de las discusiones y tema inicial a discutir," January 28, 2000. Document obtained from the Fundación Ideas para la Paz, Bogotá, June 2003.

64. "Carta Abierta al Señor Presidente de la República por el Secretario Nacional de las FARC-EP, Manuel Marulanda Vélez, Montañas de Colombia," January 29, 2000. Document obtained from the Fundación Ideas para la Paz, Bogotá, June 2003.

65. "Intervención de Raúl Reyes, Los Pozos, San Vicente de Caguán," January 29, 2000. Document obtained from the Fundación Ideas para la Paz, Bogotá, June 2003.

66. Juanita León, "Anécdota de la gira de los negociadores por Europa," *El Tiempo*, February 27, 2000.

67. "Comunicado No. 17, San Vicente de Caguán, Caquetá," March 2, 2000. Document obtained from the Fundación Ideas para la Paz, Bogotá, June 2003.

68. "Comunicado No. 9 de la Mesa Nacional de Diálogos y Negociación, Los Pozos, San Vicente de Caguán," March 10, 2000. Document obtained from the Fundación Ideas para la Paz, Bogotá, June 2003.

69. "Entrevista a Manuel Marulanda Vélez," March 15, 2000, http://six.swix.ch/farcep/Entrevistas/Entrevista_manuel_marulanda.htm, last visited March 22, 2000.

70. "Manifiesto del Movimiento Bolivariano por la Nueva Colombia," March 25, 2000, http://www.angelfire.com/nb/17m/Colombia/movbolcol.html.

71. OnLineNewsHour, "Colombia's Civil War," http://www.pbs.org/newshour/bb/latin_america/colombia/players_farc.html, posted May 2002.

72. León Valencia, 54.

73. "Memorando para la Mesa de Diálogo, Secretario del Estado Mayor Central, FARC-Ejército del Pueblo," May 11, 2000. Document obtained from the Fundación Ideas para la Paz, Bogotá, June 2003.

74. "Colombia Suspends Peace Round After Rebel Murder," Reuters, May 16, 2000.

75. "Primer Bombazo a la Mesa," communiqué of the Secretariado del Estado Major Central, FARC-Ejercito del Pueblo, Montañas de Colombia, May 17, 2000. Document obtained from the Fundación Ideas para la Paz, Bogotá, June 2003.

76. Interview 18, Bogotá, retired military officer, July 4, 2003.

77. "Memorando para la Mesa de Diálogo."

78. "Las FARC insisten en no devolver a pirata," TERRA, Noticias, September 27, 2000, http://www.terra.com.mx/noticias/nota/20000927/108358.htm.

79. Téllez, Mendes, and Lesmes, 260.

80. Fundación Ideas para la Paz, "Siguiendo el conflicto: hechos y análisis de la semana," Número 36, October 29, 2005.

81. Interview 17, Colombian political scientist, by email, December 9, 2005.

82. Interview 5, Colombian sociologist, by email, December 9, 2005.

83. León Valencia, 55–56.

84. Interview 12, former cabinet minister, Gaviria administration, Bogotá, June 28, 2003.

85. "Comunicado No. 23, San Vicente de Caguán" October 23, 2000. Document obtained from the Fundación Ideas para la Paz, Bogotá, June 2003.

86. Téllez, Mendes, and Lesmes, 270.

Chapter 5

1. Téllez, Mendes, and Lesmes, 288–89.

2. "Carta de Marulanda al Comisionado de Paz," January 17, 2001. Document obtained from the Fundación Ideas para la Paz, Bogotá, June 2003.

3. Téllez, Mendes, and Lesmes, 287.

4. Ibid., 293.

5. "El siguiente es el texto del documento suscrito hoy por el Gobierno Nacional y las Farc-EP," *El Tiempo,* February 10, 2001.

6. Ibid.

7. "Versión completa de la rueda de prensa Pastrana-Marulanda, Los Pozos (Caquetá)," February 9, 2001. Document obtained from the Fundación Ideas para la Paz, Bogotá, June 2003.

8. "Comunicado No. 25, San Vicente de Caguán" February 16, 2001. Document obtained from the Fundación Ideas para la Paz, Bogotá, June 2003.

9. "The Peace Process and the Public Hearings," *Resistencia* 25, February 2001," http://www.ciponline.org/colombia/020103.htm.

10. "Communiqué no. 27, FARC-government talks," March 9, 2001, http://www.ciponline.org/colombia/030903.htm.

11. "Communiqué no. 29, FARC-government talks," May 11, 2001, http://www.ciponline.org/colombia/051105.htm.

12. Ibid.

13. León Valencia, 60–61.

14. "FARC communiqué upon prisoner release," June 28, 2001, http://www.ciponline.org/colombia/062802.htm.

15. Gloria Castrillón Élber Gutiérrez "'Queremos ser Gobierno': FARC," *El Espectador,* http://www.anncol.com/julio_2/0702_FARCgobierno.html. ANNCOL is the New Colombian News Agency in Stockholm, Sweden. It publishes the FARC line. Here they have posted an article from *El Espectador*. Do not confuse ANNCOL with ANCOL (the Pastrana presidential website), discussed in footnote 48 in Chapter 2.

16. Téllez, Mendes, and Lesmes, 323.

17. "El Gobierno no está entregando el país," *El Tiempo,* July 8, 2001.

18. "'No se debe temer que Farc entren en política': Pastrana," *El Tiempo,* July 14, 2001.

19. "Comunicado de las FARC sobre el secuestro de Alán Jara," July 19, 2001, http://www.ciponline.org/colombia/071901.htm.

20. "FARC statement on German citizens' kidnapping," October 11, 2001, http://www.ciponline.org/colombia/082405.htm.

21. "Framework Agreement for the Resumption of the Negotiating Process between

the Government of Guatemala and the UNIDAD Revolucionaria Nacional Guatemalteca," United States Institute of Peace, Peace Agreements Digital Collection: Guatemala, http://www.usip.org/library/pa/guatemala/guat_940110.html.

22. "Gobierno lamenta que FARC hayan roto pacto de confidencialidad," ANCOL, July 23, 2001.

23. "Revelan propuestas de Gobierno y guerrilla sobre cese de fuego," *El Tiempo,* July 23, 2001.

24. "Carta de Respuesta a Camilo Gómez Alzate, Alto Comisionado para la Paz, Montañas de Colombia," August 24, 2001. Document obtained from the Fundación Ideas para la Paz, Bogotá, June 2003.

25. "Se reactivó la Mesa de Diálogo Gobierno-Farc," *El Tiempo,* September 4, 2001. (Pretelt went on to become a cabinet minister in the following government, that of Álvaro Uribe, who also took a harder line than Pastrana had.)

26. "Renuncia en comisión de Notables," *El Tiempo,* September 6, 2001.

27. Romero, 96.

28. "Renuncia en comisión de Notables," *El Tiempo,* September 6, 2001.

29. "Comunicado de Prensa de la Comisión de Personalidades, Bogotá, D.C." ANCOL, September 6, 2001. Document obtained from the Fundación Ideas para la Paz, Bogotá, June 2003.

30. "Recomendaciones de la Comisión de Personalidades a la Mesa de Diálogo y Negociación," September 19, 2001. Document obtained from the Fundación Ideas para la Paz, Bogotá, June 2003.

31. "Recomendaciones de la Comisión de Personalidades."

32. "Marcha . . . atrás," *Revista Cambio,* October 4, 2001. *Revista Cambio* is a weekly magazine published in Bogotá. Its URL is http://www.revistacambio.com/.

33. Ibid.

34. "Comunicado," October 2, 2001 (signed by Raúl Reyes, Joaquín Gómez, Simón Trinidad, Andrés París, and Carlos A. Lozada). Document obtained from the Fundación Ideas para la Paz, Bogotá, June 2003.

35. Ibid.

36. Interview 12, former cabinet minister, Gaviria administration, Bogotá, June 28, 2003.

37. "Colombian Peace Talks Rocked by Key Killing," Reuters, September 30, 2001.

38. Téllez, Montes, and Lesmes, 338.

39. "Pulso firme, bien comun y voces de colombianos decidirán la zona," ANCOL, October 3, 2001.

40. "Acuerdo de San Francisco de la Sombre entre el Gobierno y FARC-EP," ANCOL, October 5, 2001.

41. "Colombian Peace Talks Gain Momentum," Associated Press, October 6, 2001.

42. "Colombian Leader Meets Army Before Rebel Deadline," Reuters, October 5, 2001.

43. "Fuerzas militares acatarán cualquier decision del Presidente sobre zona de distension: General Fernando Tapias," ANCOL, October 5, 2001.

44. "Con mayores controles se garantiza uso correcto de la zona," ANCOL, October 7, 2001.

45. Manuel Marulanda, "Carta a los voceros de las FARC-EP," October 16, 2001. Document obtained from the Fundación Ideas para la Paz, Bogotá, June 2003.

46. Ibid.

47. "Proceso de paz, en su más grave crisis," *El Tiempo*, October 18, 2001.

48. "Memorando de los negociadores de las FARC al Gobierno," *El Tiempo*, October 18, 2001.

49. "El Gobierno espera que las FARC cumplan su palabra: Camilo Gómez," ANCOL, October 20, 2001.

50. "Gobierno califica de 'poco serias' condiciones de las FARC para continuar proceso de paz," *El Tiempo*, October 21, 2001.

51. "FARC acusa a Pastrana de negarse a dialogar," *El Espectador*, October 26, 2001.

52. León Valencia, "Los Escenarios de la guerra y la paz," *El Tiempo*, November 1, 2001.

53. Margarita Vidal, "Voto Util: La clave," *El Tiempo*, November 4, 2001.

54. "'Pastrana no ha respondido': FARC," *El Tiempo*, December 18, 2001.

Chapter 6

1. Téllez, Mendes, and Lesmes, 360.

2. "Comunicado de las Farc, para esentrabar el proceso," January 3, 2002. Document obtained from the Fundación Ideas para la Paz, Bogotá, June 2003.

3. "Comunicado Público, Montañas de Colombia," January 4, 2002, http://www.farcep.org/?node=2,1732,1.

4. Téllez, Mendes, and Lesmes, 360–61.

5. Ibid., 361.

6. "Statement of Colombian Government High Commissioner for Peace Camilo Gómez," January 9, 2002, http://www.ciponline.org/colombia/010902.htm.

7. Interview 4, Colombian historian, Bogotá, July 8, 2004.

8. "Carta a James LeMoyne, Montañas de Colombia," January 8, 2002. Document obtained from the Fundación Ideas para la Paz, Bogotá, June 2003.

9. "Comunicado de Prensa, Los Pozos, San Vicente de Caguán," January 11, 2002. Document obtained from the Fundación Ideas para la Paz, Bogotá, June 2003.

10. "FARC proposal to re-start talks," January 12, 2002, http://www.ciponline.org/colombia/011201.htm.

11. Téllez, Mendes, and Lesmes, 370.

12. Interview 18, retired military officer, Bogotá, July 4, 2003.

13. "Text of 'Accord for a timetable for the future of the Peace Process,' January 20, 2002," http://www.ciponline.org/colombia/012004.htm.

14. "Propuesta de las FARC-EP para la disminución de la intensidad del conflicto, Montañas de Colombia," February 2, 2002. Document obtained from the Fundación Ideas para la Paz, Bogotá, June 2003.

15. Ibid.

16. "Draft government cease-fire proposal," February 4, 2002, http://ciponline.org/colombia/02020403.htm.

17. Ibid.

18. "Actividades de la Mesa de Diálogo y Negociación para esta semana," ANCOL, February 11, 2002.

19. "Hemos profundizado en el tema de tregua con cese de fuegos: Gómez," ANCOL, Febrero 13, 2002.

20. Unidad de Paz, "Nueva cita para los candidatos en Los Pozos," *El Espectador,* February 14, 2002.

21. "Gobierno asegura que propuesta de tregua no implica más zonas de distension," *El Tiempo,* February 20, 2003.

22. "FARC dicen que no es suficiente una tregua para terminar la guerra," *El Tiempo,* February 20, 2002.

23. Unidad de Paz, "Nuevo choque sobre tregua entre Gobierno y Farc," *El Espectador,* February 20, 2002

24. "Farc desvían avión comercial y secuestran al senador Jorge Eduardo Gechen," *El Espectador,* February 21, 2002.

25. Téllez, Mendes, and Lesmes, 375–76.

26. "Frases del Presidente Pastrana en alocución sobre fin del proceso," ANCOL, February 20, 2002.

27. Ibid.

28. Téllez, Mendes, and Lesmes, 378.

29. "Guerrilla culpa a Pastrana," *El Espectador,* February 21, 2002.

30. "FARC Kidnap Colombian Presidential Candidate," Reuters, February 24, 2002.

31. Interview 18, retired military officer, Bogotá, July 4, 2003.

32. Interview 4, Colombian historian, Bogotá, June 10, 2003.

33. Interview 13, Colombian political scientist, Bogotá, July 1, 2003; Interview 5, Colombian sociologist, Bogotá, June 13, 2003; Interview 15, member of the Peace Commission, Bogotá, July 3, 2003.

34. Interview 11, Colombian political scientist, Bogotá, June 26, 2003; Interview 13, Colombian political scientist, Bogotá, July 1, 2003; Interview 8, official in the office of the vice presidency, Bogotá, June 19, 2003.

35. Interview 19, Colombian sociologist, by telephone from Tuscaloosa, September 6, 2003.

36. Interview 6, Colombian sociologist, Bogotá, June 14, 2003; Interview 12, former cabinet minister, Gaviria administration, Bogotá, June 28, 2003.

37. Interview 6, Colombian sociologist, Bogotá, June 14, 2003.

38. Interview 15, member of the Peace Commission, Bogotá, July 3, 2003.

39. Interview 4, Colombian historian, Bogotá, June 10, 2003.

40. Interview 19, Colombian sociologist, by telephone from Tuscaloosa, September 6, 2003.

41. Interview 18, retired military officer, Bogotá, July 4, 2003.

42. Interview 7, Colombian political scientist, Bogotá, June 19, 2003.

43. Interview 8, official in the office of the vice presidency, Bogotá, June 19, 2003.

44. Interview 12, former cabinet minister, Gaviria administration, Bogotá, June 28, 2003.

45. Interview 18, retired military officer, Bogotá, July 4, 2003.

46. Interview 5, Colombian sociologist, Bogotá, June 13, 2003.

47. Interview 19, Colombian sociologist, by telephone from Tuscaloosa, September 6, 2003

48. Interview 7, Colombian political scientist, Bogotá, June 19, 2003; Interview 10, Colombian economist, Bogotá, June 24, 2003

49. Interview 10, Colombian economist, Bogotá, June 24, 2003.

50. Interview 3, Pastrana government representative in National Thematic Committee, Bogotá, June 12, 2003.

51. Interview 9, Colombian political scientist, Bogotá, June 24, 2003.

52. Interview 3, Pastrana government representative in National Thematic Committee, Bogotá, June 9, 2003.

53. Interview 19: Colombian sociologist, Bogotá, July 7, 2004.

54. Interview 13, Colombian political scientist, Bogotá, July 1, 2003,

55. Interview 10, Colombian economist, Bogotá, June 24, 2003.

Chapter 7

1. Interview 15, member of the Peace Commission, Bogotá, July 3, 2003.

2. "Gobierno Nacional respalda gestiones con el Eln: Consejo de Paz, dispuesto a descongelar Convención," *El Tiempo*, September 8, 1998.

3. "Carta Reunión Preparatoria, Cárcel de Itagüí," September 15, 1998, http://www.eln-voces.com/comupa/pp_co_ci.htm, last visited, September 15, 1998.

4. "Documento Borrador del acta de la reunión del Comité Operativo Preparatorio de la Convención Nacional corespondiente a la sesión del 14 de septiembre de 1998 en Itagüí." Document obtained from the Fundación Ideas para la Paz, Bogotá, June 2003.

5. "Gobierno aplaza decisión de salvoconductos a Galán y Torres: Serán suspendidas las actividades militares en algún territorio del país, durante cinco días, para permitir encuentro entre voceros de la sociedad civil y comando central del Eln," *El Tiempo*, October 9, 1998.

6. "Concedido permiso a Galán y a Torres para salir de la cárcel: Abierto diálogo formal con Eln," *El Tiempo*, October 10, 1998.

7. "Definida la agenda específica para ocho meses de diálogo con el Eln," October 1998. Document obtained from the Fundación Ideas para la Paz, Bogotá, June 2003.

8. Ibid.

9. Human Rights Watch, "Colombia, Human Rights Developments," *World Report, 1999*, http://www.hrw.org/wr2k/americas-03.htm.

10. "Documento presentado por Francisco Galán y Felipe Torres, voceros del ELN, ante el Comité Operativo, contentivo de una propuesta en relación con los criterios de

selección de los participantes de la Convención Nacional," December 11, 1998. Document obtained from the Fundación Ideas para la Paz, Bogotá, June 2003.

11. "Documentos presentados por Francisco Galán y Felipe Torres, voceros del ELN, los cuales contienen las propuestas de metodología y plan de acción sugeridas por el encuentro con el COCE, Itagüí," October 8, 1998. Document obtained from the Fundación Ideas para la Paz, Bogotá, June 2003.

12. "El certamen se hará definitivamente en Colombia: ELN pide encuentro con Pastrana antes de la Convención Nacional," *El Tiempo,* January 23, 1999.

13. "Hoy, cumbre en Caracas: Eln pedirá despeje en Norte de S.," *El Tiempo,* February 9, 1999.

14. "Paralelo a la Convención buscarán acuerdos humanitarios: Gobierno y Eln crearán línea directa," *El Tiempo,* February 10, 1999.

15. "En tablas, primera cumbre de Caracas entre Eln y Gobierno: Despeje sí, pero con cese del fuego," *El Tiempo,* February 11, 1999.

16. "Sector de la sociedad civil dice que 'Gabino' cambió reglas de juego: Despeje entraba Convención del Eln," *El Tiempo,* February 12, 1999.

17. Ibid.

18. Ibid.

19. Ibid.

20. "Los caminos hacia la paz con el Eln comenzaron a desbloquearse," *El Tiempo,* February 16, 1999.

21. "Colombian Gov't Won't Talk to Rebels," Associated Press, May 31, 1999.

22. "Propuesta a Gobierno y Eln para iniciar diálogos," *El Tiempo,* August 1, 1999.

23. "Colombia's Warring Foes Meet in Caracas," Reuters, September 17, 1999.

24. María V. Cristancho, "'Solo falta el lugar,' dice 'Pablo Beltrán'," *El Tiempo,* November 10, 1999.

25. María V. Cristancho, "Sociedad civil presionará para la cita: La convención quedó para el año 2000," *El Tiempo,* December 16, 1999.

26. Unidad de Paz, "Zona de convivencia y no de despeje para el Eln: Solo falta definir fecha y lugar," *El Tiempo,* December 20, 1999.

27. "Nueva reunión con el comisionado Ricardo en el sur de Bolívar: Proceso con Eln, aún sin definiciones," *El Tiempo,* December 24, 1999.

28. "'Gobernador se opone a la paz,' Pastrana," *El Tiempo,* January 5, 2000.

29. "Protestas por possible despeje en el sur de Bolívar," *El Tiempo,* January 6, 2000.

30. "El Eln insiste en el despeje del Bolívar para volver a dialogar con el Gobierno," *El Tiempo,* February 1, 2000.

31. "Para el Eln, la zona de convivencia no puede ser ajena del conflicto y a cultivos ilícitos para celebrar la Convención Nacional," *El Tiempo,* February 2, 2000.

32. Arturo Peñalosa Pinzón, "Siete mil campesinos taparon carretera a la Costa: Con bloqueo se oponen al despeje," *El Tiempo,* February 9, 2000.

33. Édison Chacón, "Sur de Bolívar sigue siendo opción para la convención del Eln: No al despeje, sí a conviencia," *El Tiempo,* February 18, 2000.

34. "Campesinos insisten en que diálogos no sean en el sur de Bolívar," *El Tiempo,* February 25, 2000.

35. Alfredo Rangel Suárez, "El Tercer Actor: La disyuntiva del Eln," *El Tiempo,* March 3, 2000.

36. "Gobierno es quien definirá zona para Eln," *El Tiempo,* March 23, 2000.

37. Diana Lozada, "Diez obstáculos con el Eln," *El Tiempo,* March 26, 2000.

38. Comando Central, "Proceso de paz, Convención Nacional: Una propuesta para la reconstrucción de la sociedad," Montañas de Colombia, April 2000. Document obtained from the Fundación Ideas para la Paz, Bogotá, June 2003.

39. "Colombian President Announces Pact to Grant Rebels Another Demilitarized Zone," Agence France-Presse, April 25, 2000. The URL of the Agence France-Presse is http://www.afp.com/.

40. Unidad de Paz, "En firme despeje para el Eln: Gobierno decidió crear una Zona de Encuentro de 4,725 kilometros entre Bolívar y Antioquia, con verificación internacional," *El Tiempo,* April 25, 2000.

41. Unidad de Paz, "La zona de encuentro del Eln," *El Tiempo,* April 25, 2000.

42. Steven Dudley, "Colombia Sets Negotiations With a Second Rebel Group," *Washington Post,* April 28, 2000.

43. Unidad de Paz, "El Presidente está atento a las sugerencias sobre la Zona de Encuentro," *El Tiempo,* April 26, 2000.

44. Arturo Peñalosa Pinzón, "En Yondó y Cantagallo siguen voces de inconformismo: Revuelo en San Pablo por despeje," *El Tiempo,* April 26, 2000.

45. "Los pobladores se encuentran intimidados por las autodefensas y esperan a una comisión que les aclare que pasará en sus regiones," *El Tiempo,* April 28, 2000.

46. Arturo Peñalosa Pinzón, "La navegación en el río Magdalena se encuentra paralizada por la protesta de los pobladores del sur de Bolívar," *El Tiempo,* April 29, 2000.

47. Arturo Peñalosa Pinzón, "Pararon 34 municipios," *El Tiempo,* May 11, 2000.

48. Arturo Peñalosa Pinzón, "Líderes de protesta dialogaron con el Gobierno: Sí al despeje, pero con Ejército," *El Tiempo,* May 16, 2000.

49. Centro Regional de Oriente, "Cumbre sobre zona para Eln," *El Tiempo,* May 23, 2000.

50. Luis Alberto Miño, "Manifestantes no ceden de despeje para Eln," *El Tiempo,* May 24, 2000.

51. Arturo Peñalosa Pinzón, "Alto Comisionado se reunió con cúpula del Eln: Diálogos para el desbloqueo," *El Tiempo,* May 29, 2000.

52. Arturo Peñalosa Pinzón, "Levantaron tres bloqueos en troncal," *El Tiempo,* May 30, 2000.

53. "Primer Acuerdo Gobierno-Eln: Definida participación internacional," *El Tiempo,* June 20, 2000.

54. Larry Rohter, "Earmarked for Colombian Rebels, a Region Asks to Be Left Alone," *New York Times,* July 8, 2000.

55. "Colombians Bid for Peace in Geneva," Associated Press, July 24, 2000.

56. Rodrigo Pardo, "El despegue del ELN: La distancia aque va de Maguncia a Ginebra," *El Tiempo,* July 20, 2000.

57. Diana Losada C., "Eln, Gobierno y Sociedad, tras un consenso," *El Tiempo,* July 23, 2000.

58. "El ABC del Encuentro en Ginebra: Así propone el Eln el diálogo," *El Tiempo,* July 23, 2000.

59. Juan Carlos Iragorri, "El diálogo estuvo a punto de suspenderse: Sí en Genebra a la salida negociada con el Eln," *El Tiempo,* July 26, 2000.

60. Juan Carlos Iragorra, "En Suiza se perdió la oportunidad," *El Tiempo,* July 27, 2000.

61. León Valencia Agudelo, "El martes negro en Ginebra," *El Tiempo,* July 30, 2000.

62. Francisco Santos, "El fracaso de Ginebra," *El Tiempo,* July 30, 2000.

63. Juan José Ramírez, "Análisis de las propuestas que están sobre la mesa: Hay más coincidencias que diferencias," *El Tiempo,* January 12, 1999.

64. María Victoria Cristancho, "El optimismo del Gobierno frente al proceso con el Eln, contrasta con el pesimismo del segundo Comandante de esa guerrilla," *El Tiempo,* September 6, 2000.

65. "No al Despeje ratificó propuesta para el Eln," *El Tiempo,* September 12, 2000.

66. Interview 5, Colombian Sociologist, Bogotá, June 3, 2004.

67. Interview 20, Colombian political scientist, Bogotá, July 6, 2004.

68. Romero, 112.

69. Romero, 94.

Chapter 8

1. Unidad de Paz, "Industriales piden suspensión de diálogo," *El Tiempo,* September 20, 2000.

2. Unidad de Paz, "Es difícil evaluar el estado actual de las conversaciones entre el Gobierno y el Eln," *El Tiempo,* October 23, 2000.

3. "Se discuten alternativas para la Convención Nacional," *El Tiempo,* November 17, 2000.

4. "Decidirán estrategia: Más protestas conta el despeje en Bolivar," *El Tiempo,* November 5, 2000; "ASOCIPAZ: 'Eln no da muestras de querer la paz'," *El Tiempo,* November 8, 2000.

5. María Camia Morales, "Paises amigos elaboran proyecto de despeje para ELN," *El Tiempo,* December 2, 2000.

6. "Se 'descongeló' proceso con Eln," *El Tiempo,* December 18, 2000.

7. "Protestas por eventual despeje," *El Tiempo,* December 21, 2000.

8. "Nueva protesta campesina en el sur de Bolívar," *El Tiempo,* December 22, 2000.

9. "A examen, borrador de acuerdo con el Eln," *El Tiempo,* December 26, 2000.

10. "Persisten reparos a despeje para el Eln," *El Tiempo,* December 28, 2000.

11. "Colombia debe conocer el preacuerdo," *El Tiempo,* December 29, 2000.

12. Scott Wilson, "Fearful Colombians Oppose Haven for 2nd Rebel Group," *Washington Post,* January 1, 2001.

13. "Reglamento de una posible zona de encuentro no será letra muerta," ANCOL, January 12, 2001.

14. "Duro forcejeo del Gobierno para convención del Eln," *El Tiempo,* January 17, 2001.

15. "Colombians Protest Guerrilla Enclave," Associated Press, February 4, 2001.

16. Unidad de Paz, "Crisis en proceso con Eln," *El Tiempo,* February 6, 2001.

17. Interview 12, former cabinet minister, Gaviria administration, Bogotá, June 28, 2003.

18. Unidad de Paz, "Crisis en proceso con Eln," *El Tiempo,* February 6, 2001.

19. "Colombian Peasants Block Road to Protest Enclave," Reuters, February 16, 2001.

20. "Gobierno ordena desalojo de vías," *El Tiempo,* February 18, 2001.

21. "Protestors Lift Colombia Roadblocks," Reuters, February 19, 2001.

22. José Navia y Andrés Mompotes, "Levantadas las protestas," *El Tiempo,* February 21, 2001.

23. "Castaño: Sí contribuimos al bloqueo," *El Tiempo,* February 23, 2001.

24. "Eln suspende," *El Tiempo,* March 10, 2001.

25. "Gobierno y ELN reanudan contactos," *El Tiempo,* April 1, 2001.

26. "Asocipaz no acepta presiones de nadie," *El Tiempo,* April 3, 2001.

27. "Eln incumplió cita con embajadores," *El Tiempo,* April 6, 2001.

28. Arturo Peñalosa Pinzón, "Diálogo con gobierno, en punto muerto," *El Tiempo,* April 10, 2001.

29. Juan Forero, "Sanctuary for Talks Gives Way to Fierce Fighting in Colombia," *New York Times,* April 12, 2001.

30. Unidad de Paz, "Diálogo, en el atolladero," *El Tiempo,* April 16, 2001.

31. Scott Wilson, "Rightist Forces Seize Key Areas in Colombia," *Washington Post,* April 19, 2001.

32. Alfredo Rangel Suárez, "Las alternativas con el Eln: Despeje o despeje," *El Tiempo,* April 27, 2001.

33. Sergio Gómez Maseri, "Están dadas las condiciones para el despeje," *El Tiempo,* May 16, 2001.

34. "Las condiciones no son favorables," *El Tiempo,* May 17, 2001.

35. "Gente del sur de Bolívar amenaza con armarse," *El Tiempo,* May 21, 2001.

36. "Presidente reitera disposición de reunirse con voceros del ELN," ANCOL, June 7, 2001.

37. "Creo en la posibilidad de paz con Eln," *El Tiempo,* June 21, 2001.

38. "Eln dice que despeje es la única salida," *El Tiempo,* June 7, 2001.

39. León Valencia, "A un paso, Acuerdo con el Ejército de Liberación Nacional," *El Tiempo,* August 5, 2001.

40. "Colombia President Suspends Peace Talks with Rebel Group," Associated Press, August 8, 2001.

41. "Suspensión diálogos con Eln no es triunfo de autodefensas: Gómez," ANCOL, August 7, 2001.

42. "La testadurez del Eln," *El Tiempo*, August 8, 2001.

43. "Eln definitivamente no dialoga con Gobierno de Andrés Pastrana," *El Tiempo*, September 11, 2001.

44. "Proceso de paz con Eln no está roto: Pastrana," ANCOL, November 7, 2001.

45. "Eln estaría dispuesto a reactivar diálogos con el Gobierno," *El Tiempo*, November 11, 2001.

46. "Colombian Government, ELN Rebels to Meet in Cuba," Reuters, November 16, 2001.

47. "Con Acuerdo de siete puntos, gobierno y Eln reinician proceso paz," ANCOL, November 25, 2001.

48. "Acusaciones del ELN contra Bell son Calumnia Infame: Camilo Gómez," ANCOL, December 6, 2001.

49. "Nueva crisis en proceso con Eln," *El Espectador*, December 8, 2001.

50. "Colombia, Rebels End Round of Talks," Associated Press, December 15, 2001.

51. "Gobierno declare reinicio formal de proceso con el Eln," ANCOL, December 21, 2001.

52. "Colombian Rebels Decry Government," Associated Press, January 6, 2002.

53. International Crisis Group, "Colombia: The Prospects for Peace with the ELN," *Latin America Report No. 2*, Bogotá/Brussels, October 4, 2002, 18, http://www.reliefweb.int/library/documents/2002/icg-col-4oct.pdf.

54. "Eln condiciona proceso de paz a veeduría en el Catatumbo," *El Tiempo*, January 14, 2002.

55. Bibliana Mercado, "Se inicia nueva etapa de diálogos con Eln," *El Tiempo*, January 28, 2002.

56. "Declaración de la Cumbre por la Paz de la Habana (Cuba)," ANCOL, January 31, 2002.

57. Ibid.

58. "Hasta hoy hay voluntad del Eln por avanzar en el proceso de paz," ANCOL, February 26, 2002.

59. "Proceso con el Eln apunta a una tregua inmediata," *El Tiempo*, March 7, 2002.

60. "Proceso con Eln sigue andando: Alto Comisionado," ANCOL, March 6, 2002.

61. Unidad de Paz, "Se acerca posibilidad de tregua con el Eln," *El Espectador*, March 12, 2002.

62. "Comunicado del Gobierno y del Ejército de Liberación Nacional (ELN)," ANCOL, March 12, 2002.

63. León Valencia, "El Eln viro a última hora," *El Tiempo*, March 17, 2002.

64. "Financiación estatal al Eln mientras dure tregua, plantea 'Pablo Beltrán'," *El Tiempo*, March 20, 2002.

65. "Eln muestra su propuesta de tregua," *El Tiempo*, March 21, 2002.

66. "Eln responde a interrogantes sobre tregua integral," *El Espectador*, March 22, 2002.

67. "Gobierno no pagará rescate por secuestrados del Eln," *El Tiempo*, April 2, 2002.

68. Kline, *State Building*, 90–100.

69. "Gobierno y Eln difieren sobre verificación de tregua," *El Tiempo*, April 21, 2002.

70. "Eln critica demora de Gobierno en definer una tregua," *El Tiempo*, May 11, 2002.

71. "Gobierno anuncia suspensión de proceso con Eln," ANCOL, May 31, 2002.

72. "Pastrana dejó proceso de paz con el Eln en manos de Uribe," *El Tiempo*, June 1, 2002.

73. Ibid.

74. Marisol Gómez Giraldo, "Eln no firmó Acuerdo para disminuir el conflicto por presión de las FARC," *El Tiempo*, June 9, 2002.

75. "Pulso a su situación militar: Los débiles talones del movimiento 'eleno'," *El Tiempo*, February 14, 1999.

76. Interview 5, Colombian sociologist, Bogotá, June 13, 2003.

77. Interview 6, Colombian sociologist, Bogotá, June 14, 2003.

78. Ibid.

79. Rangel Suárez, "El proceso de paz con el Eln: Parálisis, 'cañazo' y tercería," *El Tiempo*, February 28, 1999.

80. Pizarro, 107.

Chapter 9

1. I do not include the Nicaraguan peace process in the analysis because the insurgency became the revolutionary government of the Sandinistas and the counterrevolutionaries were funded by the government of the United States. However, if theory building were the only concern, that case might also be considered.

2. *Fuerzas Militares*, 50.

3. Interview 7, Colombian political scientist, email response on December 13, 2005.

4. Aranguren, 245.

5. Cynthia Arnson, "Introduction," in Cynthia Arnson, ed., *Comparative Peace Processes in Latin America* (Washington: Woodrow Wilson Center Press, 1999), 19.

6. Susanne Jonas, *Of Centaurs and Doves: Guatemala's Peace Process* (Boulder, CO: Westview Press, 2000), 46.

7. "Las FARC ganan un billón de pesos al trimestre con el narcotráfico," *El Tiempo*, June 15, 2004. This estimate is higher than most, which run from US$200 to US$600 million a year.

8. Pizarro, 348.

9. Ibid.

10. Interview 18, retired military officer, Bogotá. July 4, 2003.

11. Pizarro, 343.

12. Angelika Rettberg, "The Business of Peace in Colombia: Assessing the Role of the Business Community in the Colombian Peace Process." Prepared for delivery at the 2003 meeting of the Latin American Studies Association, Dallas, TX, USA, March 27–29, 2003. It is of note, however, that the El Nogal attack came after the Pastrana government, not during it. Further it might be added that in the two and a half years following the attack there were few additional urban attacks.

13. "Los industriales responden a críticas de E.U. sobre bajo aportes impositivos para la guerra," *El Tiempo*, August 26, 2004.

14. "El conflicto le ha costado al país $16,5 billones en los últimos cinco años," *El Tiempo*, February 8, 2005.

15. Interview 5, Colombian sociologist, Bogotá, June 13, 2003.

16. Interview 12, former cabinet minister, Gaviria administration, Bogotá, June 28, 2003.

17. Interview 20, Colombian political scientist, Bogotá, July 6, 2004.

18. Interview 23, private foundation official, Bogotá, June 28, 2004.

19. Marc Chernick, "Negotiating Peace Amid Multiple Forms of Violence," in Cynthia J. Arnson, ed., *Comparative Peace Process in Latin America* (Washington, D.C.: Woodrow Wilson Center Press, 1999), 161–62.

20. Mauceri, 158–60.

21. Ibid., 162.

22. Romero, 17.

23. Ibid., 18.

24. Romero, 138.

25. Ricardo Vargas, "State, Esprit Mafioso, and Armed Conflict in Colombia," in Jo-Marie Burt and Philip Mauceri, *Politics in the Andes: Identity, Conflict, Reform* (Pittsburgh: University of Pittsburgh Press, 2004), 108–9.

26. Ibid., 116.

27. Ibid., 117.

28. Ibid., 121.

29. Ibid., 124.

30. Ibid., 125.

31. Nazih Richani, *Systems of Violence: The Political Economy of War and Peace in Colombia* (Albany: State University of New York Press, 2002), 4.

32. Ibid., chapters 3 and 4.

33. Ibid., 151–52.

34. Interview 10, Colombian economist, private foundation, Bogotá, June 24, 2003.

35. Interview 13, Colombian political scientist, Bogotá, July 1, 2003.

36. Interview 19, Colombian sociologist, Bogotá, July 7, 2004.

37. Ibid.

38. "Aprobada prórroga de ley de orden público," CNE (Centro Nacional de Noticias del Estado), December 20, 2002. The National Center of News of the State was the first name given to the presidential website during the government of Alvaro Uribe. Its URL was http://www.presidencia.gov.co.

39. "En discurso de posesión, Uribe propone 'diálogo útil' con 'cese de hostilidades'," Radio Cadena Nacional (RCN), August 8, 2002, http://www.rcn.com.co/.

40. Élber Gutiérrez y Javier Héndez, "Gobierno ofrece indulto a guerrilla y 'paras'," *El Espectador*, September 8, 2002.

41. Francis Fukuyama, *State-Building: Governance and World Order in the 21st Century* (Ithaca: Cornell University Press, 2004), 6.

Bibliography

Interviews

When approaching potential interviewees I explained the nature of the project to them and promised that I would neither use their names nor describe them in such a way that would allow informed people to identify them. I then asked the interviewees if they agreed to those conditions. All did. During the interviews I used no recording devices. On occasion I took notes, always asking the interviewees if that was all right with them. Immediately after the interviews I typed the responses. Hence any "quotations" that appear in this book are not verbatim, but my reconstruction of what the interviewees said.

1. Former official in Samper peace process, Bogotá, June 7, 2003.
2. Official at U.S. Embassy, Bogotá, June 8, 2003.
3. Pastrana government representative in National Thematic Committee, Bogotá, June 9 and 12, 2003.
4. Historian, Bogotá, June 10, 2003, and July 8, 2004.
5. Sociologist, Bogotá, June 13, 2003, June 3 and 20, 2004, and July 20, 2004; by email, December 9, 2005, and January 4 and 5, 2006.
6. Sociologist, Bogotá, June 14, 2003.

7. Political scientist, Bogotá, June 19, 2003; by email December 13, 2005.
8. Official in the office of vice presidency, Bogotá, June 19, 2003.
9. Political scientist, Bogotá, June 24, 2003.
10. Economist, private foundation, Bogotá, June 24, 2003.
11. Political scientist, private foundation, Bogotá, June 26, 2003.
12. Former cabinet minister, Gaviria administration, Bogotá, June 28, 2003.
13. Political scientist, Bogotá, July 1, 2003, and July 13, 2004.
14. Political scientist, Bogotá, July 1, 2003.
15. Member of Peace Commission, Bogotá, July 3, 2003.
16. Historian, NGO, Bogotá, July 3, 2003.
17. Journalist, Bogotá, July 3, 2003; by email December 9, 2005.
18. Retired military officer, Bogotá, July 4, 2003.
19. Sociologist, by telephone from Tuscaloosa to Bogotá, September 6, 2003; in person in Bogotá, July 7, 2004; follow-up email response to questions, October 12, 2005.
20. Political scientist, Bogotá, July 2, 2004, and July 6, 2004.
21. Private foundation official, Bogotá, July 19, 2004.
22. Private foundation official, Bogotá, June 28, 2004.
23. Private foundation official, Bogotá, June 28, 2004.

Books

Aranguren Molina, Mauricio. *Mi Confesión: Carlos Castaño revela sus secretos.* Bogotá: Oveja Negra, 2002.

Bejarano, Jesús Antonio. *Una agenda para la paz: Aproximaciones desde la teoría de la resolución de conflictos.* Bogotá: Tercer Mundo Editores, 1995.

Bushnell, David. *The Making of Modern Colombia: A Nation in Spite of Itself.* Berkeley: The University of California Press, 1993.

Fuerzas militares para la guerra: La agenda pendiente de la reforma militar. Bogotá: Fundación Seguridad y Democracia, 2003.

Fukuyama, Francis. *State-Building: Governance and World Order in the 21st Century.* Ithaca: Cornell University Press, 2004.

García Márquez, Gabriel. *Crónica de una muerte anunciada.* Bogotá: Editorial La Oveja Negra, 1981.

Geddes, Barbara. *Politician's Dilemma: Building State Capacity in Latin America.* Berkeley: University of California Press, 1994.

Giraldo Hurtado, Luis Guillermo. *Del proceso y de la paz.* Manizales, Colombia: Edir@ficas, 2001.

Hartlyn, Jonathan. *The Politics of Coalition Rule in Colombia.* Cambridge, UK: Cambridge University Press, 1988.

Jonas, Susanne. *Of Centaurs and Doves: Guatemala's Peace Process.* Boulder, CO: Westview Press, 2000.

Kline, Harvey F. *Colombia: Democracy Under Assault.* Boulder, CO: Westview Press, 1995.

———. *State Building and Conflict Resolution in Colombia, 1986–1994.* Tuscaloosa: University of Alabama Press, 1999.

Leal Buitrago, Francisco, and Juan Gabriel Tokatian, eds. *Orden Mundial y Seguridad: Nuevos Desafíos para Colombia y América Latina.* Bogotá: Tercer Mundo Editores, 1994.

Leal Buitrago, Francisco, and León Zamosc, eds. *Al filo del caos: Crisis política en la Colombia de los años 80.* Bogotá: Tercer Mundo Editores, 1990.

Phelan, John Leddy. *The Kingdom of Quito in the Seventeenth Century: Bureaucratic Politics in the Spanish Empire.* Madison: The University of Wisconsin Press, 1967.

Pizarro Leongómez, Eduardo. *Una democracia asediada: Balance y perspectivas del conflicto armado en Colombia.* Bogotá: Grupo Editorial Norma, 2004.

Richani, Nazih. *Systems of Violence: The Political Economy of War and Peace in Colombia.* Albany: State University of New York Press, 2002.

Romero, Mauricio. *Paramilitares y autodefensas 1982–2003.* Bogotá: Editorial Planeta Colombiana, 2003.

Santa, Eduardo. *Sociología Política de Colombia.* Bogotá, Tercer Mundo Editores, 1964.

Santayana, George. *Life of Reason: Reason in Common Sense.* New York: Scribner's, 1905.

Téllez, Édgar, Oscar Montes, y Jorge Lesmes. *Diario íntimo de un fracaso: Historia no contada del proceso de paz con las Farc.* Bogotá: Editorial Planeta Colombiana, 2002.

Valencia, León. *Adiós a la política, bienvenida la guerra: Secretos de un malogrado proceso de paz.* Bogotá: Intermedio Editores, 2002.

Book Chapters, Journal Articles, Other Sources

Amnesty International, "The Guatemalan Peace Process Agreements: Elements most relevant to AI's concerns," http://web.amnesty.org/library/Index/ENGAMR340241997?open&of=ENG-2M2.

Arnson, Cynthia. Introduction to *Comparative Peace Processes in Latin America,* Cynthia Arnson, ed. Washington, DC: Woodrow Wilson Center Press, 1999.

Bejarano, Ana María. "Estrategias de paz y apertura democrática: Un balance de las administraciones Betancur y Barco." In *Al filo del caos: Crisis política en la Colombia de los años 80,* edited by Francisco Leal Buitrago and León Zamosc, 57–124. Bogotá: Tercer Mundo Editores, 1990.

Chernick, Marc. "Negotiating Peace Amid Multiple Forms of Violence." In *Comparative Peace Processes in Latin America,* edited by Cynthia J. Arnson, 159–96. Washington, DC: Woodrow Wilson Center Press, 1999.

"Colombia: Paramilitares legalizados," *Rebelión,* http://www.rebelion.org/plancolombia/sodepaz090902.htm.

Comisión de Reconciliación Nacional. "Paz y reconciliación," http://www.ccncol.org/p/paz.html#comision.

"Convivir, embuchado de largo alcance" (originally published in Bogotá, *Alternativa* no. 8, March-April, 1997), http://www.derechos.org/nizkor/colombia/doc/convivir.html.

Duzán, María Jimena. "Colombia's Bloody War of Words," *Journal of Democracy*, 2, no. 1, 1991, 105.

"Fifty Years of Violence" (originally appearing in *Colombia Report*, an online journal that was published by INOTA, the Information Network of the Americas), http://www. colombiajournal.org/fiftyyearsofviolence.htm.

Guevara, Ernesto Che. "Guerrilla war, a method," *Obra Revolucionaria* (Era: Mexico, 1973), quoted on http://www.marxists.org/archive/guevara/1963/misc/guerrilla-war-method.htm.

Human Rights Watch. "Colombia: Human Rights Developments," *World Report, 1999,* http://www.hrw.org/wr2k/americas-03.htm.

"Iglesia en Colombia mediará en cita de paz en Alemania," http://www.aciprensa.com/notic1998/julio/notic386.htm

International Crisis Group, "Colombia: The Prospects for Peace with the ELN," *Latin America Report No. 2*, Bogotá/Brussels, October 4, 2002, 18, http://www.reliefweb.int/library/documents/2002/icg-col-4oct.pdf.

Kline, Harvey F. "The National Front: Historical Perspective and Overview." In *Politics of Compromise: Coalition Government in Colombia,* edited by R. Albert Berry, Ronald G. Hellman, and Mauricio Solaún, 59–103. New Brunswick, NJ: Transaction Books, 1980.

Latin America Weekly Report, 8 January 1982.

Leal Buitrago, Francisco. "Defensa y Seguridad Nacional en Colombia, 1958–1993." In *Orden Mundial y Seguridad: Nuevos Desafíos para Colombia y América Latina,* edited by Franciso Leal Buitrago and Juan Gabriel Tokatian, 131–72. Bogotá: Tercer Mundo Editores, 1994.

Lijphart, Arend. "Consociational Democracy," *World Politics* XXI (1969), 207–25.

Mauceri, Philip. "States, Elites, and the Responses to Insurgency." In *Elites in the Andes: Identity, Conflict, Reform,* edited by Jo-Marie Burt and Philip Mauceri, 146–63. Pittsburgh: University of Pittsburgh Press, 2004.

Pardo Rueda, Rafael. "The Prospects for Peace in Colombia: Lessons from Recent Experience," Inter-American Dialogue Working Paper, July 2002, http://www.thedialogue. org/publications/country_studies/colombia_pardo.pdf.

Pizarro, Eduardo. "Revolutionary Guerrilla Groups in Colombia." In *Violence in Colombia: The Contemporary Crisis in Historical Perspective,* edited by Charles Berquist, Ricardo Peñaranda, and Gonzalo Sánchez, 169–94. Wilmington, DE: Scholarly Resources Inc., 1992.

Rettberg, Angelika. "The Business of Peace in Colombia: Assessing the Role of the Business Community in the Colombian Peace Process." Prepared for delivery at the 2003 meeting of the Latin American Studies Association, Dallas, TX, March 27–29, 2003.

"United States Support for Colombia: Fact Sheet released by the Bureau of Western Hemisphere Affairs," March 28, 2000. http://www.state.gov/www/regions/wha/colombia/fs_000328_plancolombia.html.

Vargas, Ricardo. "State, Esprit Mafioso, and Armed Conflict in Colombia." In *Politics in the Andes: Identity, Conflict, Reform,* edited by Jo-Marie Burt and Philip Mauceri, 107–25. Pittsburgh: University of Pittsburgh Press, 2004.

Zambrano Pantoja, Fabio. "Contradicciones del sistema político colombiano," *Análisis Conflicto Social y Violencia en Colombia* (1988), 19–26.

Zartman, I. William. "How Civil Wars End: Questions and Methods." In *Stopping the Killing: How Civil Wars End,* edited by Roy Licklider, 3–19. New York: New York University Press, 1993.

Documents

Government

"Actividades de la Mesa de Diálogo y Negociación para esta semana," ANCOL, February 11, 2002.

"Acusaciones del ELN contra Bell son Calumnia Infame: Camilo Gómez," ANCOL, December 6, 2001.

"Con Acuerdo de siete puntos, gobierno y Eln reinician proceso paz," ANCOL, November 25, 2001.

"Declaración de la Habana (del Gobierno Nacional y del ELN)," ANCOL, December 15, 2001.

"Draft government cease-fire proposal," February 4, 2002, http://www.ciponline.org/colombia/02020403.htm

"Frases del Presidente Pastrana en alocución sobre fin del proceso," ANCOL, February 20, 2002.

"Gobierno anuncia suspensión de proceso con Eln," ANCOL, May 31, 2002.

"Gobierno declare reinicio formal de proceso con el Eln," ANCOL, December 21, 2001.

"Hasta hoy hay voluntad del Eln por avanzar en el proceso de paz," ANCOL, February 26, 2002.

"Hemos profundizado en el tema de tregua con cese de fuegos: Gómez," ANCOL, Febrero 13, 2002.

Ley 434 de 1998 (febrero 3), "Por la cual se crea el Consejo Nacional de Paz, se otorgan funciones y se dictan otras disposiciones," http://www.secretariasenado.gov.co/leyes/L0424_98.htm.

Presidencia de la República, *El camino de la paz.* Bogotá: Consejería para la reconciliación, normalización y rehabilitación, 1989.

"Presidente reitera disposición de reunirse con voceros del ELN," ANCOL, June 7, 2001.

"Proceso con Eln sigue andando: Alto Comisionado," ANCOL, March 6, 2002.

"Proceso de paz con Eln no está roto: Pastrana," ANCOL, November 7, 2001.

"Reglamento de una posible zona de encuentro no será letra muerta," ANCOL, January 12, 2001.

Speech by President Andrés Pastrana at opening of talks with FARC, January 7, 1999, http://www.ciponline.org/colombia/past1eng.htm.

"Statement of Colombian Government High Commissioner for Peace Camilo Gómez," January 9, 2002, http://www.ciponline.org/colombia/010902.htm.

"Suspensión diálogos con Eln no es triunfo de autodefensas: Gómez," ANCOL, August 7, 2001.

"Carta abierta al Doctor Andrés Pastrana Arango, Presidente de la República," December 3, 1998. Document obtained from the Fundación Ideas para la Paz, Bogotá, June 2003.

"Carta abierta a la opinión pública," http://burn.ucsd.edu/~farc-ep/Comunicados/sep2099.html, last visited, March 22, 2000. (For a while in late 1999 and early 2000 the FARC website was only available through the homepage of a professor at the University of California-San Diego.)

"Carta Abierta al Señor Presidente de la República por el Secretario Nacional de las FARC-EP, Manuel Marulanda Vélez, Montañas de Colombia," January 29, 2000. Document obtained from the Fundación Ideas para la Paz, Bogotá, June 2003.

"Carta a James LeMoyne, Montañas de Colombia," January 8, 2002. Document obtained from the Fundación Ideas para la Paz, Bogotá, June 2003.

"Carta de Marulanda al Comisionado de Paz," January 17, 2001. Document obtained from the Fundación Ideas para la Paz, Bogotá, June 2003.

"Carta de Respuesta a Camilo Gómez Alzate, Alto Comisionado para la Paz, Montañas de Colombia," August 24, 2001. Document obtained from the Fundación Ideas para la Paz, Bogotá, June 2003.

"Comunicado de las Farc, para esentrabar el proceso," January 3, 2002. Document obtained from the Fundación Ideas para la Paz, Bogotá, June 2003.

"Comunicado de las FARC sobre el secuestro de Alán Jara," July 19, 2001, http://www.ciponline.org/colombia/071901.htm.

"Comunicado Público, Montañas de Colombia," January 4, 2002, http://www.farcep.org/?node=2,1732,1.

"Entrevista a Manuel Marulanda Vélez," March 15, 2000, http://six.swix.ch/farcep/Entrevistas/Entrevista—manuel—marulanda.htm, last visited March 22, 2000.

"FARC communiqué upon prisoner release," June 28, 2001, http://www.ciponline.org/colombia/062802.htm.

"FARC proposal to re-start talks," January 12, 2002, http://www.ciponline.org/colombia/011201.htm.

"FARC statement on German citizens' kidnapping," October 11, 2001, http://www.ciponline.org/colombia/082405.htm.

"Intervención de Raúl Reyes, Los Pozos, San Vicente de Caguán," January 29, 2000. Document obtained from the Fundación Ideas para la Paz, Bogotá, June 2003.

"Intervención del Comandante Iván Ríos, Coordinador del Comité Temático en Representación de las Farc-Ep," December 4, 1999. Document obtained from the Fundación Ideas para la Paz, Bogotá, June 2003.

"Intervención del Comandante Raúl Reyes, Vocero de las Fuerzs Armadas Revolucionarias de Colombia-Ejército del Pueblo, San Vicente de Caguán," December 4, 1999. Document obtained from the Fundación Ideas para la Paz, Bogotá, June 2003.

"Manifiesto del Movimiento Bolivariano Por la Nueva Colombia," March 25, 2000. http://www.angelfire.com/nb/17m/Colombia/movbolcol.html.

Marulanda, Manuel, "Carta a los voceros de las FARC-EP," October 16, 2001. Document obtained from the Fundación Ideas para la Paz, Bogotá, June 2003.

"Memorando para la Mesa de Diálogo, Secretario del Estado Mayor Central, FARC-Ejército del Pueblo," May 11, 2000. Document obtained from the Fundación Ideas para la Paz, Bogotá, June 2003.

The Peace Process and the Public Hearings, *Resistencia* 25, February 2001, http://www.ciponline.org/colombia/020103.htm. This journal is a FARC organ.

"Plataforma para un Gobierno de Reconstrucción y Reconciliación Nacional (FARC-EP), Octava Conferencia Nacional Guerrillera," April 3, 1993, http://www.contracultural.com.ar/notas/docu2.htm.

"Primer Bombazo a la Mesa," communiqué of the Secretariado del Estado Major Central, FARC-Ejército del Pueblo, Montañas de Colombia, May 17, 2000. Document obtained from the Fundación Ideas para la Paz, Bogotá, June 2003.

"Propuesta de las FARC-EP para la disminución de la intensidad del conflicto, Montañas de Colombia," February 2, 2002. Document obtained from the Fundación Ideas para la Paz, Bogotá, June 2003.

"Saludo del comandante Manuel Marulanda Vélez en el inicio de los diálogos con las FARC. Solución política al conflicto," *Correo del Magdalena,* II Época número 99, week of the 18th to 24th of January, 1999. http://www.voces.org/info/resu99.htm, last visited, January 19, 1999.

Government-FARC Jointly

"Accord for a Timetable for the Future of the Peace Process," January 20, 2002, http://www.ciponline.org/colombia/012004.htm.

"Acuerdo de Caquetania" is the commonly used name for the "Comunicado del Presidente Andrés Pastrana y Manuel Marulanda de las FARC, 2 de mayo de 1999," http://www.ciponline.org/colombia/990502.htm.

"Acuerdo de San Francisco de la Sombra entre el Gobierno y FARC-EP," ANCOL, October 5, 2001.

"Communiqué no. 27, FARC-government talks," March 9, 2001. http://www.ciponline.org/colombia/030903.htm.

"Communiqué no. 29, FARC-government talks," May 11, 2001, http://www.ciponline.org/colombia/051105.htm.

"Comunicado," October 2, 2001 (signed by Raúl Reyes, Joaquín Gómez, Simón Trinidad, Andrés París, and Carlos A. Lozada). Document obtained from the Fundación Ideas para la Paz, Bogotá, June 2003.

"Comunicado del Presidente Andrés Pastrana y Manuel Marulanda de las FARC," May 2, 1999 (signed in Caquetania and commonly known as the "Acuerdo de Caquetania"), http://www.ciponline.org/colombia/990502.htm.

"Comunicado de Prensa de la Comisión de Personalidades, Bogotá, D.C.," ANCOL, September 6, 2001. Document obtained from the Fundación Ideas para la Paz, Bogotá, June 2003.

"Communicado de Prensa, Los Pozos, San Vicente de Caguán," January 11, 2002. Document obtained from the Fundación Ideas para la Paz, Bogotá, June 2003.

Comunicado de Tregua de las Farc, Montañas de Colombia," December 20, 1999. Document obtained from the Fundación Ideas para la Paz, Bogotá, June 2003.

"Comunicado No. 3 de la Mesa de Diálogo y Negociación, San Vicente de Caguán," November 5, 1999. Document obtained from the Fundación Ideas para la Paz, Bogotá, June 2003.

"Comunicado No. 4, La Machaca, San Vicente de Caguán," April 21, 1999. Document obtained from the Fundación Ideas para la Paz, Bogotá, June 2003.

"Comunicado No. 5, La Machaca, San Vicente de Caguán," April 25, 1999. Document obtained from the Fundación Ideas para la Paz, Bogotá, June 2003.

"Comunicado No. 6, de la Mesa Nacional de Diálogo y Negociación, La Machaca, San Vicente de Caguán," December 18, 1999. Document obtained from the Fundación Ideas para la Paz, Bogotá, June 2003.

"Comunicado No. 6, La Machaca, San Vicente de Caguán," April 30, 1999. Document obtained from the Fundación Ideas para la Paz, Bogotá, June 2003.

"Comunicado No. 8, Los Pozos, San Vicente de Caguán, 28 de enero del 2000. Comunicado de los voceros del Gobierno Nacional y de las FARC-EP en la mesa de diálogo y negociación, Methdología de las discusiones y tema inicial a discutir," January 28, 2000. Document obtained from the Fundación Ideas para la Paz, Bogotá, June 2003.

"Comunicado No. 9 de la Mesa Nacional de Diálogos y Negociación, Los Pozos, San Vicente de Caguán," March 10, 2000. Document obtained from the Fundación Ideas para la Paz, Bogotá, June 2003.

"Comunicado No. 17, San Vicente de Caguán, Caquetá," March 2, 2000. Document obtained from the Fundación Ideas para la Paz, Bogotá, June 2003.

"Comunicado No. 23, San Vicente de Caguán," October 23, 2000. Document obtained from the Fundación Ideas para la Paz, Bogotá, June 2003.

"Comunicado No. 25, San Vicente de Caguán," February 16, 2001. Document obtained from the Fundación Ideas para la Paz, Bogotá, June 2003.

"Recomendaciones de la Comisión de Personalidades a la Mesa de Diálogo y Negociación," September 19, 2001. Document obtained from the Fundación Ideas para la Paz, Bogotá, June 2003.

"Versión completa de la rueda de prensa Pastrana-Marulanda, Los Pozos (Caquetá)," February 9, 2001. Document obtained from the Fundación Ideas para la Paz, Bogotá, June 2003.

ELN

"Carta Reunión Preparatoria, Cárcel de Itagüí," September 15, 1998, http://www.eln-voces.com/comupa/pp_co_ci.htm, last visited September 15, 1998.

"Comando Central del ELN, Montañas de Colombia," March 26, 1998, http://www.eln-voces.com/comupa/pp_co_rv.htm, last visited March 30, 1998.

Comando Central, "Proceso de Paz, Convención Nacional: Una propuesta para la reconstrucción de la sociedad," Montañas de Colombia, April 2000. Document obtained from the Fundación Ideas para la Paz, Bogotá, June 2003.

Dirección Nacional, Unión Camilista Ejercito de Liberación Nacional, "Una Propuesta Urgente para Colombia," Montañas de Colombia, February 2, 1996, http://www.eln-voces.com/historia/pp_co_ch.htm, last visited February 17, 1996.

"Documento Borrador del acta de la reunion del Comité Operativo Preparatorio de la Convención Nacional corespondiente a la sesión del 14 de septiembre de 1998 en Itagüí." Document obtained from the Fundación Ideas para la Paz, Bogotá, June 2003.

"Documento presentado por Francisco Galán y Felipe Torres, voceros del ELN, ante el Comité Operativo, contentivo de una propuesta en relación con los criterios de selección de los participantes de la Convención Nacional," December 11, 1998. Document obtained from the Fundación Ideas para la Paz, Bogotá, June 2003.

"Documentos presentados por Francisco Galán y Felipe Torres, voceros del ELN, los cuales contienen las propuestas de metodología y plan de acción sugeridas por el encuentro con el COCE, Itagüí," October 8, 1998. Document obtained from the Fundación Ideas para la Paz, Bogotá, June 2003.

"Propuesta de convención nacional del Eln a las primeras jornadas por la paz y los derechos humanos en Colombia, Madrid-España," December 12, 1997, http://www.eln-voces.com/comupa/pp_co_jp.htm, last visited December 11, 1999.

Government-ELN Jointly

"Acuerdo de Puerta del Cielo con el ELN," July 15, 1998, http://www.ciponline.org/colombia/cielo.htm.

"Comunicado del Gobierno y del Ejército de Liberación Nacional (ELN)," ANCOL, March 12, 2002.

"Declaración de la Cumbre por la Paz de la Habana (Cuba)," ANCOL, January 31, 2002.

"Declaración de Viana," February 9, 1998, http://www.ideaspaz.org/proyecto03/boletines/download/boletin03/viana.doc.

"Definida la agenda específica para ocho meses de diálogo con el Eln," October 1998. Document obtained from the Fundación Ideas para la Paz, Bogotá, June 2003.

"Government and ELN reaffirm Pre-agreement for Peace Document," Santafé de Bogotá, ANCOL, March 27th, 1998.

General Websites

ANCOL (Colombian News Agency) was the name of the presidential website during the Pastrana presidency. Its URL was http://www.presidencia.gov.co/.

ANNCOL (New Colombia News Agency) is an association of Latin American and European journalists founded in 1996. ANNCOL is based in Stockholm, Sweden, and has since May 1998 been providing on-line news about Colombia as an organ for FARC. Its URL is http://www.anncol.org/.

Associated Press's (AP) URL is http://www.ap.org/.

The Center for International Policy, a liberal think tank staffed by former diplomats and peace activists, has been concerned with U.S. policy in Central America, Cuba, and Colombia since its founding in 1975. Its URL is http://www.ciponline.org.

CNE, the National Center of News of the State (Centro Nacional de Noticias del Estado) was the first name given to the presidential website during the government of Alvaro Uribe. Its URL was http://www.presidencia.gov.co/ (and this remains the URL of Uribe's current presidential website).

ELN's URL is http://www.eln-voces.com.

El Espectador is a biweekly newspaper published in Bogotá. Its URL is http://www.elespectador.com/html/i_portals/index.php.

El Tiempo is a daily newspaper published in Bogotá. Its URL is http://eltiempo.terra.com.co/.

FARC's URL is http://www.farc-ep.ch/ or http://www.farcep.org.

New York Times' URL is http://www.nytimes.com/.

Radio Cadena Nacional (National Radio Network) publishes a daily webpage with http://www.rcn.com.co/noticia.php3?nt=12056 as its URL.

Reuters' URL is http://today.reuters.com/news/home.aspx.

Revista Cambio is a weekly magazine published in Bogotá. Its URL is http://www.revistacambio.com/.

Semana is a weekly magazine published in Bogotá. Its URL is http://semana.terra.com.co/.

Washington Post's URL is http://www.washingtonpost.com/

Index

Accompanying nations, 36
Acuerdo de Caquetanía, 69, 75, 93, 115
Acuerdo de la Puerta del Cielo, 128
Acuerdo de San Francisco de la Sombra, 105–107, 114, 118
Agreement of Aguas Claras, 136
Agreement of Colombia, 155–156
Agreement of Heaven's Gate, 38–39
Agreement of Los Pozos, 92–93. *See also* Los Pozos
ANDI, 148. *See also* Asociación Nacional de Industriales; National Association of Industrialists
Annan, Kofi, 184
Araúnoguera, Consulo, 103–105, 107
Asociación Civil para la Paz de Colombia, 136–137, 148. *See also* Asociapaz
Asociación Nacional de Industriales, 148. *See also* ANDI; National Association of Industrialists
Asociapaz, 136–137, 148, 153. *See also* Asociación Civil para la Paz de Colombia
AUC, 171–172; and drug trade, 42; attack in southern Bolívar during Geneva meeting, 142; seized region Pastrana planned for demilitarized zone. *See also* Autodefensas Unidas de Colombia
Autodefensas Unidas de Colombia, 42. *See also* AUC

Barco, President Virgilio, 3; peace process, 18–19
Barrancabermeja, 132
Beltrán, Pablo, 133, 151; insists on encounter zone, 154; finances for ELN, 160; *See also* Ramírez Pineda, Israel
Betancourt, Ingrid, 122
Betancur, President Belisario, 3, 174, 178; peace process of, 17–18
Bolívar, Department of, 131
Bolivarian militias, 181
Bonnet, General Manuel José, 32, 46
Borrero Mansilla, Armando, 61, 63, 144
Botero Zea, Fernando, 28, 31
Businessmen of Coercion, 177–178

Cali cartel, 15; money to Samper campaign, 27–28

Cantagallo, mayor of, 148
Caquetá, 81
Castaño, Carlos, 14, 40, 58, 81, 137, 145, 151; book, 42; capture not enough for FARC, 62; formation of paramilitary groups, 41
Castaño, Fidel, 114
Castaño, Jesús, 41
Catholic Church, Colombian, 34, 157; Bishops Conference form National Conciliation Commission, 35
Catholic Church, German, 34
Cazadores Battalion, 52, 54, 55, 70
Cease-fire, 20, 115; exchange of proposals between government and FARC, July 2000, 85; FARC announces at end of 1999, 79; FARC position end of 1998, 56; FARC proposes bilateral in May 2000, 84; government and FARC proposals, 97–99; government position at the end of 1998, 56; government proposes six-month cease-fire, 119; government puts agreement first in January 2002, 118; proposals exchanged in January 2002, 119
Cepeda Ulloa, Fernando, 41, 63
Coordinadora Guerrillera Simón Bolívar (CGSB), 20
Chernick, Marc, 176
Civic police, 149
Civil society, 38, 100, 133, 148, 149, 160. See also Facilitating Commission of Civil Society
Coexistence zone, ELN, 133; Bolívar opposition to, 133. See also demilitarized zone, ELN
Colombian War System, 175–183
Comando Central (COCE, Central Command), 33, 133
Commission of Notables, 92, 100–103, 114; agreements, 100–103; established, 95
Common agenda, 69, 71–74, 79
Communist Party, 10
Communitarian Cooperatives of Rural Vigilance, 40–41. See also CONVIVIR

Constituent Assembly, 16; Commission of Notables proposes, 101–102; FARC proposes, 59
Constitutional Court, 40–41
CONVIVIR, 35. See also Communitarian Cooperatives of Rural Vigilance
Cortés, Elvira, 84
Costa Rica, 32, 36
Cuba, 10, 11, 172

Death to Kidnappers, 15
Decisions, first years of independence: elite political game, 9; legal system, 6–7; use of violence, 7–9
Declaration of Cauca, 18
Declaration of Geneva, 126, 141–142
Declaration of Havana, 157–159
Declaration of the Peace Summit, 157, 159
Decree 3398, 13
De la Calle, Humberto, 151
Demilitarized zone, ELN, 139; AUC role in, 136, 139; attempts to set up ELN zone, 135–136; blockade, 140; Bolívar opposition to, 134, Bolivar protest, 150–151; ELN fails to appear for meeting, 152; ELN suspends talks, 151; Pastrana announces preliminary agreement, 138; popular consultations, 141. See also coexistence zone, ELN
Demilitarized zone, FARC, 130; agreement, 52; announced, 54; Colombian military wanted, 70; extended February 1999, 68; extended June 1999, 75; extended February 2001, 92; extended until January 31, 2001, 88; FARC proposal to President Samper, 29, military opposition to, 29, 31; rules for, 76; verification, 54
Disunited Elite, 177
Dossier of paramilitarism, 64
Drugs, 2, 10, 14, 16, 35
Duzán, María Jimena, 29

Egeland, Jan, 110
Ejército de liberación nacional (ELN), 2, 3, 10, 11; breaks Viana Agreement, 36–

37; Central Command, 128, 157; invited to join Commission of Notables proposal, 102. *See also* ELN

Elections, October 2000, 87

El Nogal, 174

El Salvador, 168, 170–173

ELN (Ejército de liberación nacional), 2, 11, 17, 23; Central Command (Comando Central, COCE), 33; financing, 144; income from extortion and kidnapping, 172; meets with government in Havana (December 2005–January 2006), 184; secondary role for Pastrana, 162. *See also* Ejército de liberación nacional

Escobar, Pablo, 16

Espinosa Meola, Rodolfo, 53

Esprit Mafioso, 178–179

Faceless justice system, 46

Facilitating Commission of Civil Society, 148

Failed state, 26

FARC (Fuerzas armadas revolucionarias de Colombia): agenda January 2002, 118; attacks on towns 83; blocks, 44; Boliviarian militias, 44; change of strategy, 43–45; Decalogue, 56–57; desire to have civil society participation in agreements, 60; Eight National Conference, 43–44; El Billar attack, 44; evaluation of peace process in February 2001, 93–94; freezing of negotiations in January 2001, 91; hijacks domestic airliner, 120; income from drugs, 172–173; leadership letter to the national government (October 2001), 108–109; membership of Viana meeting, 37; Miraflores attack, 44; Mitú attack, 44; participation in Heaven's Gate Agreement, 38–39; platform of ten social and polticial reforms, 44; presents dossier of paramilitarism, 64; prolonged war strategy, 43; public communiqués, January 2002, 113; relation of fronts with central command,

86; statement that Pastrana should be removed, 96, 97; war of movements strategy, 43–45, 181

FARC, freeze of negotiations, 20; by government, 85; by FARC, 76–77, 87; caused by paramilitary activities, 62–63, first, 62–63

Friendly Countries, 148, 149, 159

Friendly governments, 94–95

Fuerzas armadas revolucionarias de Colombia, 3, 10, *See also* FARC

Fukuyama, Francis, 185

Gabino, 131

Galán, Franciso, 127

Galán, Luis Carlos, 16

García, Antonio, 128, 130, 132, 142, 160; less optimistic after Geneva meeting

García-Peñña, Daniel, 36, 152

Gechem Turbay, Jorge, 120

Geddes, Barbara, 9, 25

Geneva, civil society in meeting, 141; ELN government and civil society meeting in, 141

German development workers, 98, 99

Giraldo, Luis Guillermo, 87

Giraldo, Monsignor Alberto, 114

Gómez, Alfonso, 53

Gómez, Camilo, 9; considers Rodríguez statement to be "vile slander," 156; ELN final straw, 162; Geneva meeting, 142; meets with Asociapaz, 148; meets with ELN leaders, 148; named high commissioner, 84; optimism in November 2001 statement about San Francisco agreement, 106; refuses to paying ELN kidnapping ransoms, 160; reports progress toward cease-fire in January 2002 meeting, 119; statement to FARC in October 2001, 109; states on January 9, 2002 that 48 hours have begun, 113; states that ELN needs to unfreeze process, 153; suspension of talks not victory of Asociapaz, 154; travels to Bolivar to talk to protesters, 140

Gómez, Hernán, 42
Gómez Martínez, Ana Mercedes, 100, 107
González, Mauricio, 149
Government and ELN joint commu-
    niqué on March 12, 2002, 159–160;
    ELN meet in Cuba on December 2001,
    156–157; meet in Puerto Ordaz, Vene-
    zuela, 154
Government response to FARC agenda
    in January 2002, 118
Guatemala, 25, 73, 100, 168, 170–173

Heaven's Gate, Agreement of, 132
Hernández, General Rafael, 74
Holmes Trujillo, Carlos, 30, 33
Honor Witness, 114
Humanitarian exchange, FARC, 95–96;
    ELN, 184

Idealism, 20. *See also* volunteerism
International Commission of Accompa-
    niment, 115
International humanitarian law in
    Heaven's Gate Agreement, 39
International verification commission, 133
Irish Republican Army, 97, 99

Jacobo Arenas Column, 100
Jara, Alán, 98
Joint news conferences, Pastrana and
    Marulanda, 93

Kidnapping, 10; ELN commercial air
    flight, 132–133; Cali mass, 132–133;
    FARC, 96, 98; increased, 83; states
    not policy, 106

La Macarena, 32
La Uribe, 30, 32
Law 35 of 1982, 17
Law 48, 13
Law 548 of 1999, 183
Leal Buitrago, Francisco, 9
Lemos Simmonds, Carlos, 53
LeMoyne, James, 114
Leyva Durán, Álvaro, 49–50, 66
Liberal party, 46, 53

Lloreda, Minister of Defense Rodrigo,
    74, 181
Los Pozos, 81, 114. *See also* Agreement of
    Los Pozos
Los Tangueros, 41

M-19. *See* Nineteenth of April Movement
Machuca, Antioquia, 130
Magdalena, Department of, 179
Mainz, Germany, 38, 50–51
Marquetalia, 10
Martínez, Celso, 149, 153
Martínez, Néstor Humberto, 78
Marulanda Vélez, Manuel, 10, 50; biogra-
    phy, 50; explanation of not being at
    first meeting, 59; failure to appear at
    first meeting, 58; interview about
    Movimiento Bolivariano por la Nueva
    Colombia, 83; letter to negotiators in
    October 2001, 107; letter to Pastrana
    in January 2001, 91; letter to President
    Pastrana in October 2001, 108; open
    letter to Pastrana in January 2000, 80–
    81; posturing before opening meeting,
    57; proposes another European trip,
    91; surprise visit in January 2000 to
    negotiating table, 80; threatens to end
    prisoner exchange, 91; wants law for
    prisoner exchange, 61. *See also* Pedro
    Antonio Marín; Tirofijo
Matallana, General José Joaquín, 32
Mauceri, Philip, 177, 183
Mechanism of financing, proposed by
    Commission of Notables, 101
Medellín cartel, 15, 41
Medina, Santiago, 28
Meeting, Gómez and Marulanda, 88
Meeting, Valle del Rio Verde, 128–129
Meetings of Andrés Pastrana and
    Tirofijo, first, 51
Mejía, María Emma, 52–53
Mesetas, 32
Mexico, 36
Mexico City conversations, 50
Military, "Plan B" to retake demilitarized
    zone, 92
Mitterrand, Danielle, 45–46

Mora, General Jorge Enrique, 68, 150
Morales, municipality of, 131–132
Moreno, Samuel, 142
Movimiento Bolivariano por la Nueva Colombia, 83

National Association of Industrialists, 100, 148
National Association of Merchants, 100
National Committee of Peace, 32
National Convention, 133, 138, 139, 149, 175; friends and facilitators of process, 140–141; international verification in, 139; operating committee produces draft in September 1998, 127–128; postponed due to conflict about location, 131–132; preparatory commission, 128
National Convention, 34–35, 37–38; Constituent Assembly from, 38; national agreement from, 38
National Council of Peace, 38, 127
National Dialogue, 17–18; to intensify work, 106
National Front, 9
National Thematic Committee, 60, 78–79, 83, 94
Negative tie, 167, 169, 175
Negotiations with ELN, 149
Negotiations with FARC: government agrees to delay verifying commission, 77; process agreements, 69; progress report at end of 1999, 79; three parallel tracks, 87; Tour of Europe, 82–83; verifying commission, 75; violation of confidential agreement, 76
Nicolás Rodríguez Bautista, 39, *See also* Gabino
Nineteenth of April Movement (M-19), 10, 12, 17
No al despeje, 145, 153. *See also* No to the Disarmament
Notables, 105, 106, 115, 118
No to the Disarmament, 145. *See also* No al despeje

Operation Bolívar, 150
Oquist, Paul, 178

ORDEN, 171, 172. *See also* Republican National Organization; Organización Republicana Nacional
Organización Republicana Nacional, 171. *See also* ORDEN; Republican National Organization
Ossa Escobar, Carlos, 61
Otero, Ariel, 14

Palacio de Justicia, 12
Parallel table for prisoner exchange, 59
Paramilitaries, Proposal by Commission of Notables, 103
Paramilitarism, 35
Paramilitary groups, 12–13, 14, 69, 175, 183; demobilized during Gaviria presidency, 39; during Samper presidency, 39–43; growth of, 43. *See also* paramilitary squads
Paramilitary squads, 3, 6–7, 175. *See also* paramilitary groups
Pardo, Rafael, 19–21
Pardo, Rodrigo, 141
París, Andrés, 114
Pastrana, President Andrés, 41; announces trip to demilitarized zone with other presidential candidates, 104; biography, 51; cancels September 30, 2001, meeting with FARC, 105; considers ELN negotiations going well after Geneva meeting, 144; declares end of FARC negotiations, 120–121; deplores end of Serpa march, 104; ELN process continuing after talk with Bolívar leaders, 149–150; first negotiating team, 52–53; inaugural speech, 52; January 2002 speech, FARC proposals not acceptable, 114; meeting with generals, 74; place in history, 68; posturing before opening meeting, 57; prepared to meet with ELN leaders, 154; response to Bolívar governor, 133–134; second meeting with Marulanda, 74; statement at opening meeting with FARC, 58–59; suspends talks with ELN on August 7, 2001, 154; threatens FARC with end of demilitarized zone, 68;

trails Serpa in first round of 1998 presidential election, 49

Peasant Self-Defense Groups of Córdoba and Urabá, 40, 42; Autodefensas Campesinas de Córdoba y Urabá (ACCU), 41–42

Pedro Antonio Marín, 51. *See also* Marulanda Vélez, Manuel; Tirofijo

Pérez, Henry, 14

Pérez Martínez, Manuel, 23, 34, 162; death of, 39

Peru, 177

Pizarro Leongómez, Eduardo, 1, 165, 167, 173, 174

Plan Colombia, 55–56, 80, 83, 84, 86, 125, 174; criticized by Tirofijo, 81

Political archipelagoes, 1, 2, 5, 15, 22, 176, 185

Political power, 20

Politician's dilemma, 9

Popular Army of Liberation, 10

Presidential Directive No. 3, 64

Presidential election of 1998, 50–51

Pretalt de la Vega, Sabas, 100

Procedural agreements, ELN, 144

Puerto Wilches, 132

Putumayo, 86, 179

Raad Hernández, Miguel, 133

Rambos, Arnubio, 85

Ramírez, Juan José, 60

Ramírez, Rubén Darío, 60–61

Ramírez Ocampo, Augusto, 139

Ramírez Pineda, Israel, 133

Rangel, Alfredo, 63, 137, 153, 164

Rational actor assumptions, 167

Reincorporation, 36

Republican National Organization, 171. *See also* ORDEN; Organización Republicana Nacional

Restrepo Santamaría, Nicanor, 53

Rettberg, Angelika, 174

Reyes, Raúl, 50; announces first freezing, 62; discusses economic problems, 77; gives goals of National Thematic Committee, 77–78; gives reason Tirofijo not at opening meeting, 58; insists that verifying commission be later, 75; January 2000 report on accomplishments in demilitarized zone, 81; meets with Ricardo, 77; proposes that Pastrana be removed, 97; states that cease-fire to be discussed in April and May 2002, 112–113

Ricardo, Víctor G. (High Commissioner), 56, 68, 74, 128, 137; announces resignation, 84; meets with Reyes, 77; gives conciliatory speech, 77; travels to Bolívar to meeting with ELN leader Beltrán, 133; writes to Marulanda, 64

Richani, Nazih, 177, 179–180, 183

Rincón, Felipe, 76

Ríos, Iván, 100

Ríos, José Noé, 36

Rio Verde, 132

Rodríguez, Nicolás: actions of government raise questions of sincerity, 157; suggests connection between military and paramilitaries, 156

Rodríguez Gacha, José Gonzalo, 16

Rodríguez Orejuela, Gilberto, 28

Rodríguez Orejuela, Miguel, 28

Rojas, Jairo, 50

Rojas Pinilla, Gustavo, 12

Romero, Mauricio, 145, 177–178, 183

Safford, Frank, 1

Samper, Ernesto, 23, 26, 173; beginning of talks with ELN, 33–39; Congress, does not impeach, 29; "First Days for Peace and Human Rights" meeting, 34–35; confusion in government, 45; drug money to campaign, 45; failure with FARC, 29–33; military opposition, 45; paramilitary growth during presidency, 45

San Pablo, municipality of, 131–132

Santa Rosa, municipality of, 131–132;

Santos, Francisco, 142

Santos, Juan Manuel, 45–46, 53, 169

School for Advanced International Studies, 169

Serpa, Horacio, 40, 49, 53; march to demilitarized zone, 103–104, 107

Simití, municipality of, 131–132;
Simón Bolívar Guerrilla Coordinator,
    19. *See also* Coordinadora Guerrillera
    Simón Bolívar (CGSB)
Soviet Union, 172
Spain, 36
Spanish and Portuguese colonies, 5–6
Suárez Briceño, Jorge, 50; announces tax,
    84, threatens kidnapping, 61, 96

Tapias, General Fernando, 74, 107
Theme I, 22–23, 27 29, 30–31, 66, 175
Theme Ia, 22
Theme Ib, 22, 74, 88, 96, 150, 162
Theme Ic 22, 86, 90, 105, 112, 132
Theme Id, 22, 126, 132, 134, 147, 148,
    150, 162
Theme Ie, 22, 147
Theme II, 22, 23–24, 27, 31, 52, 68–69
Theme IIa, 22
Theme IIb, 22, 84, 87
Theme III, 22, 24, 27, 53, 55, 66
Theme IIIa 22, 90, 146
Theme IIIb, 22, 66, 117, 121
Theme IIIc, 22, 76, 90, 100, 104, 105, 109,
    112, 131, 147, 151, 162
Theme IV, 22, 25, 52
Theme V, 22, 52, 66, 70, 87, 90, 93, 114,
    112, 129, 140, 149, 162
Timetable, January 2002, 116–117
Timetable, January 20, 2002, 114–115
Tirofijo, 10; biography, 51–52; imper-
    tinence speak first, 57. *See also*
    Marulanda Vélez, Manuel; Pedro
    Antonio Marín
Tlaxcala, 20
Torres, Felipe, 127
Truce: Betancur government with M-19,
FARC, and ELN, 17; between ELN and
government, proposed by the Decem-
ber 2001 Declaration of Havana, 159;
between FARC and government, pro-
posed by Commission of Notables,
102; proposals of ELN and govern-
ment in April, 2002, 160–161
Turbay, Diego, 88

United Nations, 50, 110, 114, 157, 159, 184
United States, 159
Uribe, Juan Gabriel, 107, 109
Uribe, President Álvaro, 173, 181, 183
U.S. Drug Enforcement Agency, 16

Valdivieso, Alfonso, 28
Valencia, León, 68, 110, 160
Valencia, President Guillermo León, 10, 13
Valencia Cossio, Fabio, 53, 71
Valencia Tovar, General Alvaro, 57–58
Vargas, Ricardo, 177, 178–179, 183
Vargas Lleras, Germán, 53
Vargas Velásquez, Alejo 75
Venezuela, 36
Viana, Prearrangement of, 35–36,
Vidal, Margarita, 110
Villa Nueva Colombia, 81–82
Vista Hermosa, 32
Volunteerism, 20. *See also* idealism

War System, 179–180
War, Costs of, 174–175
Working tables between Betancur gov-
    ernment and M-19, 18–19; with ELN,
    136–137

Zartman, I. William, 167